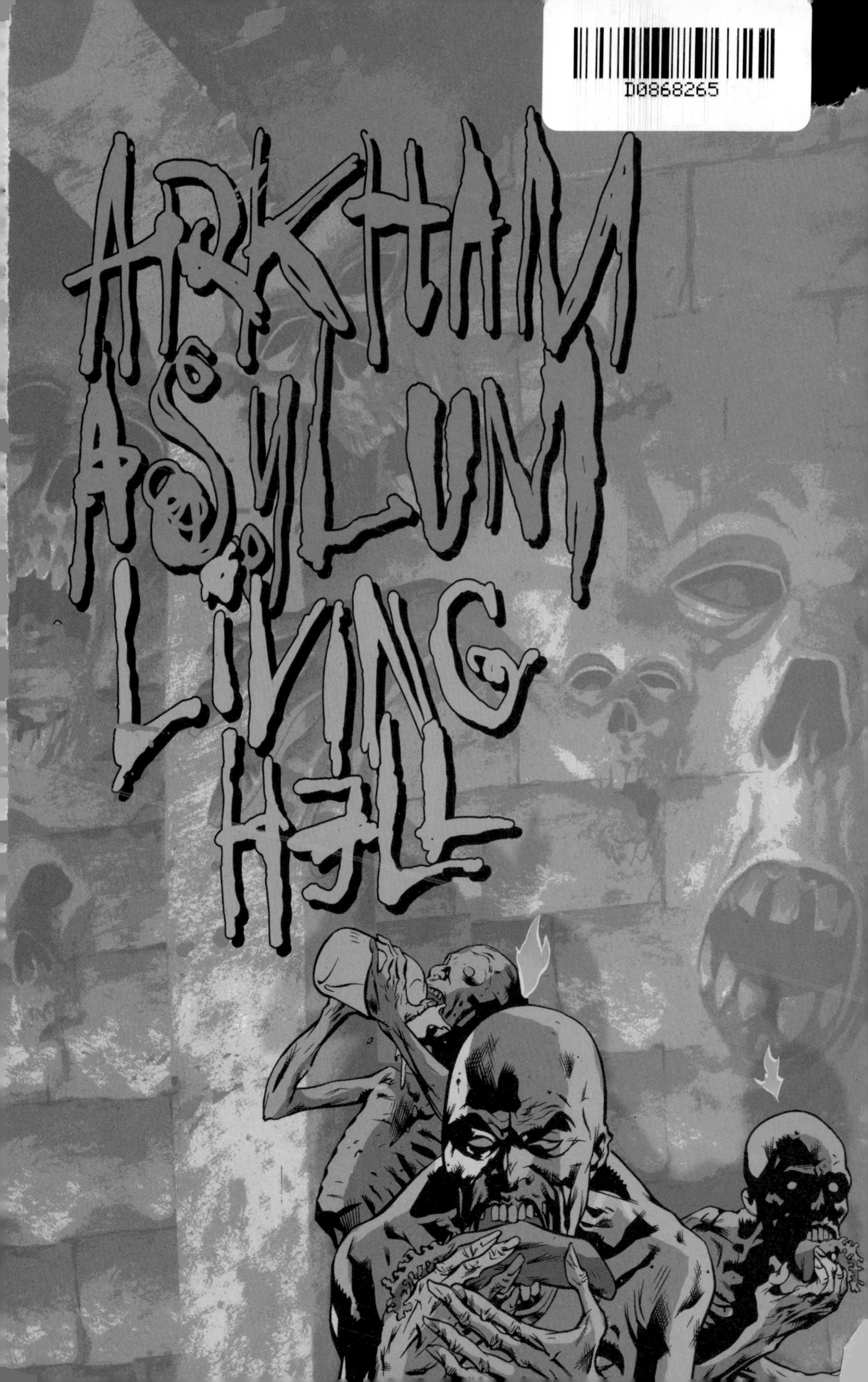
ARKHAM
ASYLUM
LIVING
HELL

DC Comics, 1700 Broadway, New York, NY 10019
A Warner Bros. Entertainment Company
Printed in Canada. First Printing.
ISBN: 1-4012-0193-8
Cover art by Eric Powell

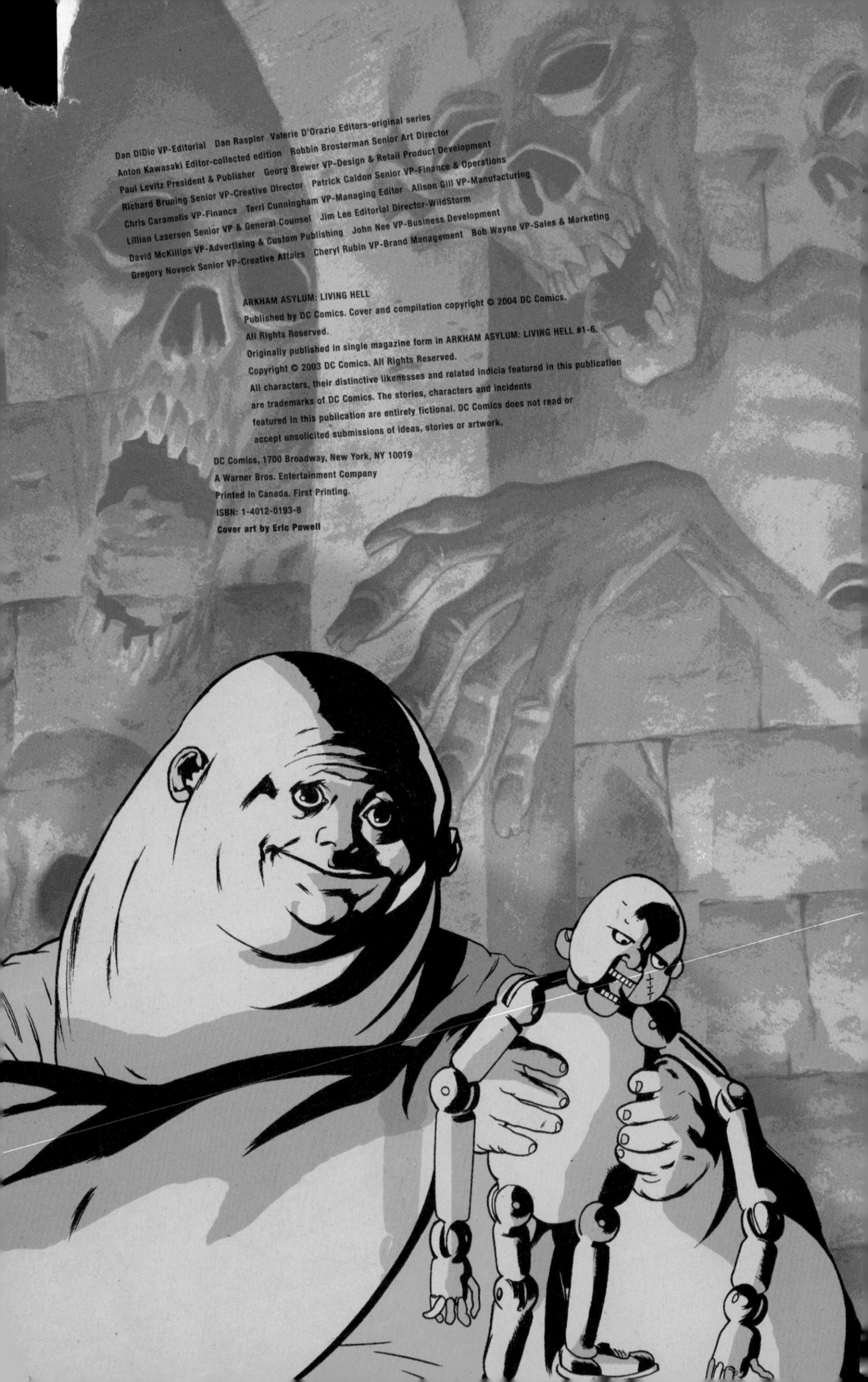

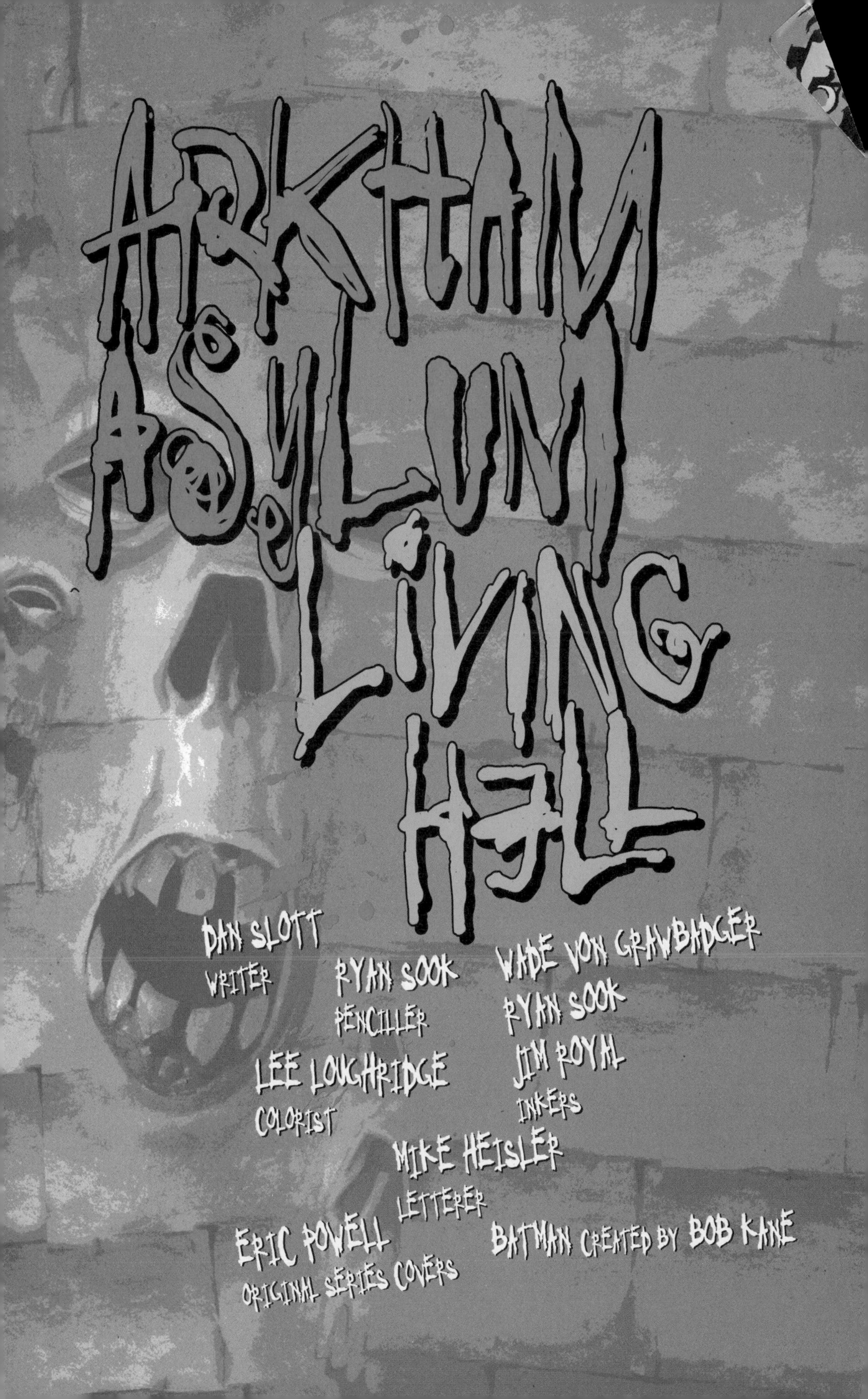
ARKHAM ASYLUM
LIVING HELL
DAN SLOTT
WRITER
RYAN SOOK
PENCILLER
WADE VON GRAWBADGER
RYAN SOOK
JIM ROYAL
INKERS
LEE LOUGHRIDGE
COLORIST
MIKE HEISLER
LETTERER
ERIC POWELL
ORIGINAL SERIES COVERS
BATMAN CREATED BY BOB KANE

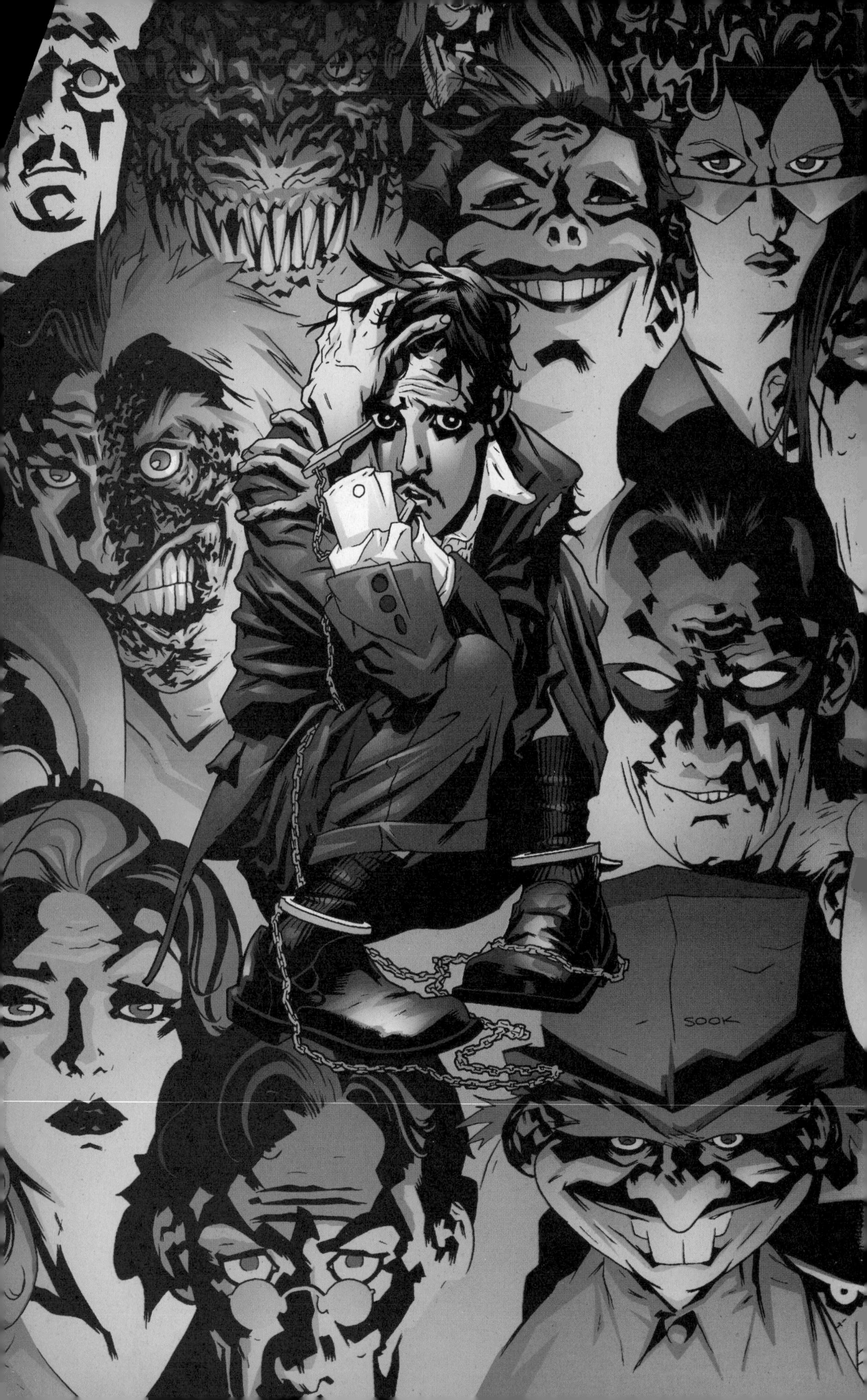
SOOK

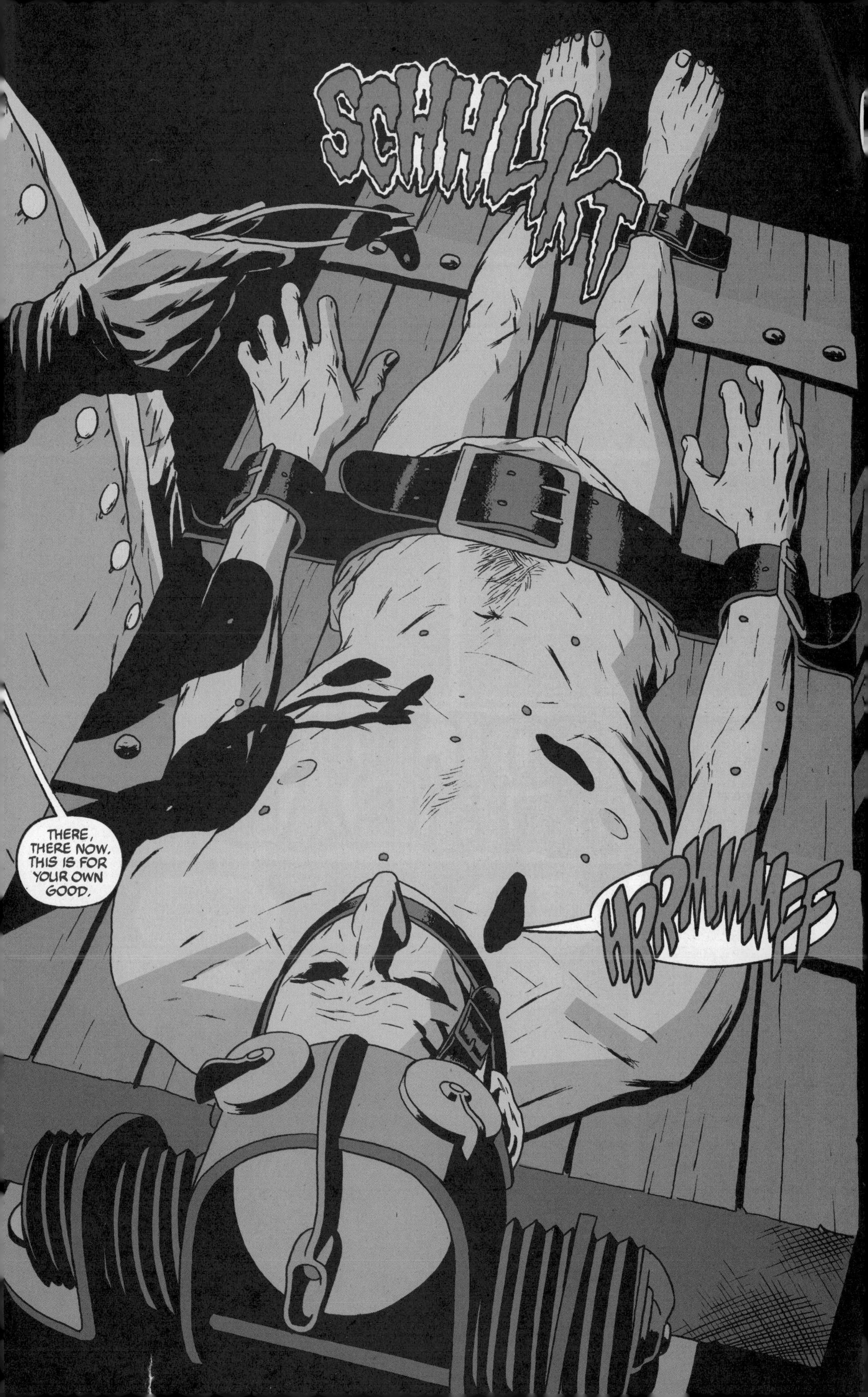
SCHHLAKT
THERE, THERE NOW. THIS IS FOR YOUR OWN GOOD.
HRRMMMFF

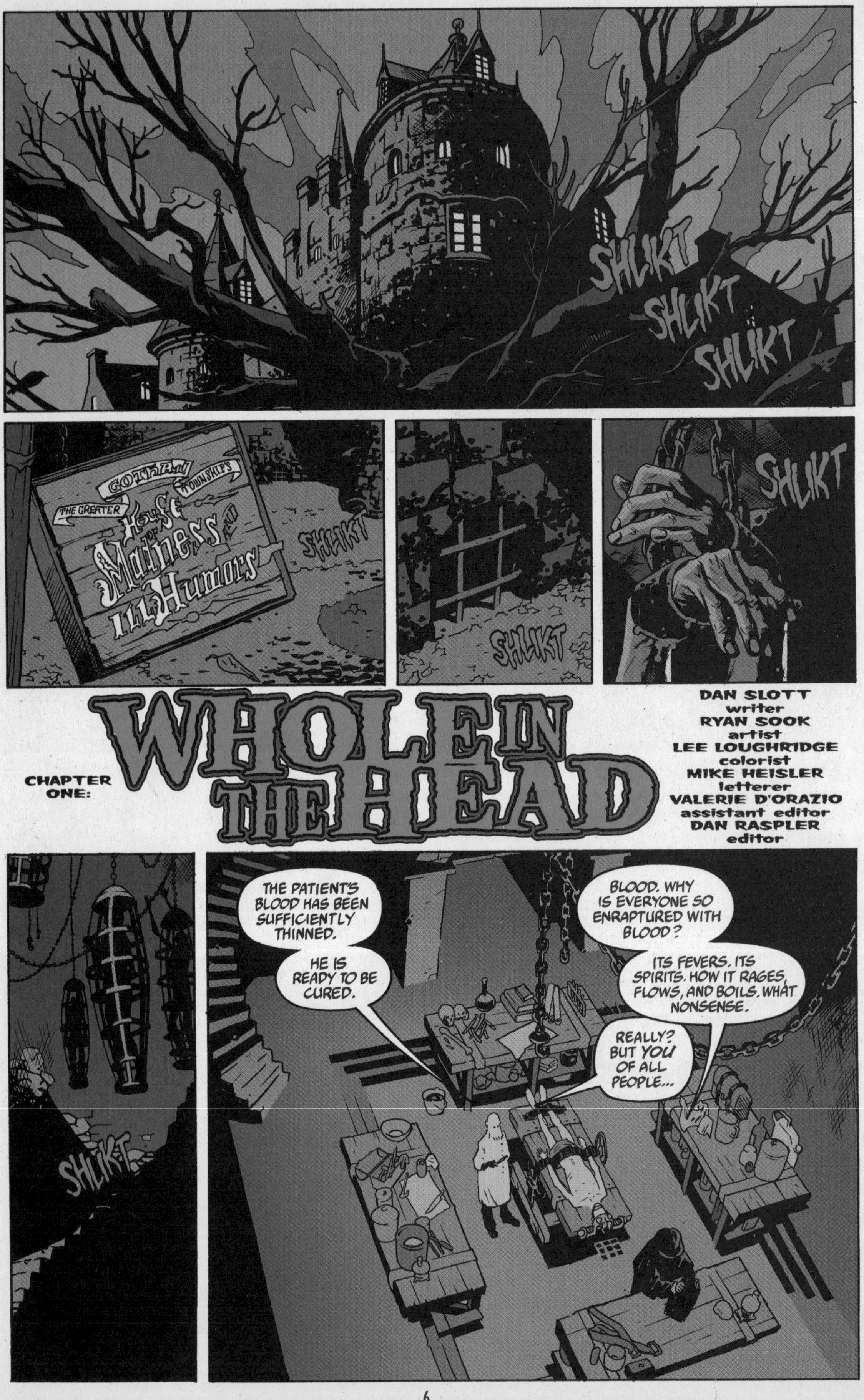
SHLIKT
SHLIKT
SHLIKT
THE GREATER GOTHAM TOWNSHIP'S
HOUSE FOR MADNESS AND ILL HUMORS
SHLIKT
SHLIKT
SHLIKT
CHAPTER ONE:
WHOLE IN THE HEAD
DAN SLOTT writer
RYAN SOOK artist
LEE LOUGHRIDGE colorist
MIKE HEISLER letterer
VALERIE D'ORAZIO assistant editor
DAN RASPLER editor
SHLIKT
THE PATIENT'S BLOOD HAS BEEN SUFFICIENTLY THINNED.
HE IS READY TO BE CURED.
BLOOD. WHY IS EVERYONE SO ENRAPTURED WITH BLOOD?
ITS FEVERS. ITS SPIRITS. HOW IT RAGES, FLOWS, AND BOILS. WHAT NONSENSE.
REALLY? BUT YOU OF ALL PEOPLE...

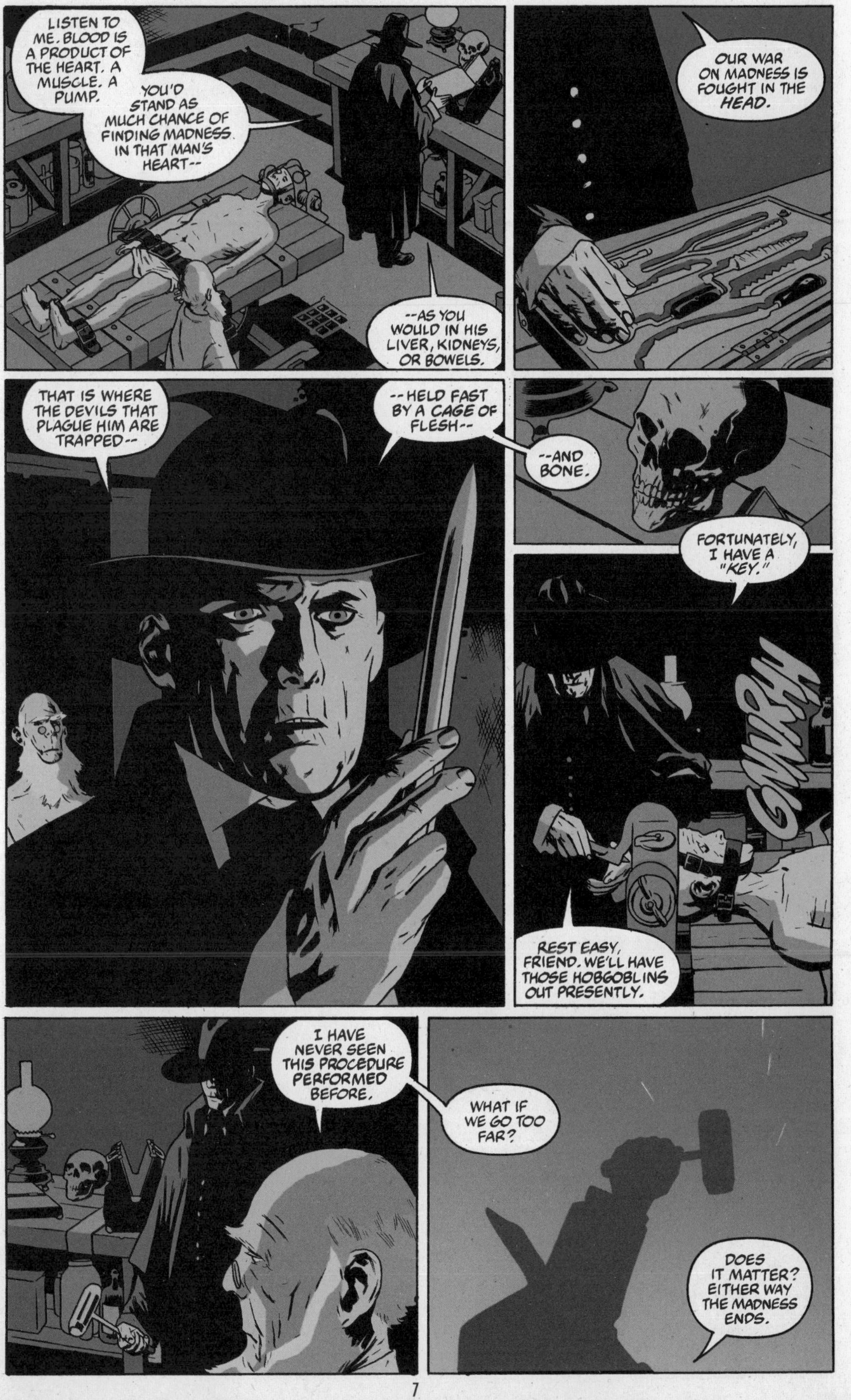
LISTEN TO ME. BLOOD IS A PRODUCT OF THE HEART. A MUSCLE. A PUMP.
YOU'D STAND AS MUCH CHANCE OF FINDING MADNESS IN THAT MAN'S HEART--
--AS YOU WOULD IN HIS LIVER, KIDNEYS, OR BOWELS.
OUR WAR ON MADNESS IS FOUGHT IN THE HEAD.
THAT IS WHERE THE DEVILS THAT PLAGUE HIM ARE TRAPPED--
--HELD FAST BY A CAGE OF FLESH--
--AND BONE.
FORTUNATELY, I HAVE A "KEY."
GNNRH
REST EASY, FRIEND. WE'LL HAVE THOSE HOBGOBLINS OUT PRESENTLY.
I HAVE NEVER SEEN THIS PROCEDURE PERFORMED BEFORE.
WHAT IF WE GO TOO FAR?
DOES IT MATTER? EITHER WAY THE MADNESS ENDS.

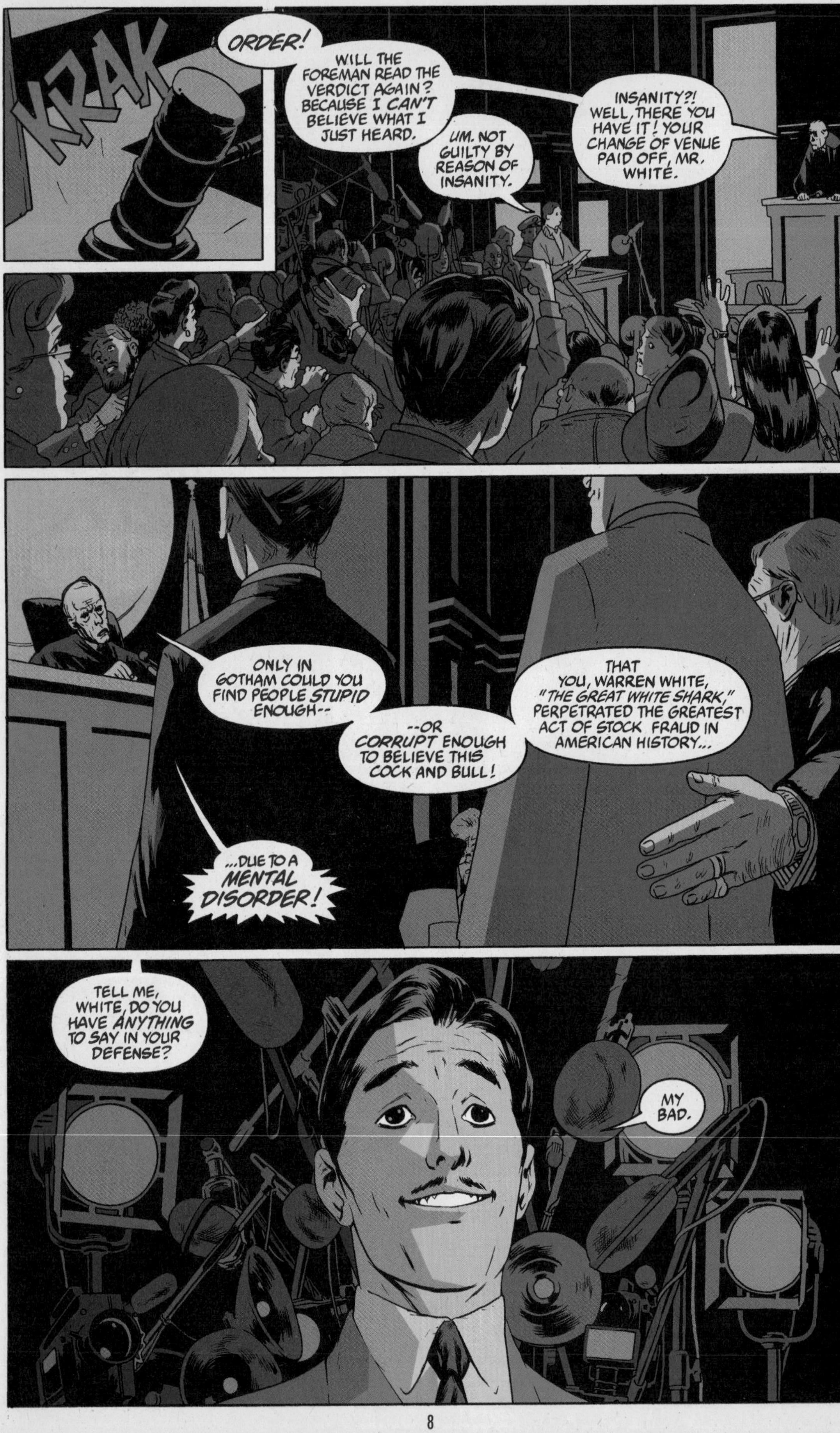
KRAK
ORDER!
WILL THE FOREMAN READ THE VERDICT AGAIN? BECAUSE I CAN'T BELIEVE WHAT I JUST HEARD.
UM. NOT GUILTY BY REASON OF INSANITY.
INSANITY?! WELL, THERE YOU HAVE IT! YOUR CHANGE OF VENUE PAID OFF, MR. WHITE.
ONLY IN GOTHAM COULD YOU FIND PEOPLE STUPID ENOUGH--
--OR CORRUPT ENOUGH TO BELIEVE THIS COCK AND BULL!
THAT YOU, WARREN WHITE, "THE GREAT WHITE SHARK," PERPETRATED THE GREATEST ACT OF STOCK FRAUD IN AMERICAN HISTORY...
...DUE TO A MENTAL DISORDER!
TELL ME, WHITE, DO YOU HAVE ANYTHING TO SAY IN YOUR DEFENSE?
MY BAD.

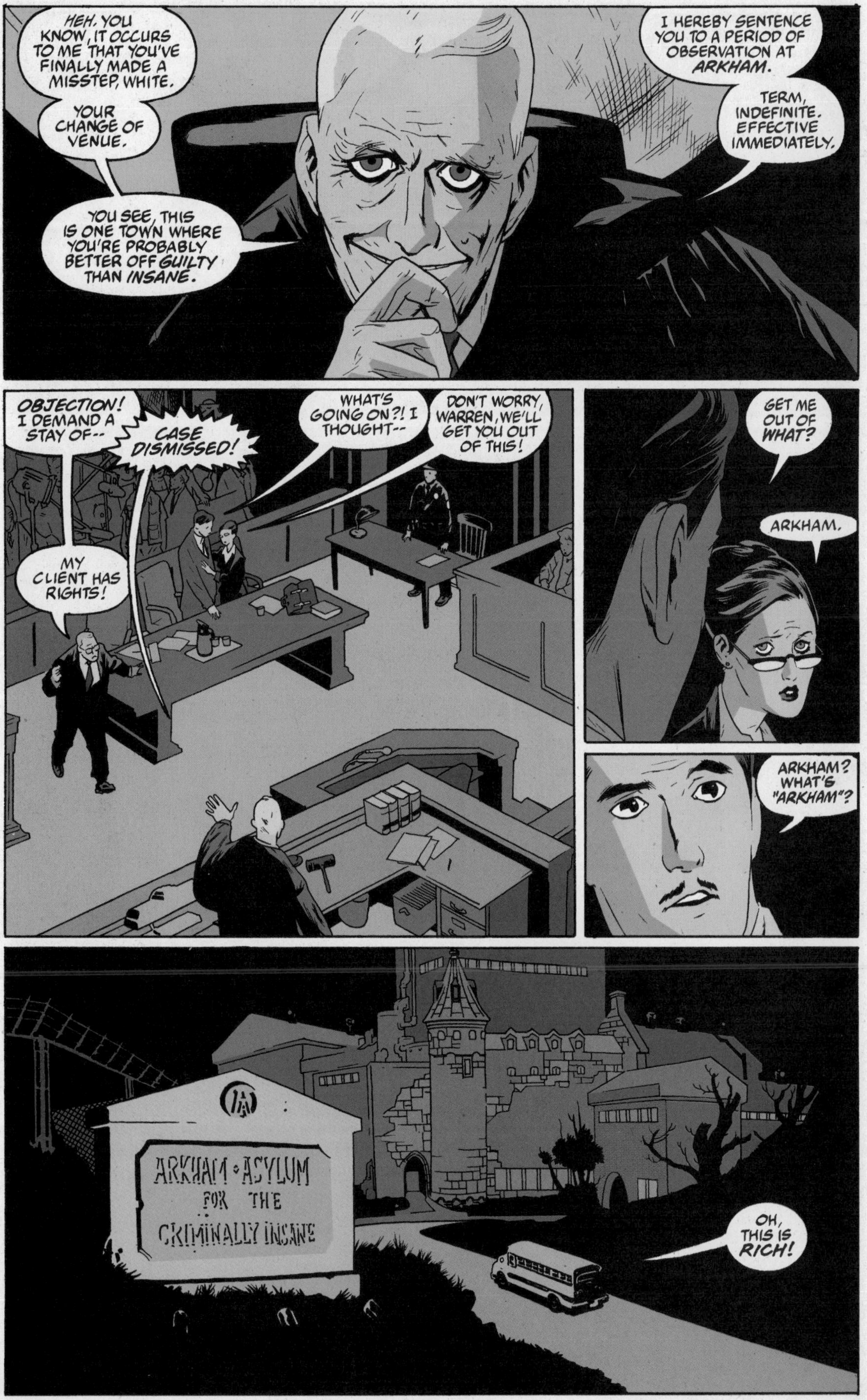
HEH. YOU KNOW, IT OCCURS TO ME THAT YOU'VE FINALLY MADE A MISSTEP, WHITE.
YOUR CHANGE OF VENUE.
YOU SEE, THIS IS ONE TOWN WHERE YOU'RE PROBABLY BETTER OFF GUILTY THAN INSANE.
I HEREBY SENTENCE YOU TO A PERIOD OF OBSERVATION AT ARKHAM.
TERM, INDEFINITE. EFFECTIVE IMMEDIATELY.
OBJECTION! I DEMAND A STAY OF--
CASE DISMISSED!
MY CLIENT HAS RIGHTS!
WHAT'S GOING ON?! I THOUGHT--
DON'T WORRY, WARREN, WE'LL GET YOU OUT OF THIS!
GET ME OUT OF WHAT?
ARKHAM.
ARKHAM? WHAT'S "ARKHAM"?
ARKHAM ASYLUM FOR THE CRIMINALLY INSANE
OH, THIS IS RICH!

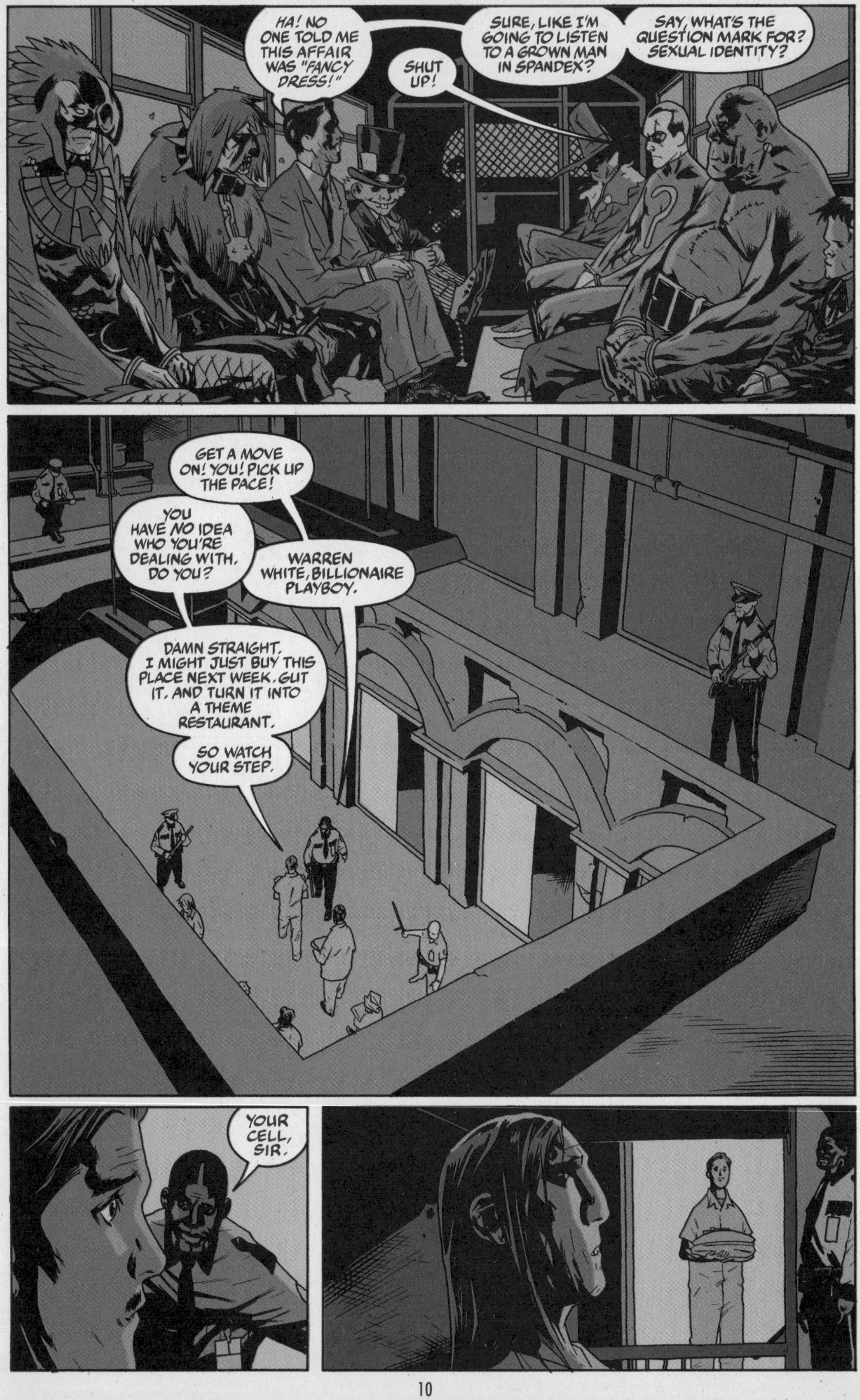
HA! NO ONE TOLD ME THIS AFFAIR WAS "FANCY DRESS!"
SHUT UP!
SURE, LIKE I'M GOING TO LISTEN TO A GROWN MAN IN SPANDEX?
SAY, WHAT'S THE QUESTION MARK FOR? SEXUAL IDENTITY?
GET A MOVE ON! YOU! PICK UP THE PACE!
YOU HAVE NO IDEA WHO YOU'RE DEALING WITH, DO YOU?
WARREN WHITE, BILLIONAIRE PLAYBOY.
DAMN STRAIGHT. I MIGHT JUST BUY THIS PLACE NEXT WEEK. GUT IT. AND TURN IT INTO A THEME RESTAURANT.
SO WATCH YOUR STEP.
YOUR CELL, SIR.

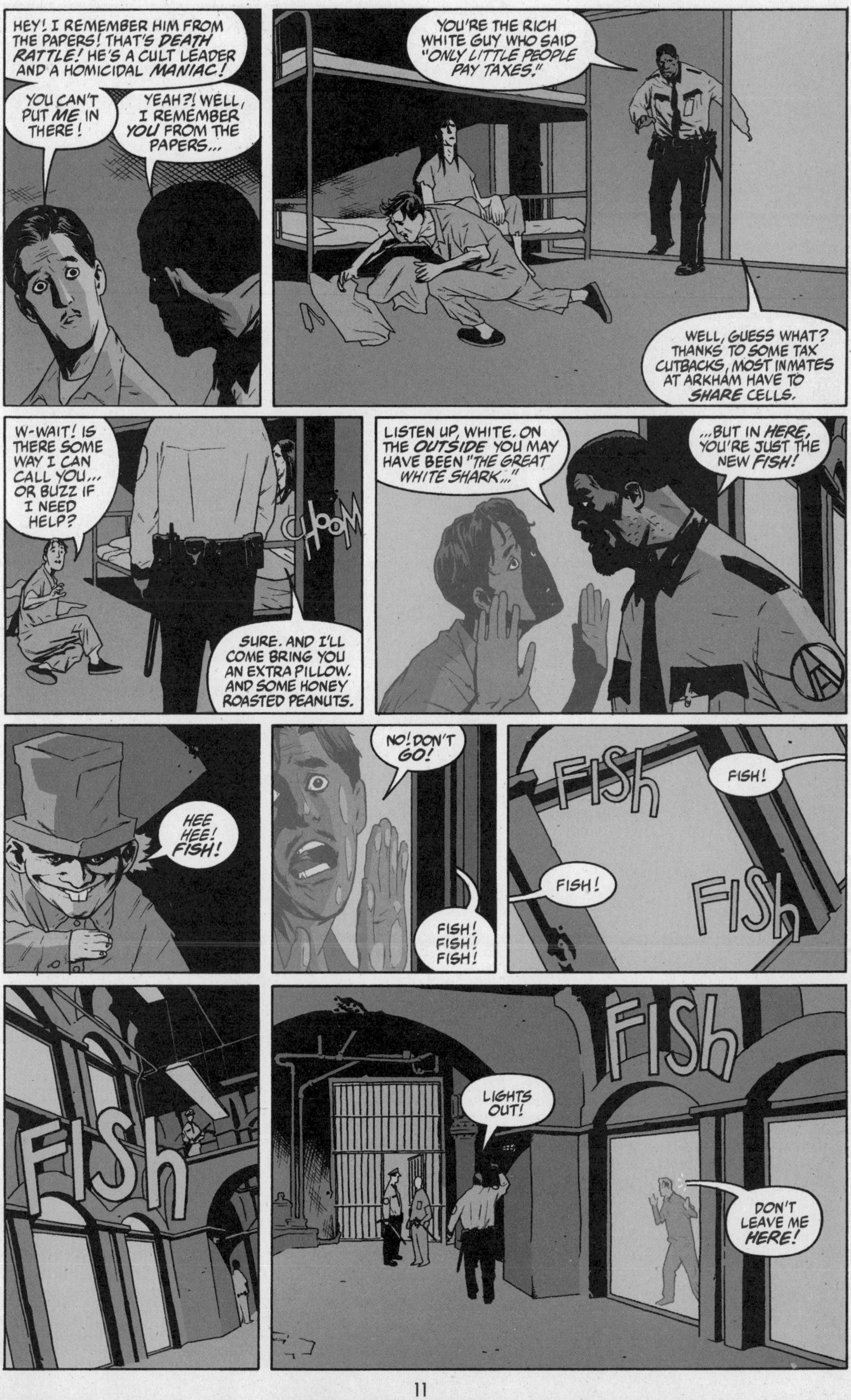
HEY! I REMEMBER HIM FROM THE PAPERS! THAT'S DEATH RATTLE! HE'S A CULT LEADER AND A HOMICIDAL MANIAC!
YOU CAN'T PUT ME IN THERE!
YEAH?! WELL, I REMEMBER YOU FROM THE PAPERS...
YOU'RE THE RICH WHITE GUY WHO SAID "ONLY LITTLE PEOPLE PAY TAXES."
WELL, GUESS WHAT? THANKS TO SOME TAX CUTBACKS, MOST INMATES AT ARKHAM HAVE TO SHARE CELLS.
W-WAIT! IS THERE SOME WAY I CAN CALL YOU... OR BUZZ IF I NEED HELP?
CHOOM
SURE. AND I'LL COME BRING YOU AN EXTRA PILLOW. AND SOME HONEY ROASTED PEANUTS.
LISTEN UP, WHITE. ON THE OUTSIDE YOU MAY HAVE BEEN "THE GREAT WHITE SHARK..."
...BUT IN HERE, YOU'RE JUST THE NEW FISH!
HEE HEE! FISH!
NO! DON'T GO!
FISH! FISH! FISH!
FISH
FISH!
FISH!
FISH
FISH
FISH
LIGHTS OUT!
DON'T LEAVE ME HERE!

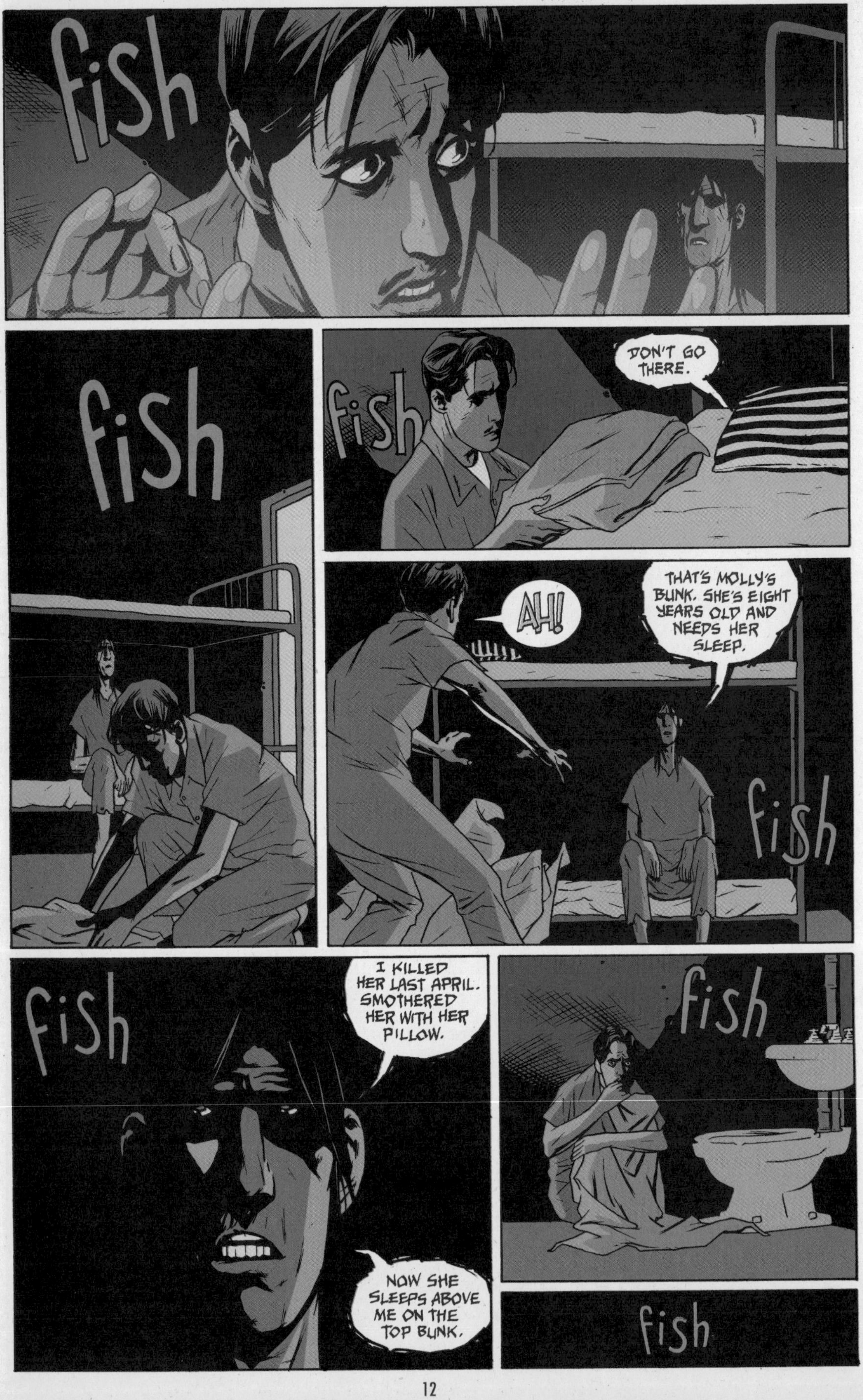
fish
fish
fish
DON'T GO THERE.
AH!
THAT'S MOLLY'S BUNK. SHE'S EIGHT YEARS OLD AND NEEDS HER SLEEP.
fish
fish
I KILLED HER LAST APRIL. SMOTHERED HER WITH HER PILLOW.
NOW SHE SLEEPS ABOVE ME ON THE TOP BUNK.
fish
fish

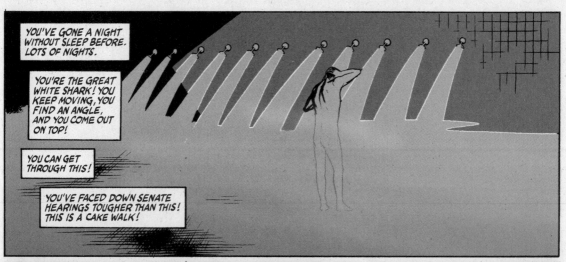

YOU'VE GONE A NIGHT WITHOUT SLEEP BEFORE. LOTS OF NIGHTS.

YOU'RE THE GREAT WHITE SHARK! YOU KEEP MOVING, YOU FIND AN ANGLE, AND YOU COME OUT ON TOP!

YOU CAN GET THROUGH THIS!

YOU'VE FACED DOWN SENATE HEARINGS TOUGHER THAN THIS! THIS IS A CAKE WALK!

YOU'VE GOT MONEY, CONNECTIONS, YOU'LL BE OUT OF HERE IN NO TIME.

IS HE CLEAN?

SILLY BOY, THAT'S WHY I'M HERE.

NO WEAPONS OR CONTRABAND, I CHECKED.

RIGHT DOWN TO MY WHOOPEE CUSHION.

I'LL BE KEEPING AN EYE ON YOU, SO NO FUNNY STUFF...

...JOKER.

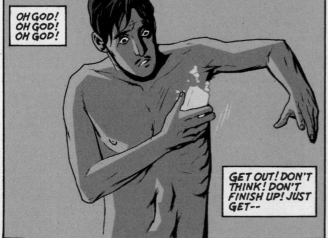

OH GOD! OH GOD! OH GOD!

GET OUT! DON'T THINK! DON'T FINISH UP! JUST GET--

SQUP

WAP!

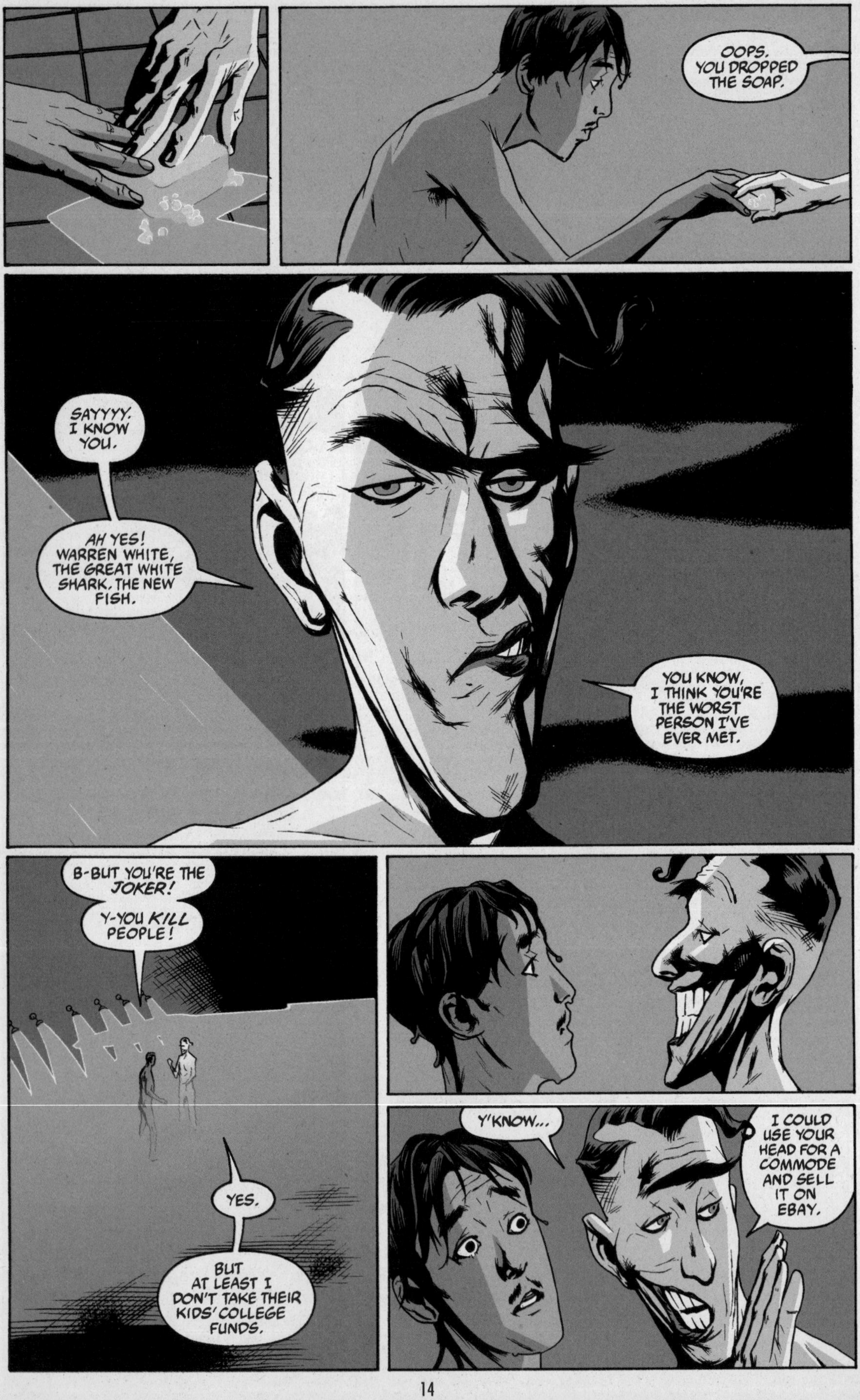
OOPS. YOU DROPPED THE SOAP.
SAYYYY. I KNOW YOU.
AH YES! WARREN WHITE, THE GREAT WHITE SHARK. THE NEW FISH.
YOU KNOW, I THINK YOU'RE THE WORST PERSON I'VE EVER MET.
B-BUT YOU'RE THE JOKER!
Y-YOU KILL PEOPLE!
YES.
BUT AT LEAST I DON'T TAKE THEIR KIDS' COLLEGE FUNDS.
Y'KNOW...
I COULD USE YOUR HEAD FOR A COMMODE AND SELL IT ON EBAY.

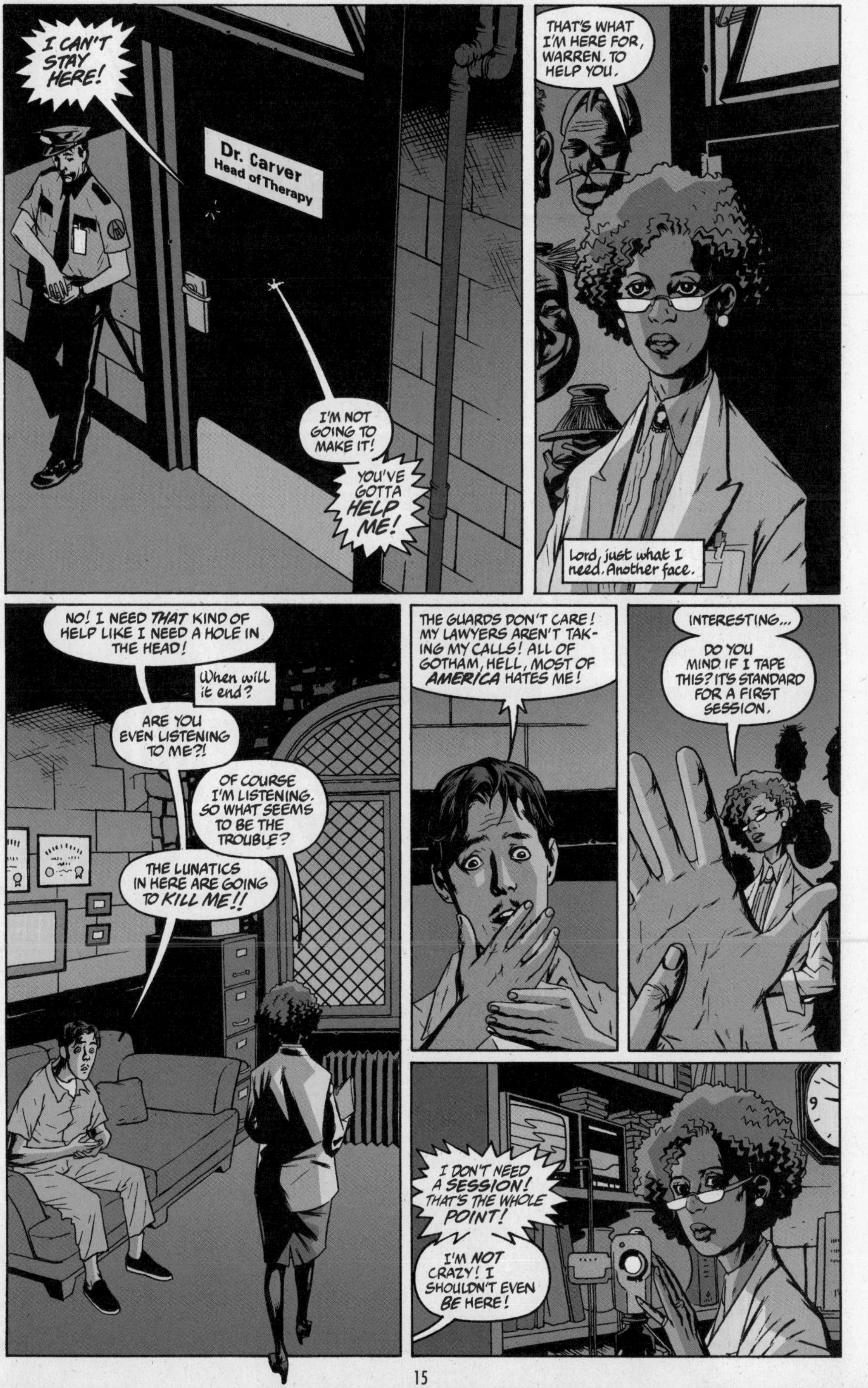
I CAN'T STAY HERE!
Dr. Carver
Head of Therapy
I'M NOT GOING TO MAKE IT!
YOU'VE GOTTA HELP ME!
THAT'S WHAT I'M HERE FOR, WARREN. TO HELP YOU.
Lord, just what I need. Another face.
NO! I NEED THAT KIND OF HELP LIKE I NEED A HOLE IN THE HEAD!
When will it end?
ARE YOU EVEN LISTENING TO ME?!
OF COURSE I'M LISTENING. SO WHAT SEEMS TO BE THE TROUBLE?
THE LUNATICS IN HERE ARE GOING TO KILL ME!!
THE GUARDS DON'T CARE! MY LAWYERS AREN'T TAKING MY CALLS! ALL OF GOTHAM, HELL, MOST OF AMERICA HATES ME!
INTERESTING...
DO YOU MIND IF I TAPE THIS? IT'S STANDARD FOR A FIRST SESSION.
I DON'T NEED A SESSION! THAT'S THE WHOLE POINT!
I'M NOT CRAZY! I SHOULDN'T EVEN BE HERE!

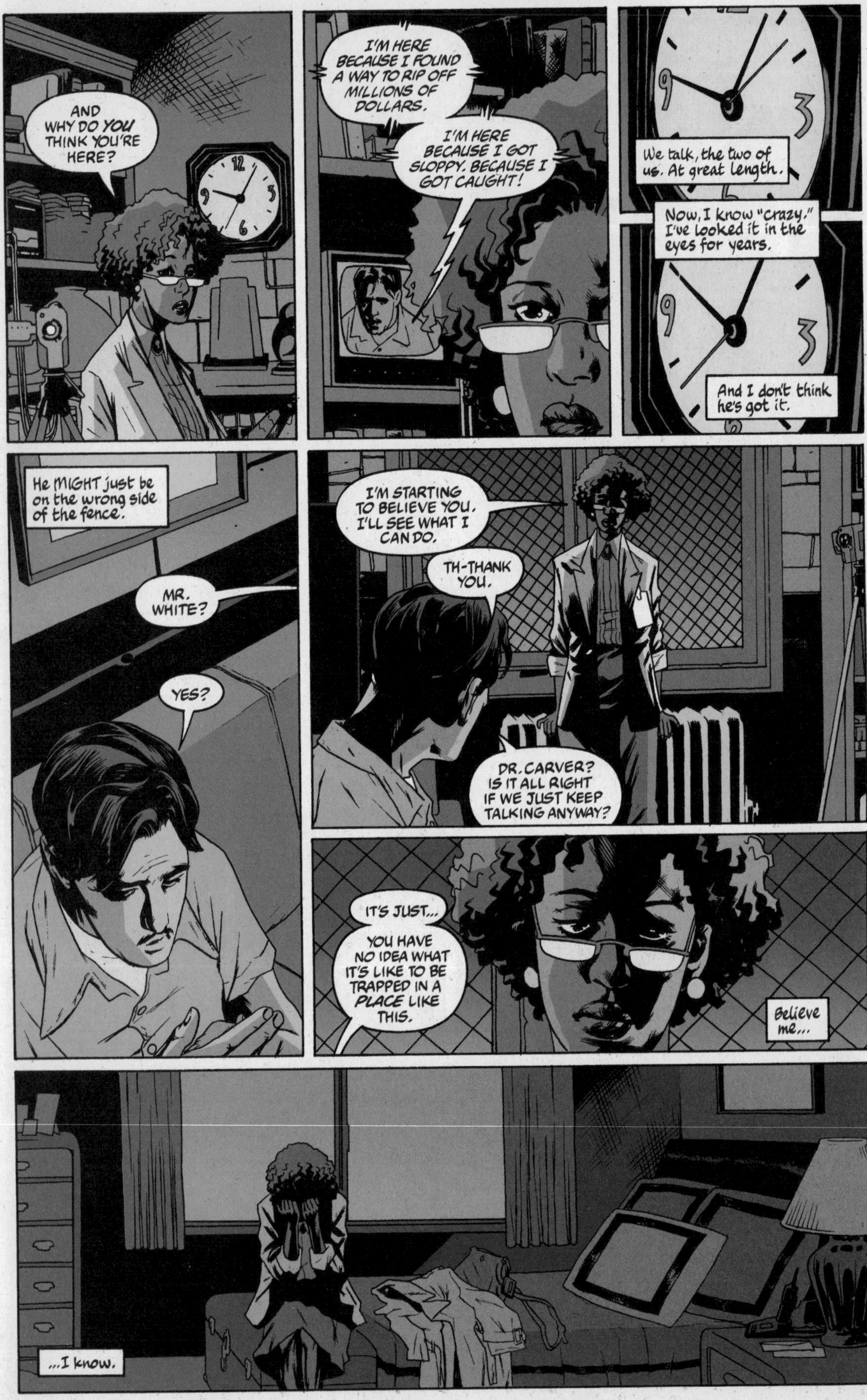
AND WHY DO YOU THINK YOU'RE HERE?
I'M HERE BECAUSE I FOUND A WAY TO RIP OFF MILLIONS OF DOLLARS.
I'M HERE BECAUSE I GOT SLOPPY. BECAUSE I GOT CAUGHT!
We talk, the two of us. At great length.
Now, I know "crazy." I've looked it in the eyes for years.
And I don't think he's got it.
He MIGHT just be on the wrong side of the fence.
MR. WHITE?
YES?
I'M STARTING TO BELIEVE YOU. I'LL SEE WHAT I CAN DO.
TH-THANK YOU.
DR. CARVER? IS IT ALL RIGHT IF WE JUST KEEP TALKING ANYWAY?
IT'S JUST...
YOU HAVE NO IDEA WHAT IT'S LIKE TO BE TRAPPED IN A PLACE LIKE THIS.
Believe me...
...I know.

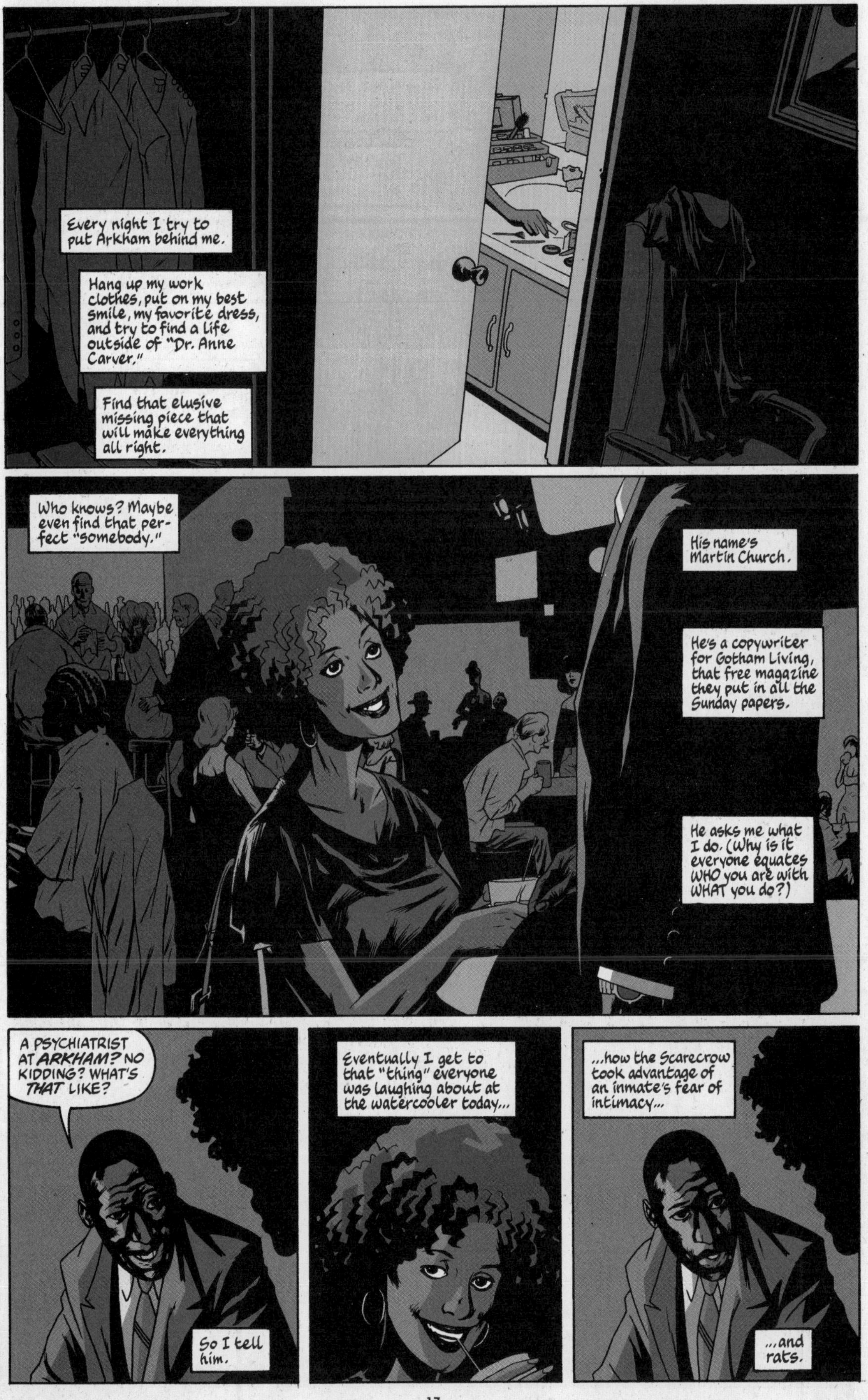
Every night I try to put Arkham behind me.
Hang up my work clothes, put on my best smile, my favorite dress, and try to find a life outside of "Dr. Anne Carver."
Find that elusive missing piece that will make everything all right.
Who knows? Maybe even find that perfect "somebody."
His name's Martin Church.
He's a copywriter for Gotham Living, that free magazine they put in all the Sunday papers.
He asks me what I do. (Why is it everyone equates WHO you are with WHAT you do?)
A PSYCHIATRIST AT ARKHAM? NO KIDDING? WHAT'S THAT LIKE?
So I tell him.
Eventually I get to that "thing" everyone was laughing about at the watercooler today...
...how the Scarecrow took advantage of an inmate's fear of intimacy...
...and rats.

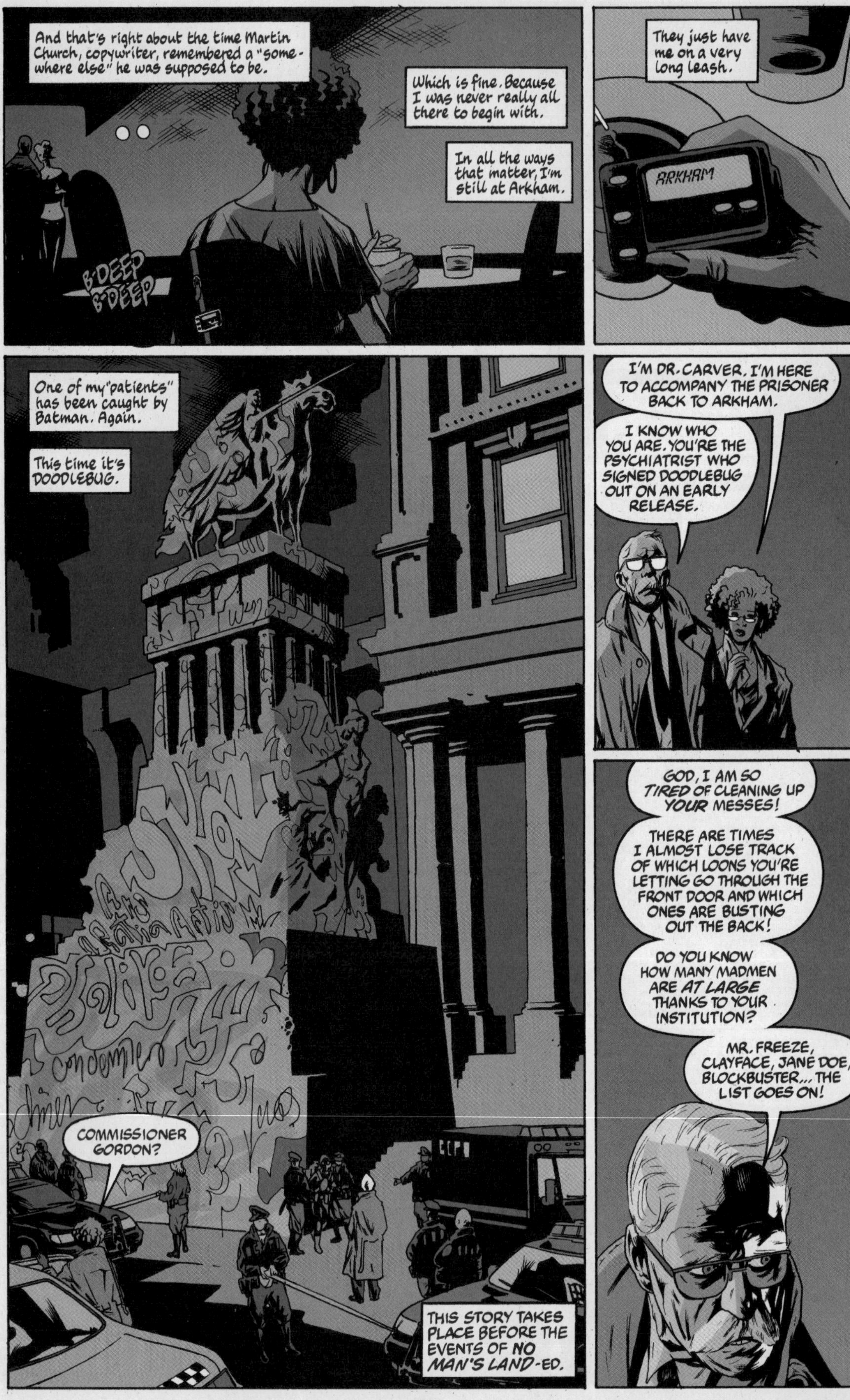
And that's right about the time Martin Church, copywriter, remembered a "somewhere else" he was supposed to be.
Which is fine. Because I was never really all there to begin with.
In all the ways that matter, I'm still at Arkham.
B-DEEP B-DEEP
They just have me on a very long leash.
ARKHAM
One of my "patients" has been caught by Batman. Again.
This time it's DOODLEBUG.
COMMISSIONER GORDON?
THIS STORY TAKES PLACE BEFORE THE EVENTS OF NO MAN'S LAND -ED.
I'M DR. CARVER. I'M HERE TO ACCOMPANY THE PRISONER BACK TO ARKHAM.
I KNOW WHO YOU ARE. YOU'RE THE PSYCHIATRIST WHO SIGNED DOODLEBUG OUT ON AN EARLY RELEASE.
GOD, I AM SO TIRED OF CLEANING UP YOUR MESSES!
THERE ARE TIMES I ALMOST LOSE TRACK OF WHICH LOONS YOU'RE LETTING GO THROUGH THE FRONT DOOR AND WHICH ONES ARE BUSTING OUT THE BACK!
DO YOU KNOW HOW MANY MADMEN ARE AT LARGE THANKS TO YOUR INSTITUTION?
MR. FREEZE, CLAYFACE, JANE DOE, BLOCKBUSTER... THE LIST GOES ON!

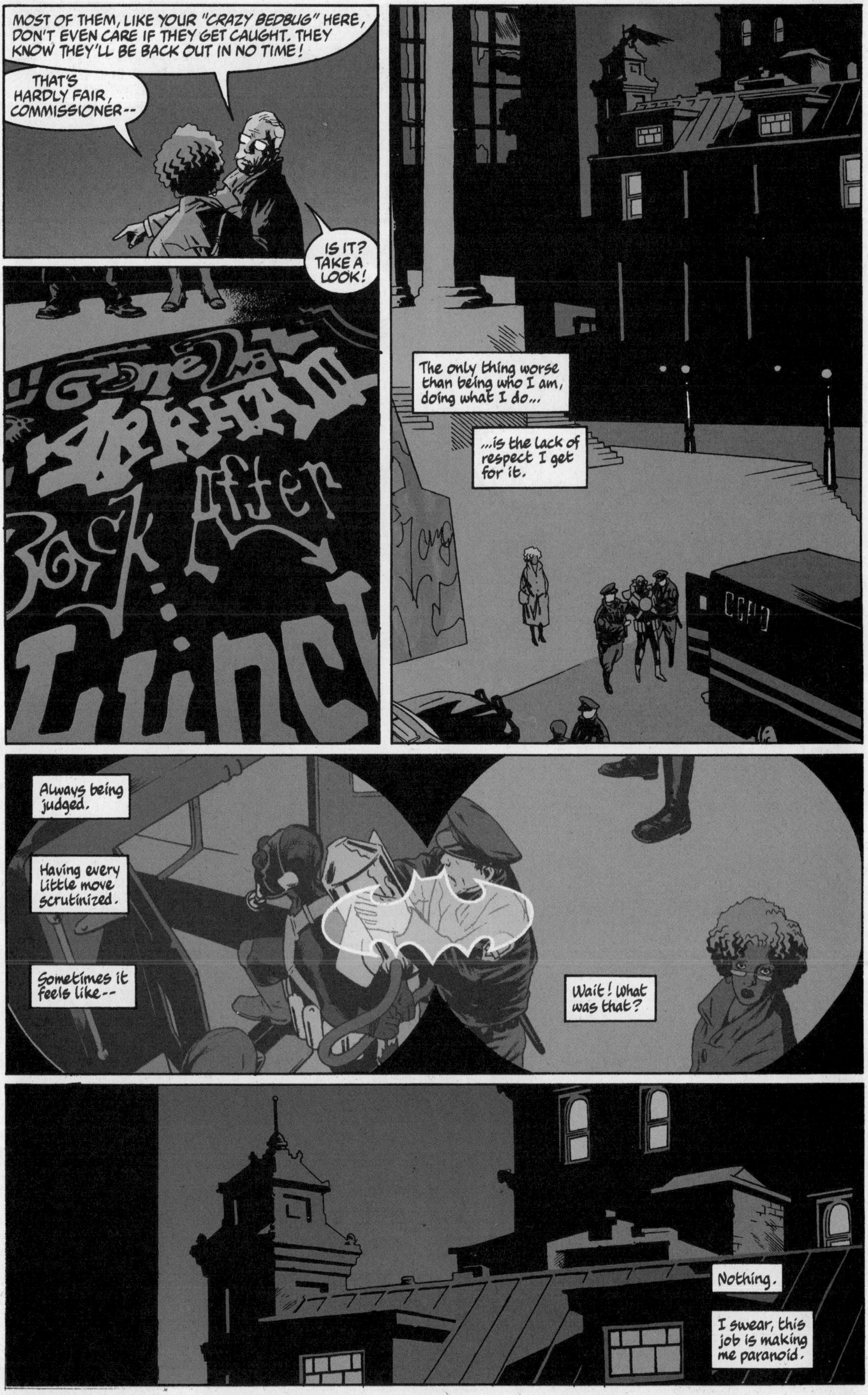

MOST OF THEM, LIKE YOUR "CRAZY BEDBUG" HERE, DON'T EVEN CARE IF THEY GET CAUGHT. THEY KNOW THEY'LL BE BACK OUT IN NO TIME!
THAT'S HARDLY FAIR, COMMISSIONER--
IS IT? TAKE A LOOK!
The only thing worse than being who I am, doing what I do...
...is the lack of respect I get for it.
Always being judged.
Having every little move scrutinized.
Sometimes it feels like--
Wait! What was that?
Nothing.
I swear, this job is making me paranoid.

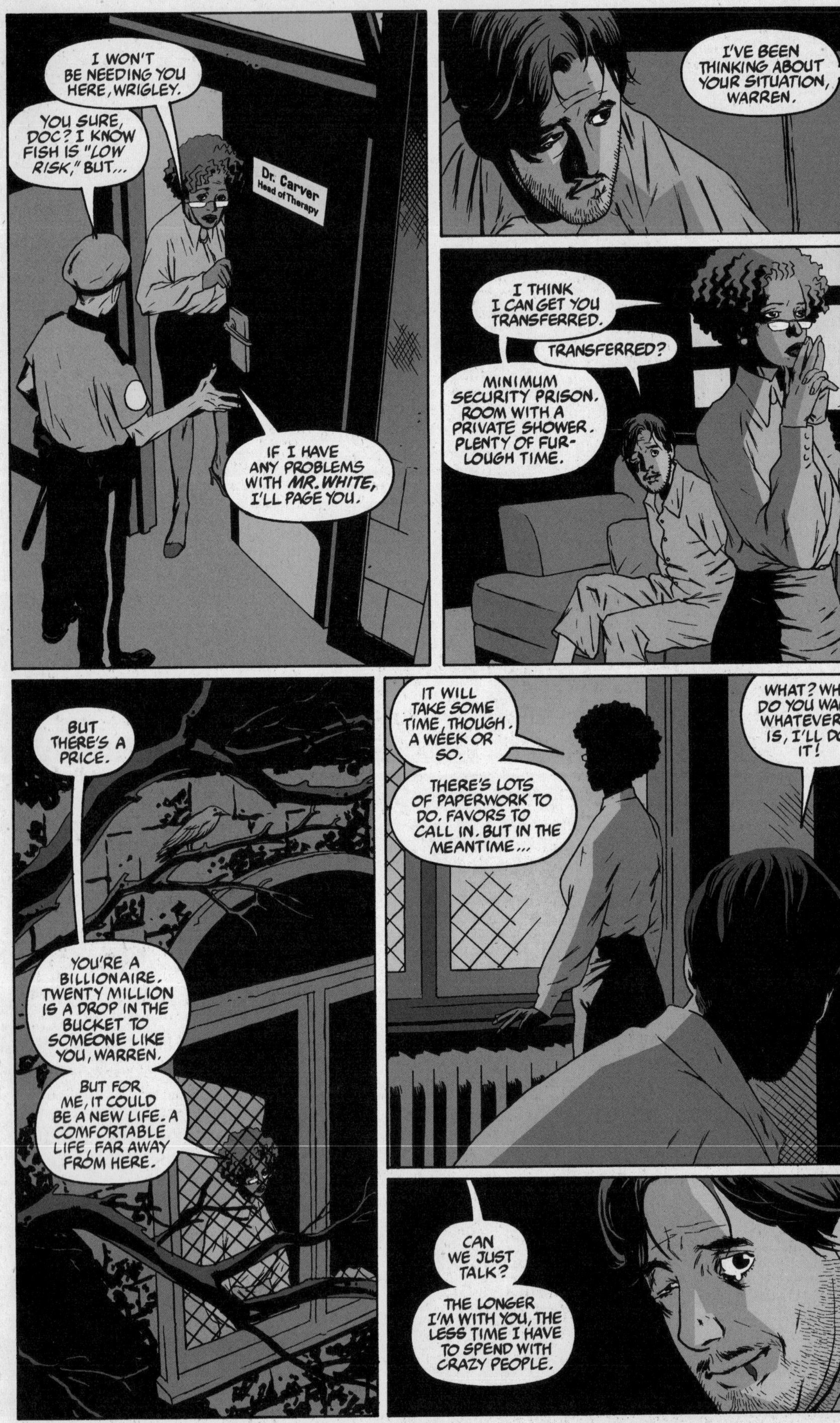
I WON'T BE NEEDING YOU HERE, WRIGLEY.
YOU SURE, DOC? I KNOW FISH IS "LOW RISK," BUT...
Dr. Carver Head of Therapy
IF I HAVE ANY PROBLEMS WITH MR. WHITE, I'LL PAGE YOU.
I'VE BEEN THINKING ABOUT YOUR SITUATION, WARREN.
I THINK I CAN GET YOU TRANSFERRED.
TRANSFERRED?
MINIMUM SECURITY PRISON. ROOM WITH A PRIVATE SHOWER. PLENTY OF FURLOUGH TIME.
BUT THERE'S A PRICE.
YOU'RE A BILLIONAIRE. TWENTY MILLION IS A DROP IN THE BUCKET TO SOMEONE LIKE YOU, WARREN.
BUT FOR ME, IT COULD BE A NEW LIFE. A COMFORTABLE LIFE, FAR AWAY FROM HERE.
IT WILL TAKE SOME TIME, THOUGH. A WEEK OR SO.
THERE'S LOTS OF PAPERWORK TO DO. FAVORS TO CALL IN. BUT IN THE MEANTIME...
WHAT? WHAT DO YOU WANT? WHATEVER IT IS, I'LL DO IT!
CAN WE JUST TALK?
THE LONGER I'M WITH YOU, THE LESS TIME I HAVE TO SPEND WITH CRAZY PEOPLE.

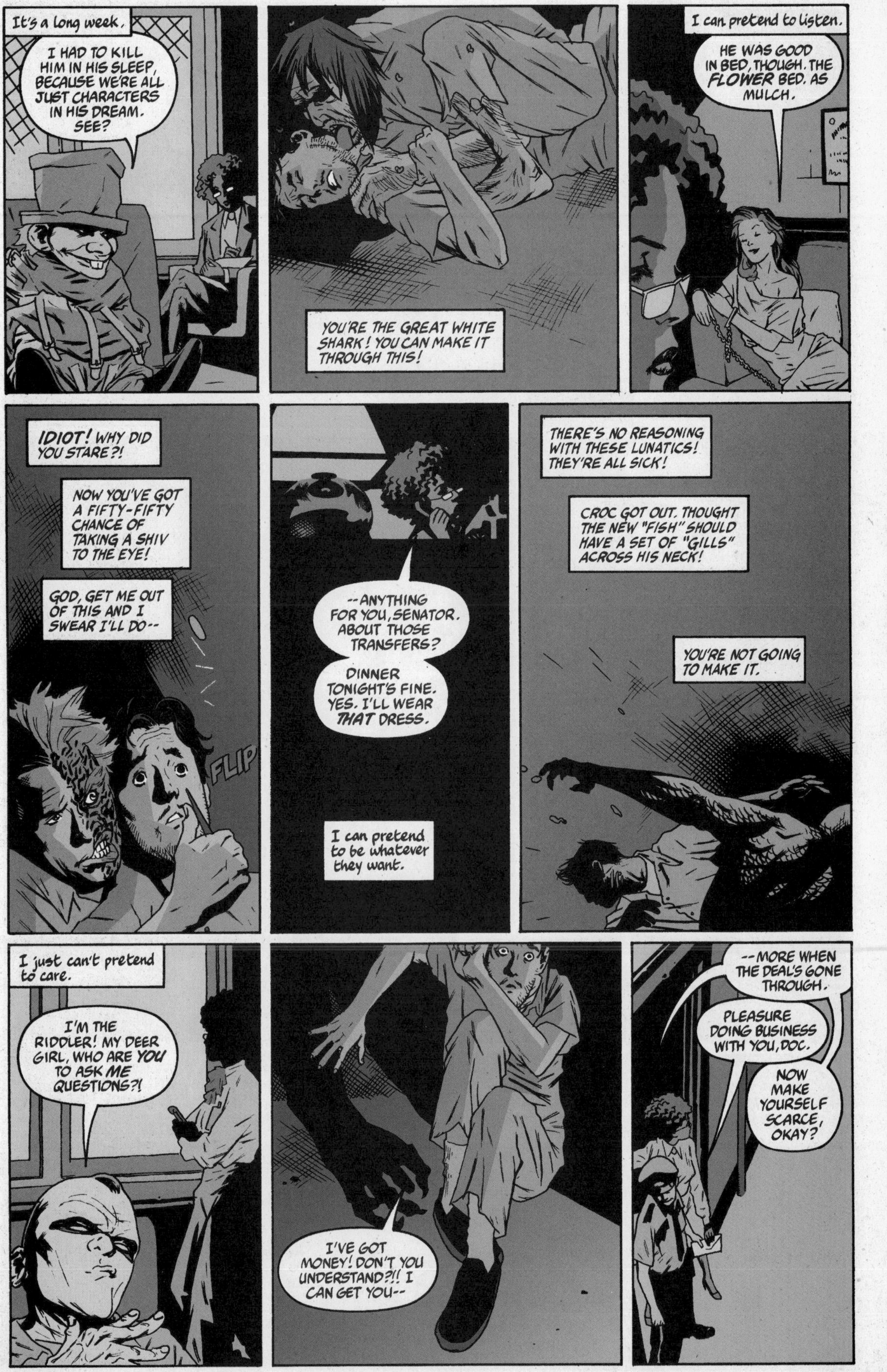
It's a long week.
I HAD TO KILL HIM IN HIS SLEEP, BECAUSE WE'RE ALL JUST CHARACTERS IN HIS DREAM. SEE?
YOU'RE THE GREAT WHITE SHARK! YOU CAN MAKE IT THROUGH THIS!
I can pretend to listen.
HE WAS GOOD IN BED, THOUGH. THE FLOWER BED. AS MULCH.
IDIOT! WHY DID YOU STARE?!
NOW YOU'VE GOT A FIFTY-FIFTY CHANCE OF TAKING A SHIV TO THE EYE!
GOD, GET ME OUT OF THIS AND I SWEAR I'LL DO--
FLIP
--ANYTHING FOR YOU, SENATOR. ABOUT THOSE TRANSFERS?
DINNER TONIGHT'S FINE. YES. I'LL WEAR THAT DRESS.
I can pretend to be whatever they want.
THERE'S NO REASONING WITH THESE LUNATICS! THEY'RE ALL SICK!
CROC GOT OUT. THOUGHT THE NEW "FISH" SHOULD HAVE A SET OF "GILLS" ACROSS HIS NECK!
YOU'RE NOT GOING TO MAKE IT.
I just can't pretend to care.
I'M THE RIDDLER! MY DEER GIRL, WHO ARE YOU TO ASK ME QUESTIONS?!
I'VE GOT MONEY! DON'T YOU UNDERSTAND?!! I CAN GET YOU--
--MORE WHEN THE DEAL'S GONE THROUGH.
PLEASURE DOING BUSINESS WITH YOU, DOC.
NOW MAKE YOURSELF SCARCE, OKAY?

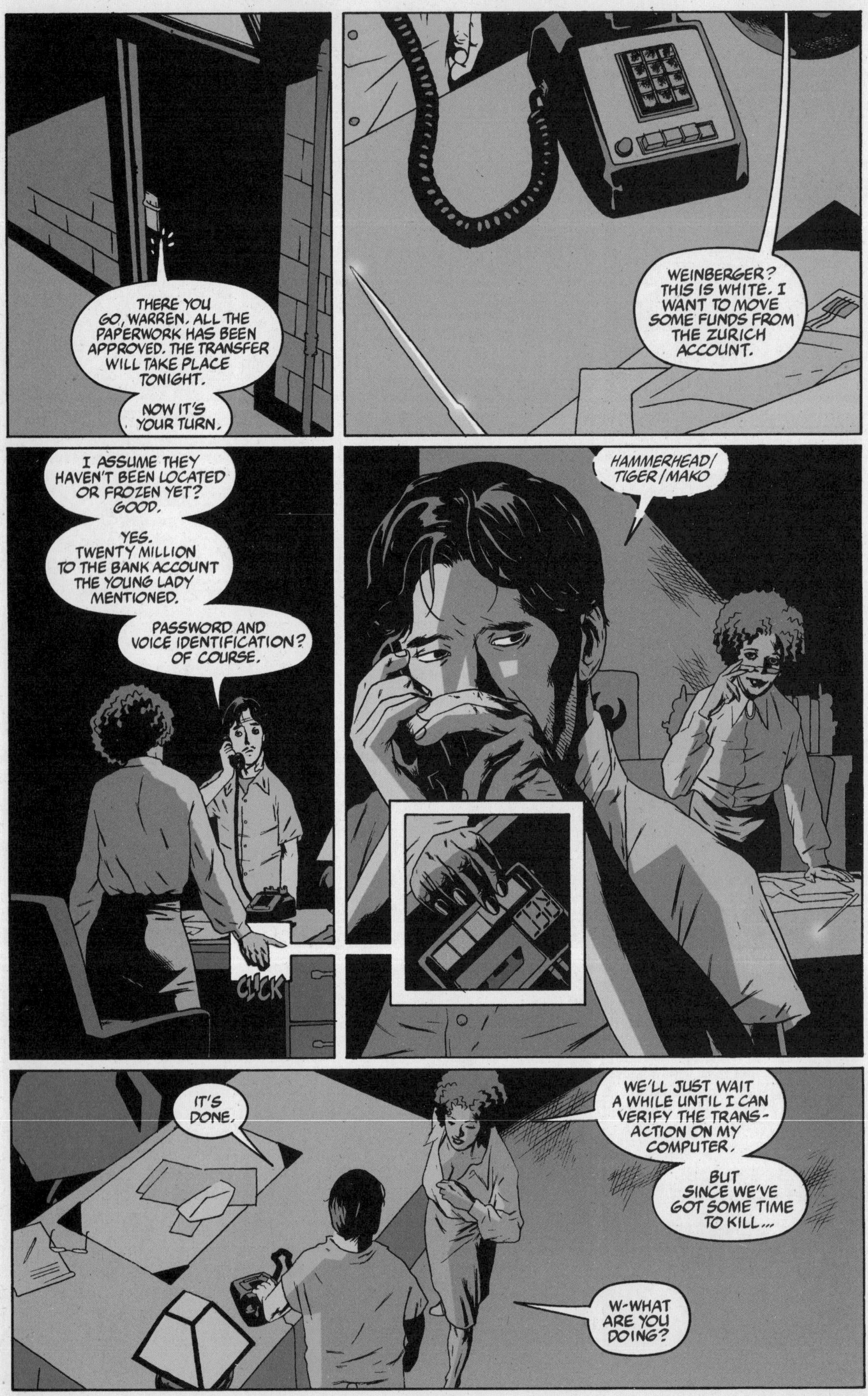
THERE YOU GO, WARREN. ALL THE PAPERWORK HAS BEEN APPROVED. THE TRANSFER WILL TAKE PLACE TONIGHT.
NOW IT'S YOUR TURN.
WEINBERGER? THIS IS WHITE. I WANT TO MOVE SOME FUNDS FROM THE ZURICH ACCOUNT.
I ASSUME THEY HAVEN'T BEEN LOCATED OR FROZEN YET? GOOD.
YES. TWENTY MILLION TO THE BANK ACCOUNT THE YOUNG LADY MENTIONED.
PASSWORD AND VOICE IDENTIFICATION? OF COURSE.
CLICK
HAMMERHEAD/ TIGER/ MAKO
IT'S DONE.
WE'LL JUST WAIT A WHILE UNTIL I CAN VERIFY THE TRANS-ACTION ON MY COMPUTER.
BUT SINCE WE'VE GOT SOME TIME TO KILL...
W-WHAT ARE YOU DOING?

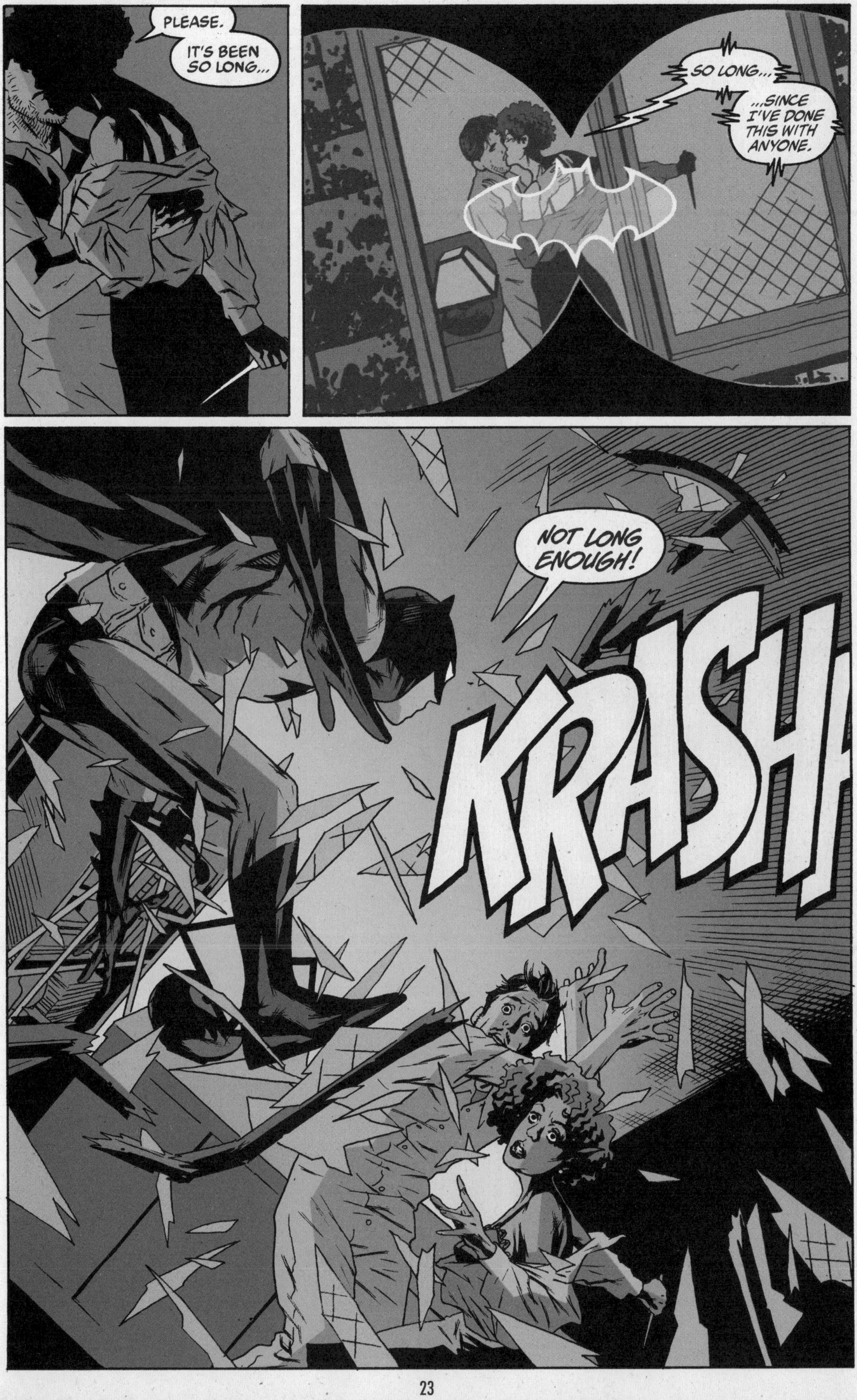
PLEASE.
IT'S BEEN SO LONG...
SO LONG...
...SINCE I'VE DONE THIS WITH ANYONE.
NOT LONG ENOUGH!
KRASH

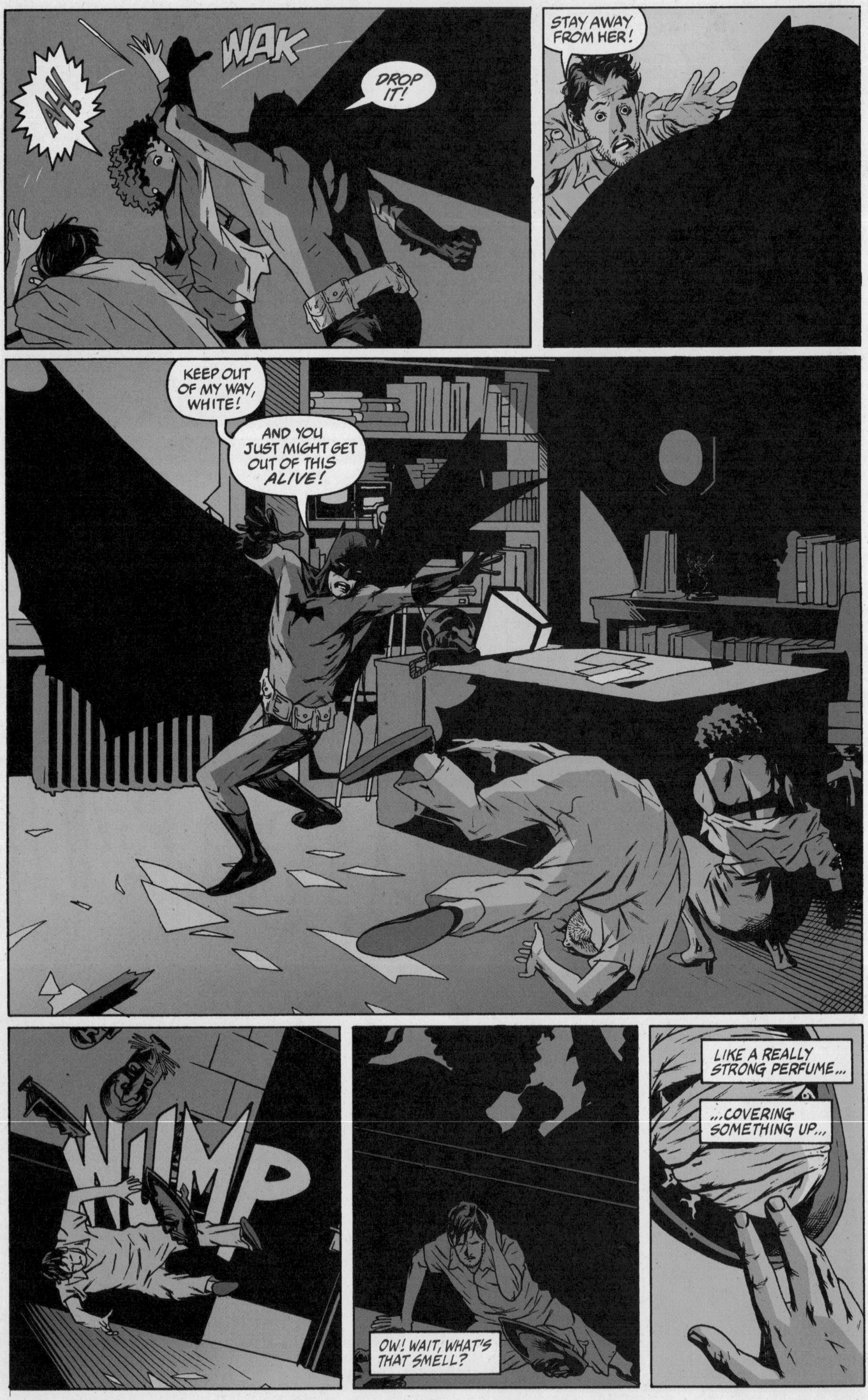
AH!
WAK
DROP IT!
STAY AWAY FROM HER!
KEEP OUT OF MY WAY, WHITE!
AND YOU JUST MIGHT GET OUT OF THIS ALIVE!
WUMP
OW! WAIT, WHAT'S THAT SMELL?
LIKE A REALLY STRONG PERFUME...
...COVERING SOMETHING UP...

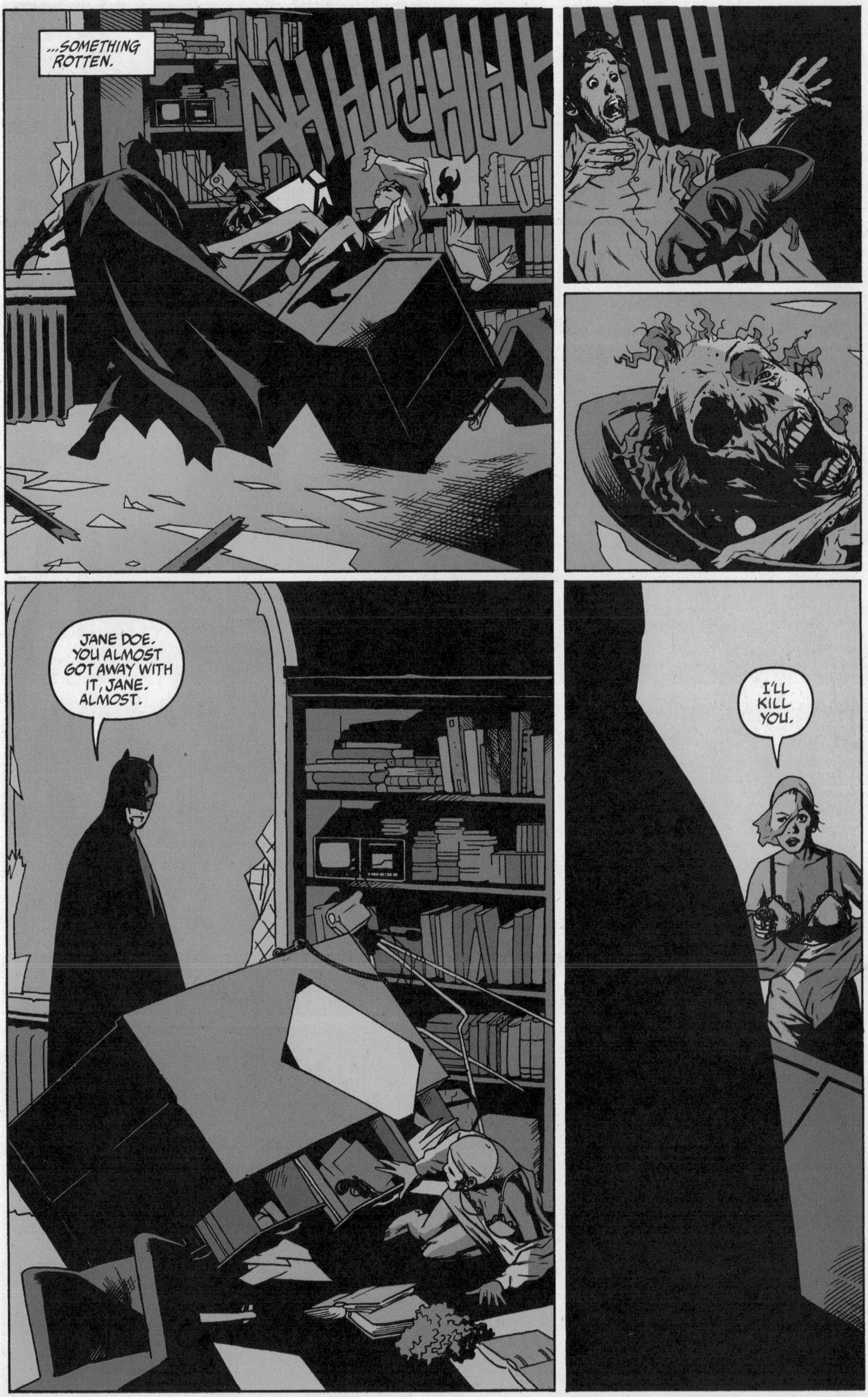
...SOMETHING ROTTEN.
AHHHHHHHHHHHHH
JANE DOE. YOU ALMOST GOT AWAY WITH IT, JANE. ALMOST.
I'LL KILL YOU.

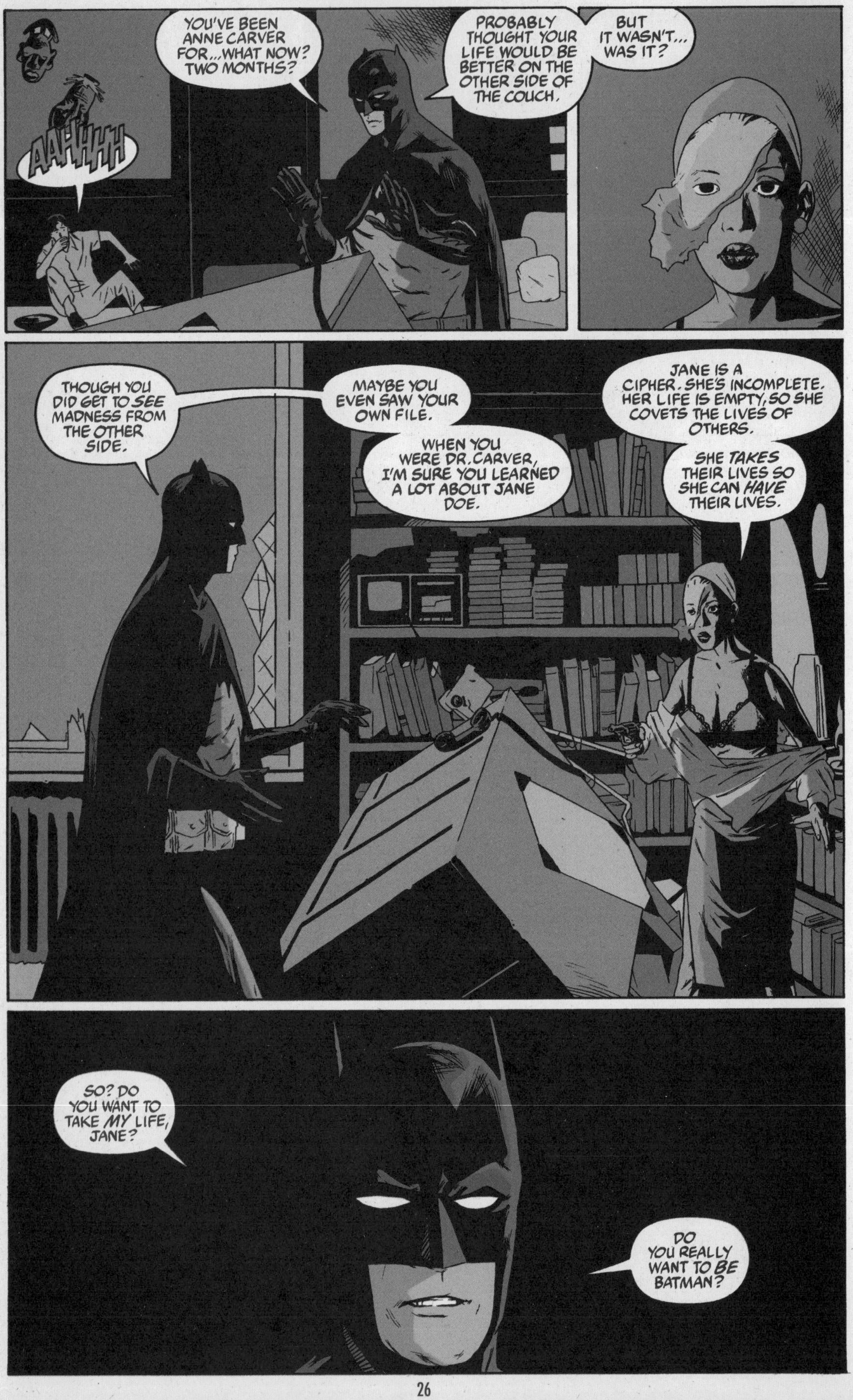
AAHHHH
YOU'VE BEEN ANNE CARVER FOR... WHAT NOW? TWO MONTHS?
PROBABLY THOUGHT YOUR LIFE WOULD BE BETTER ON THE OTHER SIDE OF THE COUCH.
BUT IT WASN'T... WAS IT?
THOUGH YOU DID GET TO SEE MADNESS FROM THE OTHER SIDE.
MAYBE YOU EVEN SAW YOUR OWN FILE.
WHEN YOU WERE DR. CARVER, I'M SURE YOU LEARNED A LOT ABOUT JANE DOE.
JANE IS A CIPHER. SHE'S INCOMPLETE. HER LIFE IS EMPTY, SO SHE COVETS THE LIVES OF OTHERS.
SHE TAKES THEIR LIVES SO SHE CAN HAVE THEIR LIVES.
SO? DO YOU WANT TO TAKE MY LIFE, JANE?
DO YOU REALLY WANT TO BE BATMAN?

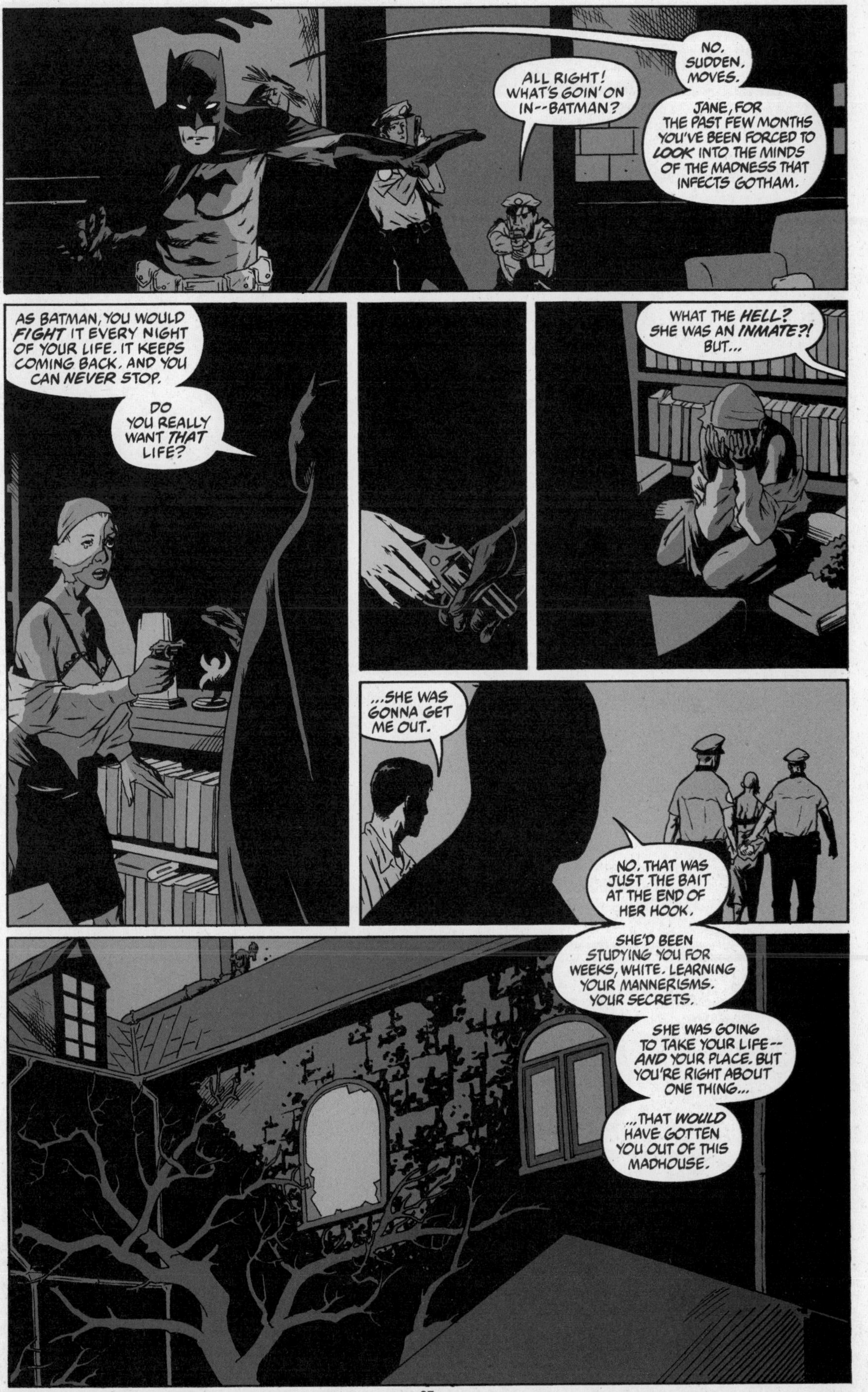
ALL RIGHT! WHAT'S GOIN' ON IN--BATMAN?
NO, SUDDEN, MOVES.
JANE, FOR THE PAST FEW MONTHS YOU'VE BEEN FORCED TO LOOK INTO THE MINDS OF THE MADNESS THAT INFECTS GOTHAM.
AS BATMAN, YOU WOULD FIGHT IT EVERY NIGHT OF YOUR LIFE. IT KEEPS COMING BACK. AND YOU CAN NEVER STOP.
DO YOU REALLY WANT THAT LIFE?
WHAT THE HELL? SHE WAS AN INMATE?! BUT...
...SHE WAS GONNA GET ME OUT.
NO. THAT WAS JUST THE BAIT AT THE END OF HER HOOK.
SHE'D BEEN STUDYING YOU FOR WEEKS, WHITE. LEARNING YOUR MANNERISMS. YOUR SECRETS.
SHE WAS GOING TO TAKE YOUR LIFE-- AND YOUR PLACE. BUT YOU'RE RIGHT ABOUT ONE THING...
...THAT WOULD HAVE GOTTEN YOU OUT OF THIS MADHOUSE.

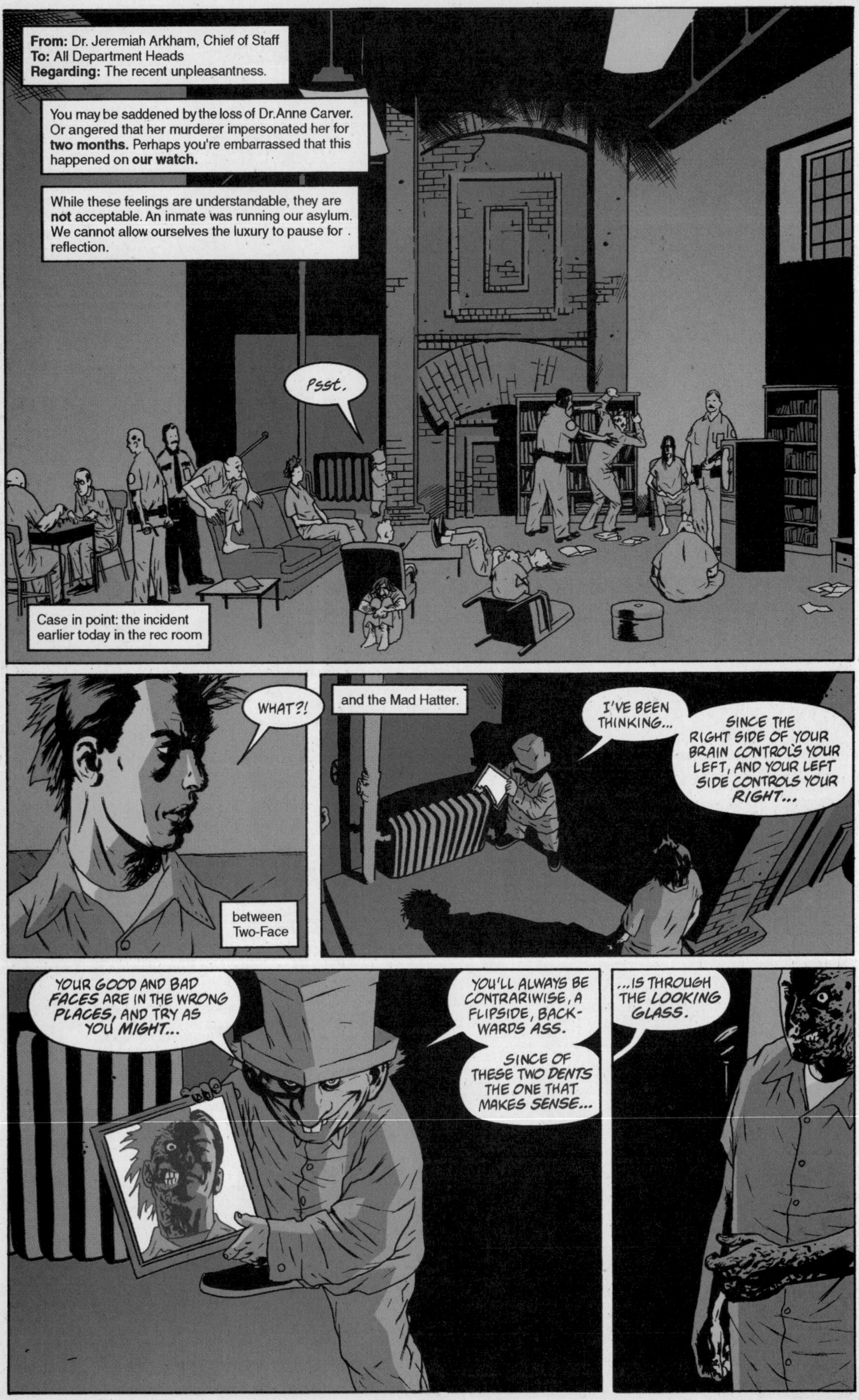
From: Dr. Jeremiah Arkham, Chief of Staff
To: All Department Heads
Regarding: The recent unpleasantness.
You may be saddened by the loss of Dr. Anne Carver. Or angered that her murderer impersonated her for two months. Perhaps you're embarrassed that this happened on our watch.
While these feelings are understandable, they are not acceptable. An inmate was running our asylum. We cannot allow ourselves the luxury to pause for reflection.
Psst.
Case in point: the incident earlier today in the rec room
WHAT?!
between Two-Face
and the Mad Hatter.
I'VE BEEN THINKING...
SINCE THE RIGHT SIDE OF YOUR BRAIN CONTROLS YOUR LEFT, AND YOUR LEFT SIDE CONTROLS YOUR RIGHT...
YOUR GOOD AND BAD FACES ARE IN THE WRONG PLACES, AND TRY AS YOU MIGHT...
YOU'LL ALWAYS BE CONTRARIWISE, A FLIPSIDE, BACKWARDS ASS.
SINCE OF THESE TWO DENTS THE ONE THAT MAKES SENSE...
...IS THROUGH THE LOOKING GLASS.

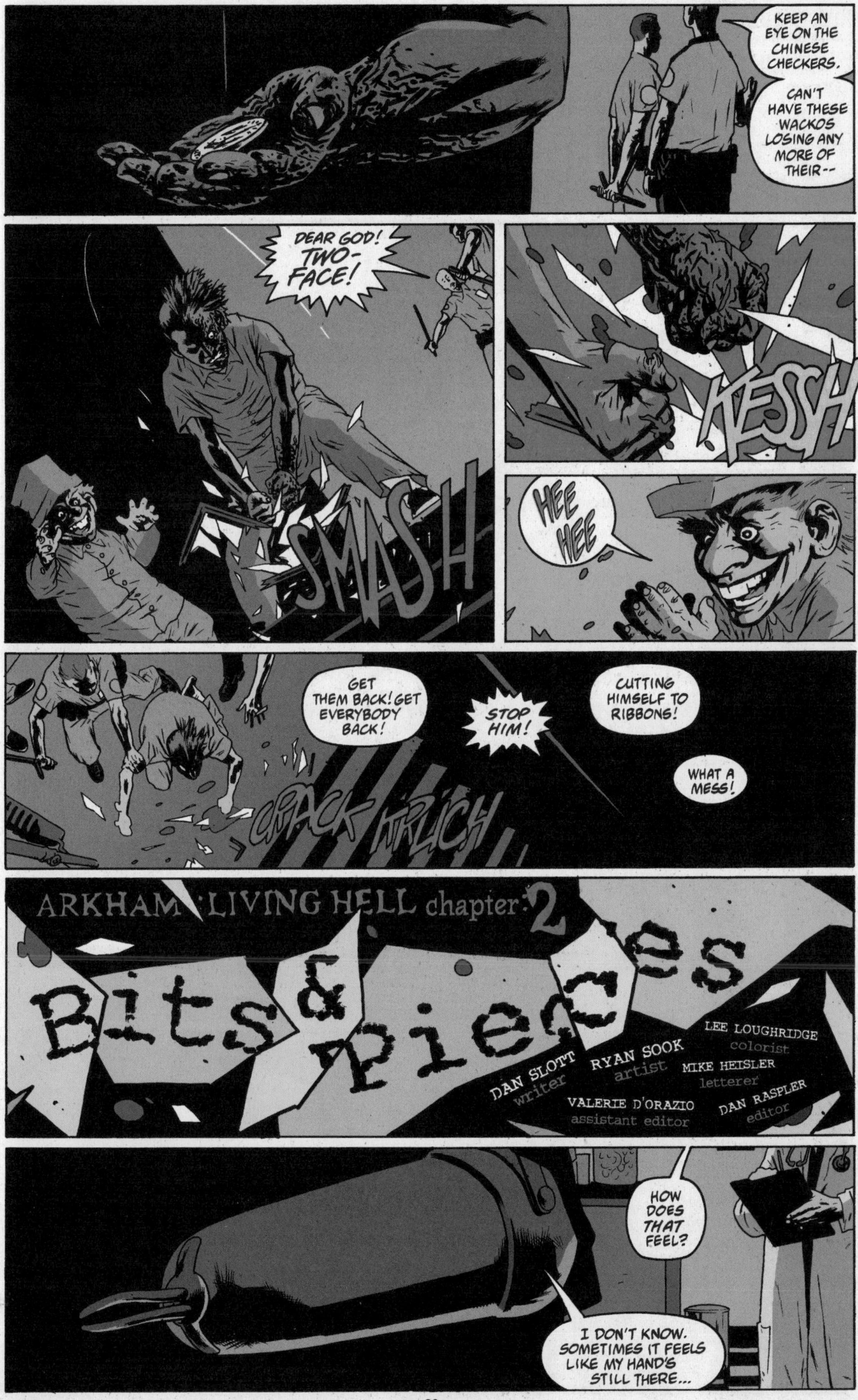
KEEP AN EYE ON THE CHINESE CHECKERS.
CAN'T HAVE THESE WACKOS LOSING ANY MORE OF THEIR--
DEAR GOD! TWO-FACE!
SMASH
KESSH
HEE HEE
GET THEM BACK! GET EVERYBODY BACK!
STOP HIM!
CUTTING HIMSELF TO RIBBONS!
WHAT A MESS!
CRACK KRUCH
ARKHAM: LIVING HELL chapter: 2
Bits & pieces
DAN SLOTT writer
RYAN SOOK artist
LEE LOUGHRIDGE colorist
MIKE HEISLER letterer
VALERIE D'ORAZIO assistant editor
DAN RASPLER editor
HOW DOES THAT FEEL?
I DON'T KNOW. SOMETIMES IT FEELS LIKE MY HAND'S STILL THERE...

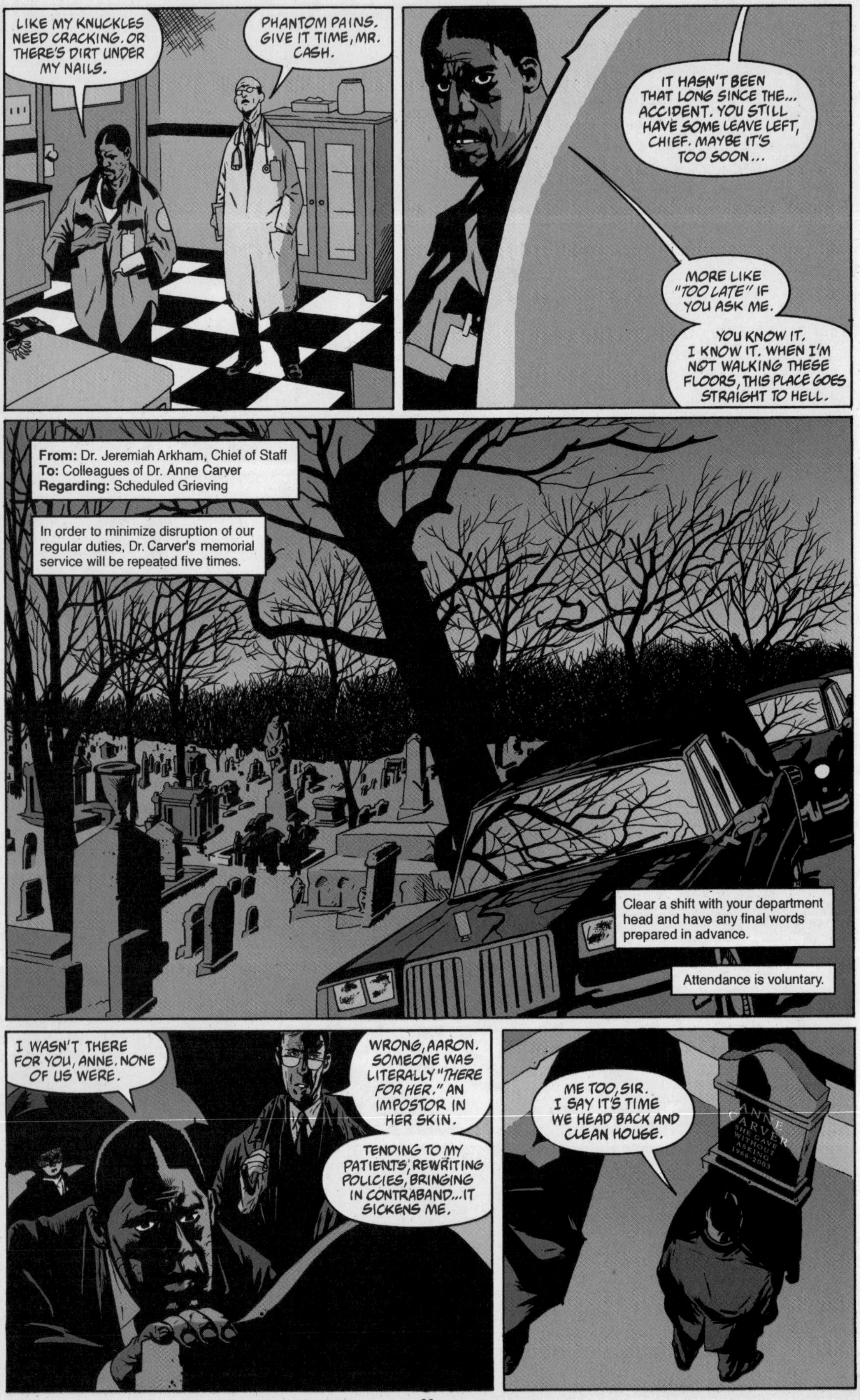
LIKE MY KNUCKLES NEED CRACKING. OR THERE'S DIRT UNDER MY NAILS.
PHANTOM PAINS. GIVE IT TIME, MR. CASH.
IT HASN'T BEEN THAT LONG SINCE THE... ACCIDENT. YOU STILL HAVE SOME LEAVE LEFT, CHIEF. MAYBE IT'S TOO SOON...
MORE LIKE "TOO LATE" IF YOU ASK ME.
YOU KNOW IT. I KNOW IT. WHEN I'M NOT WALKING THESE FLOORS, THIS PLACE GOES STRAIGHT TO HELL.
From: Dr. Jeremiah Arkham, Chief of Staff
To: Colleagues of Dr. Anne Carver
Regarding: Scheduled Grieving
In order to minimize disruption of our regular duties, Dr. Carver's memorial service will be repeated five times.
Clear a shift with your department head and have any final words prepared in advance.
Attendance is voluntary.
I WASN'T THERE FOR YOU, ANNE. NONE OF US WERE.
WRONG, AARON. SOMEONE WAS LITERALLY "THERE FOR HER." AN IMPOSTOR IN HER SKIN.
TENDING TO MY PATIENTS, REWRITING POLICIES, BRINGING IN CONTRABAND... IT SICKENS ME.
ME TOO, SIR. I SAY IT'S TIME WE HEAD BACK AND CLEAN HOUSE.
ANNE CARVER
SHE GAVE WITHOUT ASKING
1966-2003

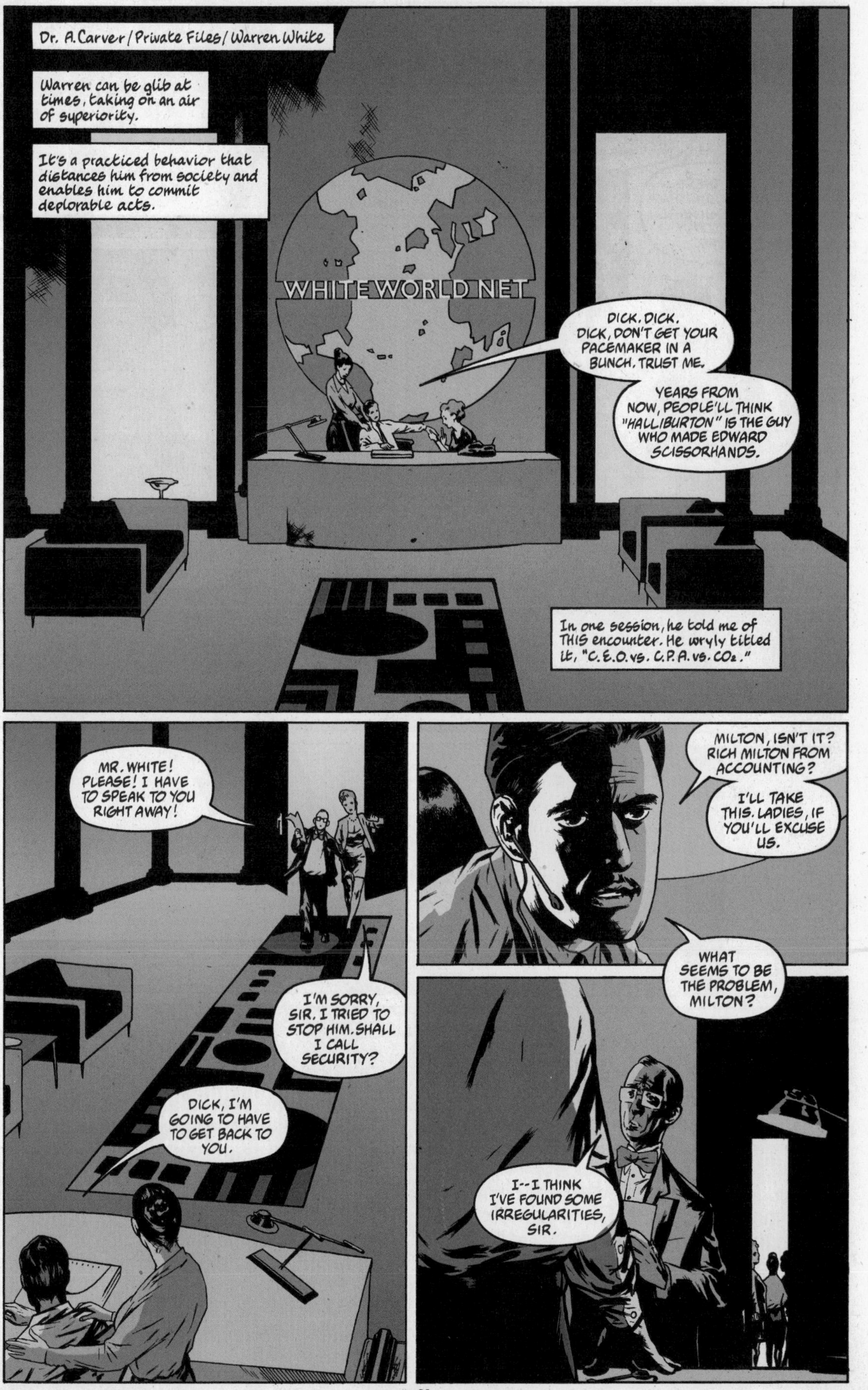
Dr. A.Carver / Private Files / Warren White
Warren can be glib at times, taking on an air of superiority.
It's a practiced behavior that distances him from society and enables him to commit deplorable acts.
WHITE WORLD NET
DICK. DICK. DICK, DON'T GET YOUR PACEMAKER IN A BUNCH. TRUST ME.
YEARS FROM NOW, PEOPLE'LL THINK "HALLIBURTON" IS THE GUY WHO MADE EDWARD SCISSORHANDS.
In one session, he told me of THIS encounter. He wryly titled it, "C.E.O. vs. C.P.A. vs. CO_2."
MR. WHITE! PLEASE! I HAVE TO SPEAK TO YOU RIGHT AWAY!
I'M SORRY, SIR. I TRIED TO STOP HIM. SHALL I CALL SECURITY?
DICK, I'M GOING TO HAVE TO GET BACK TO YOU.
MILTON, ISN'T IT? RICH MILTON FROM ACCOUNTING?
I'LL TAKE THIS. LADIES, IF YOU'LL EXCUSE US.
WHAT SEEMS TO BE THE PROBLEM, MILTON?
I--I THINK I'VE FOUND SOME IRREGULARITIES, SIR.

GROSS IRREGULARITIES, ACTUALLY. QUESTIONABLE ACCOUNTING. MILLIONS OF DOLLARS OUT OF PLACE.

THANK YOU FOR BRINGING THIS TO MY ATTENTION. OF COURSE, I'LL HAVE TO REVIEW ALL THE FILES.

BUT THAT'S JUST IT, SIR. THIS FILE APPEARS TO BE THE ONLY RECORD.

ODD. WHY IS IT ON RED PAPER?

SECURITY PRECAUTION, MR. WHITE. IT MAKES IT TOO HARD TO PHOTOCOPY--

AND THE PAPER TRAIL, MILTON. WHERE DOES IT END?

WITH ME, SIR, OR, RATHER NOW, WITH YOU.

NO. IT ENDS WITH YOU.

BZZZZ

By Warren's account, the man just stood there, stock still -- watching his future go into the shredder.

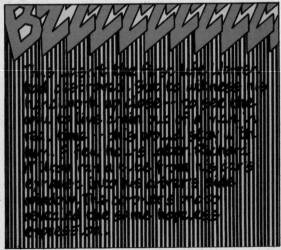

This wasn't the first life Warren had destroyed. But to witness his handiwork up close -- to see the will to live drain out of a man in real time -- this would stay with him. A few hours later, Richard Milton ran a tube from his car's exhaust into his driver's side window. The coroner's photo revealed the same hopeless expression.

BZZZZZZZZZ

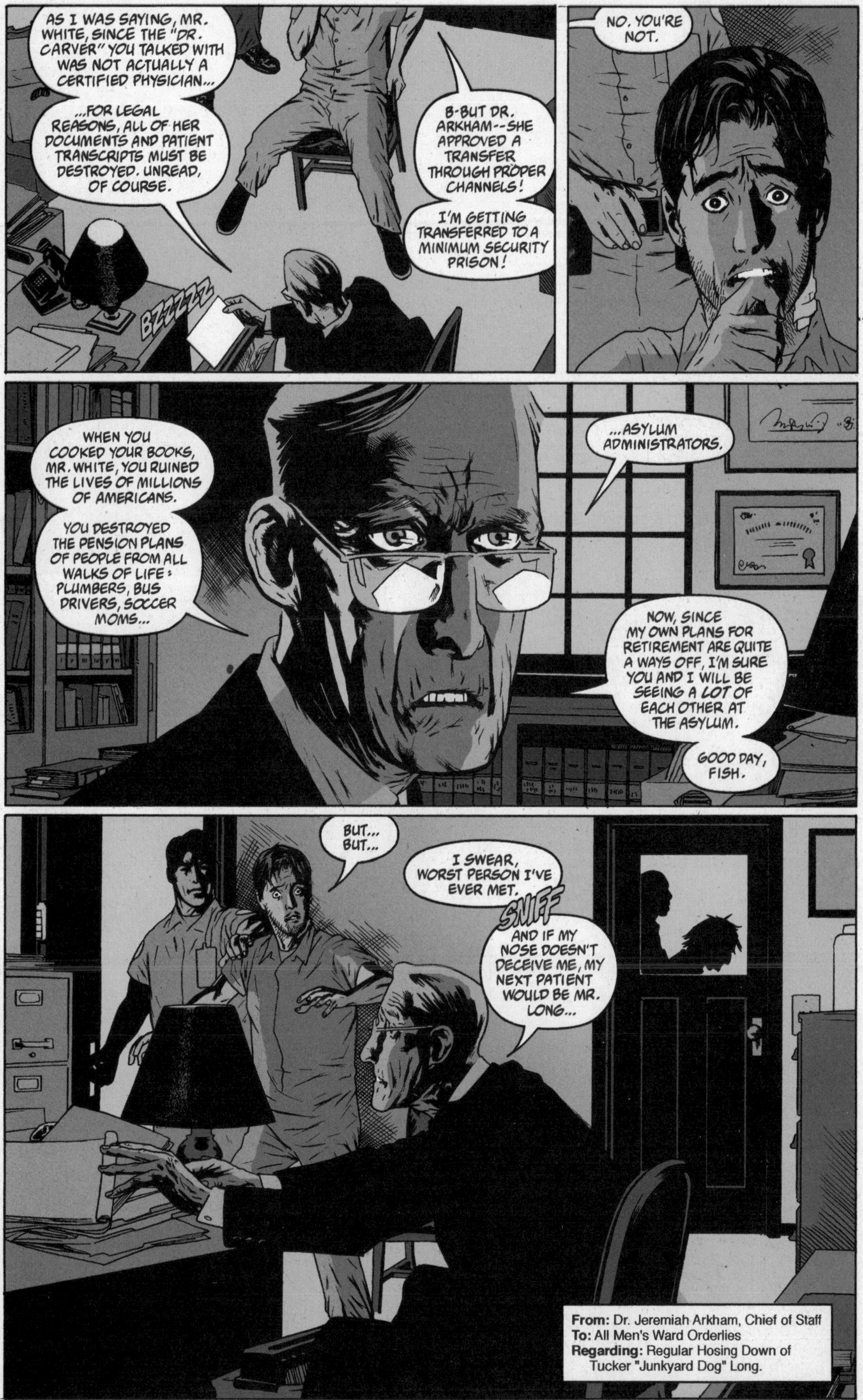
AS I WAS SAYING, MR. WHITE, SINCE THE "DR. CARVER" YOU TALKED WITH WAS NOT ACTUALLY A CERTIFIED PHYSICIAN...
...FOR LEGAL REASONS, ALL OF HER DOCUMENTS AND PATIENT TRANSCRIPTS MUST BE DESTROYED. UNREAD, OF COURSE.
B-BUT DR. ARKHAM--SHE APPROVED A TRANSFER THROUGH PROPER CHANNELS!
I'M GETTING TRANSFERRED TO A MINIMUM SECURITY PRISON!
BZZZZZZ
NO. YOU'RE NOT.
WHEN YOU COOKED YOUR BOOKS, MR. WHITE, YOU RUINED THE LIVES OF MILLIONS OF AMERICANS.
YOU DESTROYED THE PENSION PLANS OF PEOPLE FROM ALL WALKS OF LIFE: PLUMBERS, BUS DRIVERS, SOCCER MOMS...
...ASYLUM ADMINISTRATORS.
NOW, SINCE MY OWN PLANS FOR RETIREMENT ARE QUITE A WAYS OFF, I'M SURE YOU AND I WILL BE SEEING A LOT OF EACH OTHER AT THE ASYLUM.
GOOD DAY, FISH.
BUT... BUT...
I SWEAR, WORST PERSON I'VE EVER MET.
SNIFF
AND IF MY NOSE DOESN'T DECEIVE ME, MY NEXT PATIENT WOULD BE MR. LONG...
From: Dr. Jeremiah Arkham, Chief of Staff
To: All Men's Ward Orderlies
Regarding: Regular Hosing Down of Tucker "Junkyard Dog" Long.

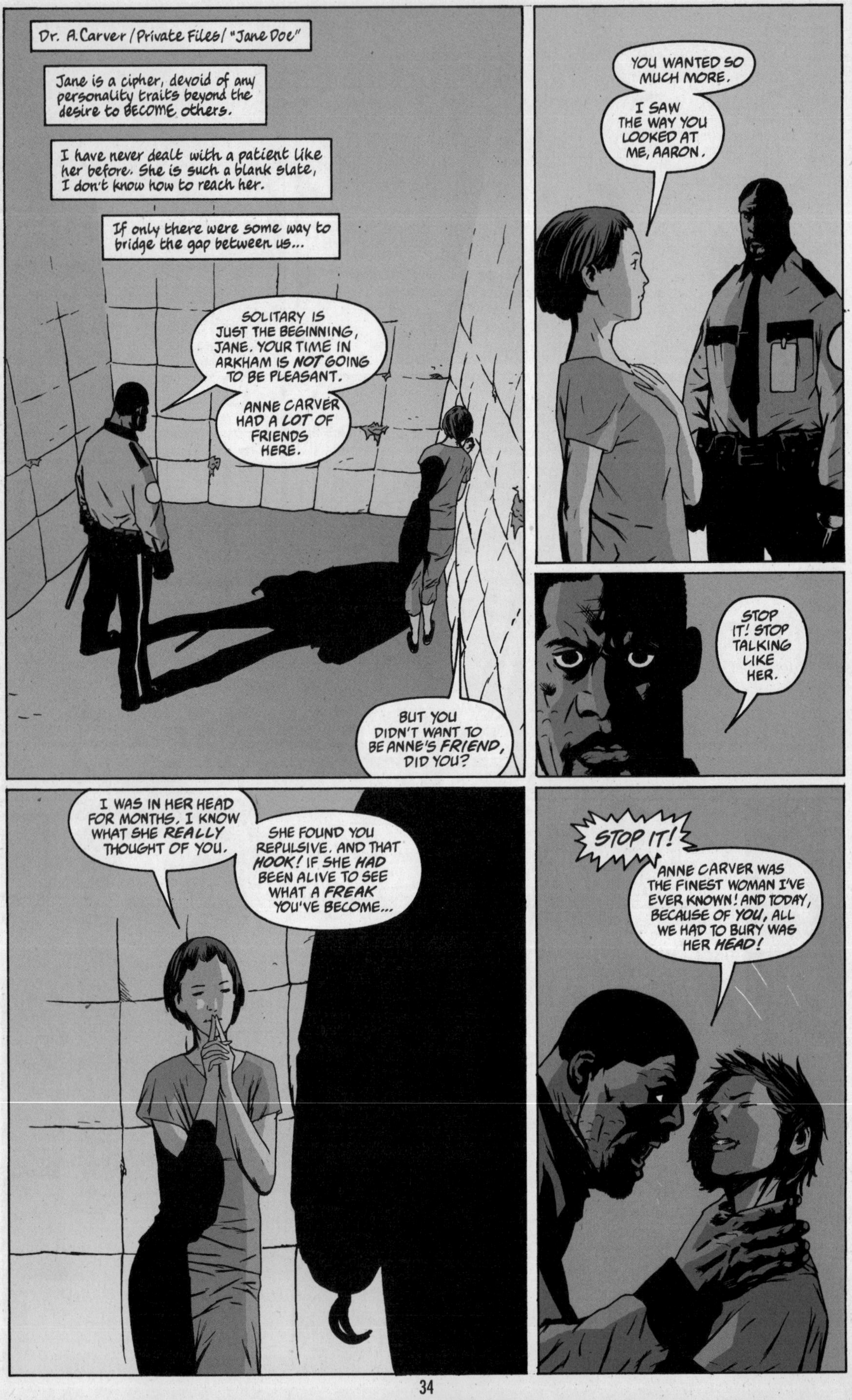
Dr. A.Carver / Private Files / "Jane Doe"
Jane is a cipher, devoid of any personality traits beyond the desire to BECOME others.
I have never dealt with a patient like her before. She is such a blank slate, I don't know how to reach her.
If only there were some way to bridge the gap between us...
SOLITARY IS JUST THE BEGINNING, JANE. YOUR TIME IN ARKHAM IS NOT GOING TO BE PLEASANT.
ANNE CARVER HAD A LOT OF FRIENDS HERE.
BUT YOU DIDN'T WANT TO BE ANNE'S FRIEND, DID YOU?
YOU WANTED SO MUCH MORE.
I SAW THE WAY YOU LOOKED AT ME, AARON.
STOP IT! STOP TALKING LIKE HER.
I WAS IN HER HEAD FOR MONTHS. I KNOW WHAT SHE REALLY THOUGHT OF YOU.
SHE FOUND YOU REPULSIVE. AND THAT HOOK! IF SHE HAD BEEN ALIVE TO SEE WHAT A FREAK YOU'VE BECOME...
STOP IT!
ANNE CARVER WAS THE FINEST WOMAN I'VE EVER KNOWN! AND TODAY, BECAUSE OF YOU, ALL WE HAD TO BURY WAS HER HEAD!

WHAT DID YOU *DO*, JANE?! WHAT DID YOU DO WITH THE *BODY*?!!

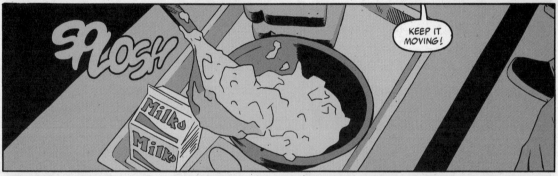

SPLOSH

Milk

Milk

KEEP IT MOVING!

CHICKEN.

OUTTA CHICKEN.

WHAT THE HELL IS THIS?

MYSTERY MEAT.

ALL NIGHT, GUY'S IN THE BUNK UNDA' ME, WON'T SHUT UP.

HE'S SAYIN' "BATMAN THIS, BATMAN THAT." WON'T SHUT UP!

NO MYSTERY TO ME.

SO WHAT *IS* IT, NYGMA?

IT'S WHAT KILLER CROC FORGOT TO FLUSH.

SO I TELLS HIM TO *SHUT UP!*

WHICH HE DON'T. SO YOU KNOW WHAT I DO?

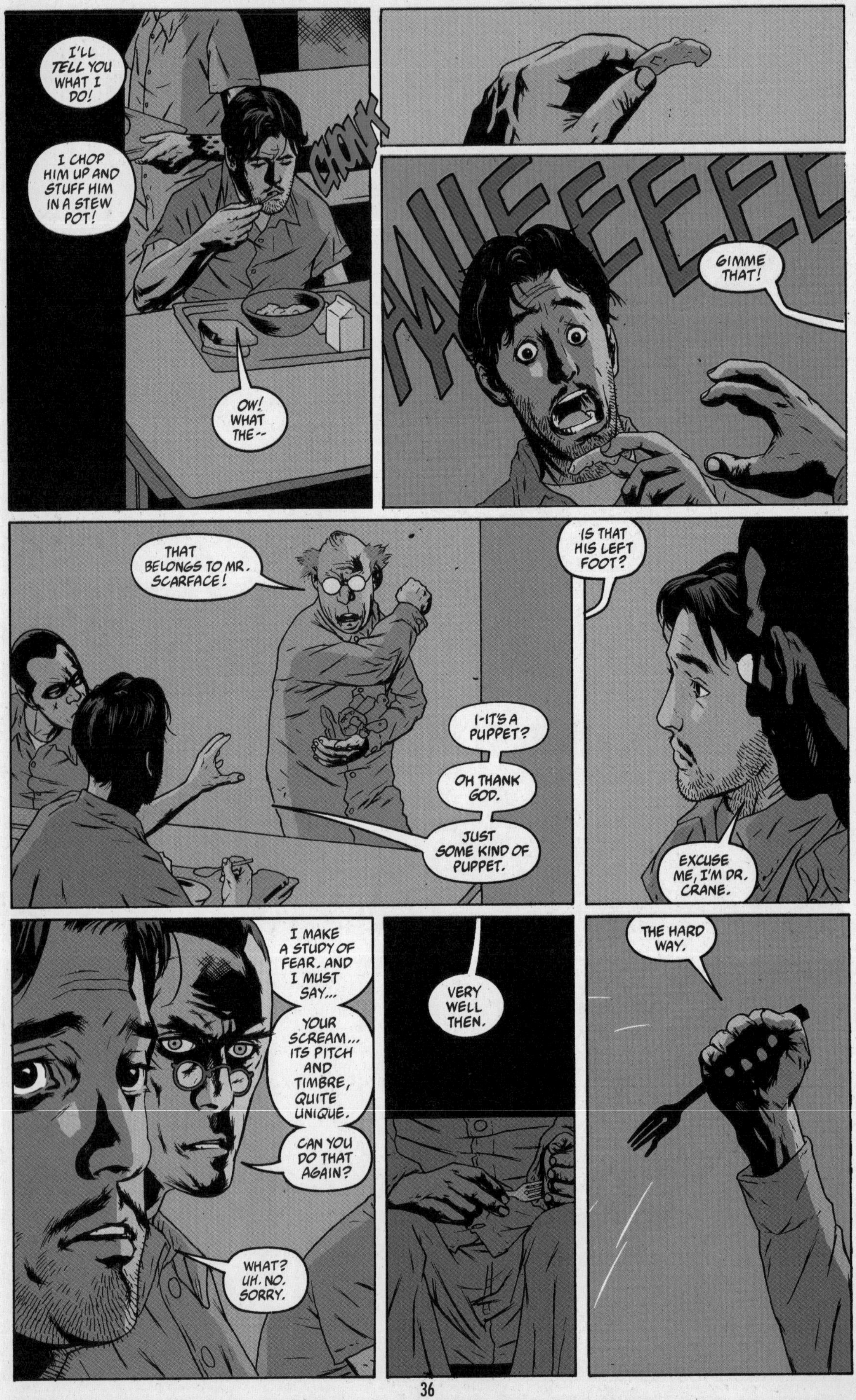
I'LL TELL YOU WHAT I DO!
CHOMK
I CHOP HIM UP AND STUFF HIM IN A STEW POT!
OW! WHAT THE--
AAIIEEEEE
GIMME THAT!
THAT BELONGS TO MR. SCARFACE!
IS THAT HIS LEFT FOOT?
I-IT'S A PUPPET?
OH THANK GOD.
JUST SOME KIND OF PUPPET.
EXCUSE ME, I'M DR. CRANE.
I MAKE A STUDY OF FEAR. AND I MUST SAY...
YOUR SCREAM... ITS PITCH AND TIMBRE, QUITE UNIQUE.
CAN YOU DO THAT AGAIN?
WHAT? UH. NO. SORRY.
VERY WELL THEN.
THE HARD WAY.

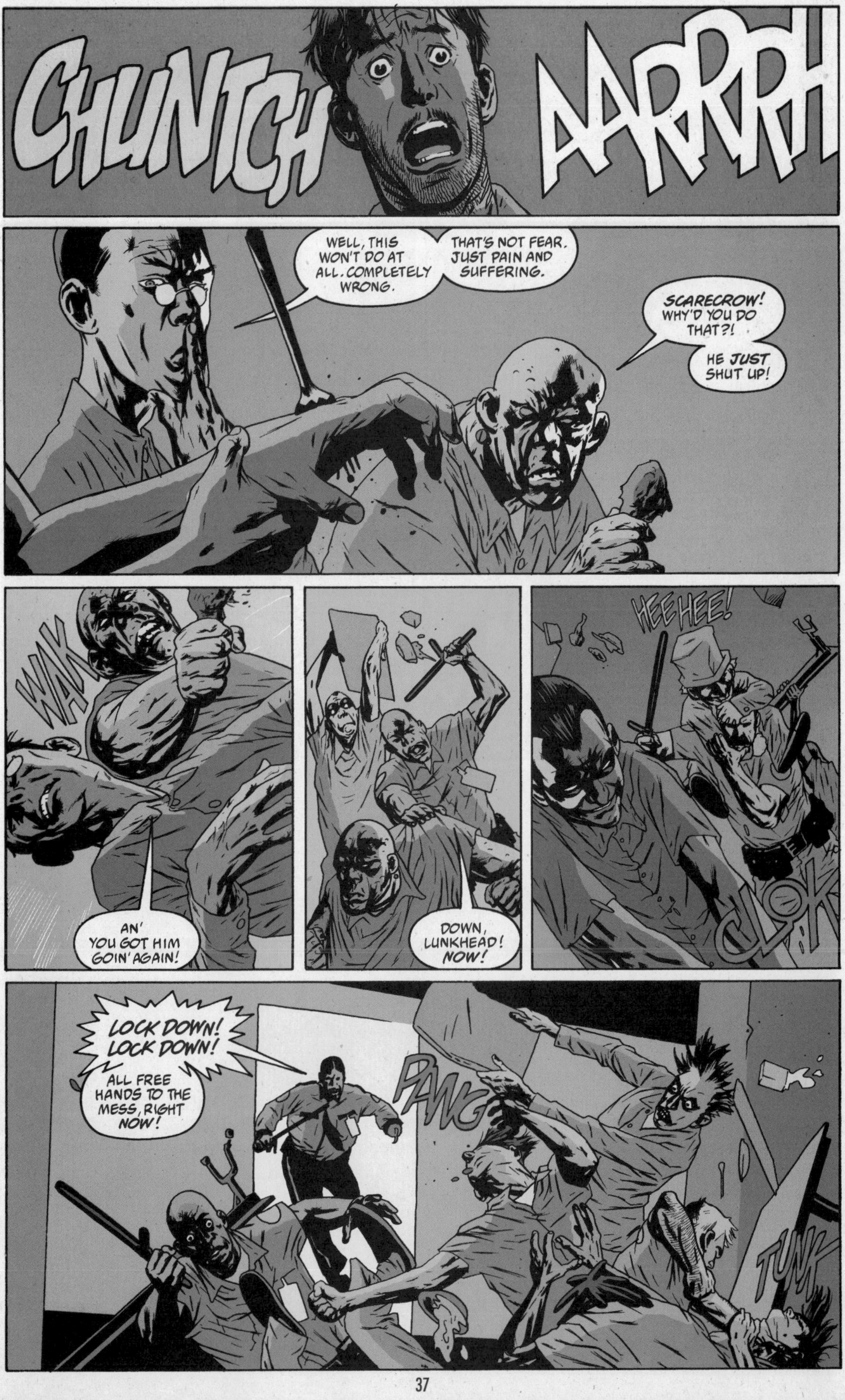
CHUNTCH
AARRRRH
WELL, THIS WON'T DO AT ALL. COMPLETELY WRONG.
THAT'S NOT FEAR. JUST PAIN AND SUFFERING.
SCARECROW! WHY'D YOU DO THAT?!
HE JUST SHUT UP!
WAK
AN' YOU GOT HIM GOIN' AGAIN!
DOWN, LUNKHEAD! NOW!
HEE HEE!
CLOK
LOCK DOWN! LOCK DOWN!
ALL FREE HANDS TO THE MESS, RIGHT NOW!
PANG
TUNK

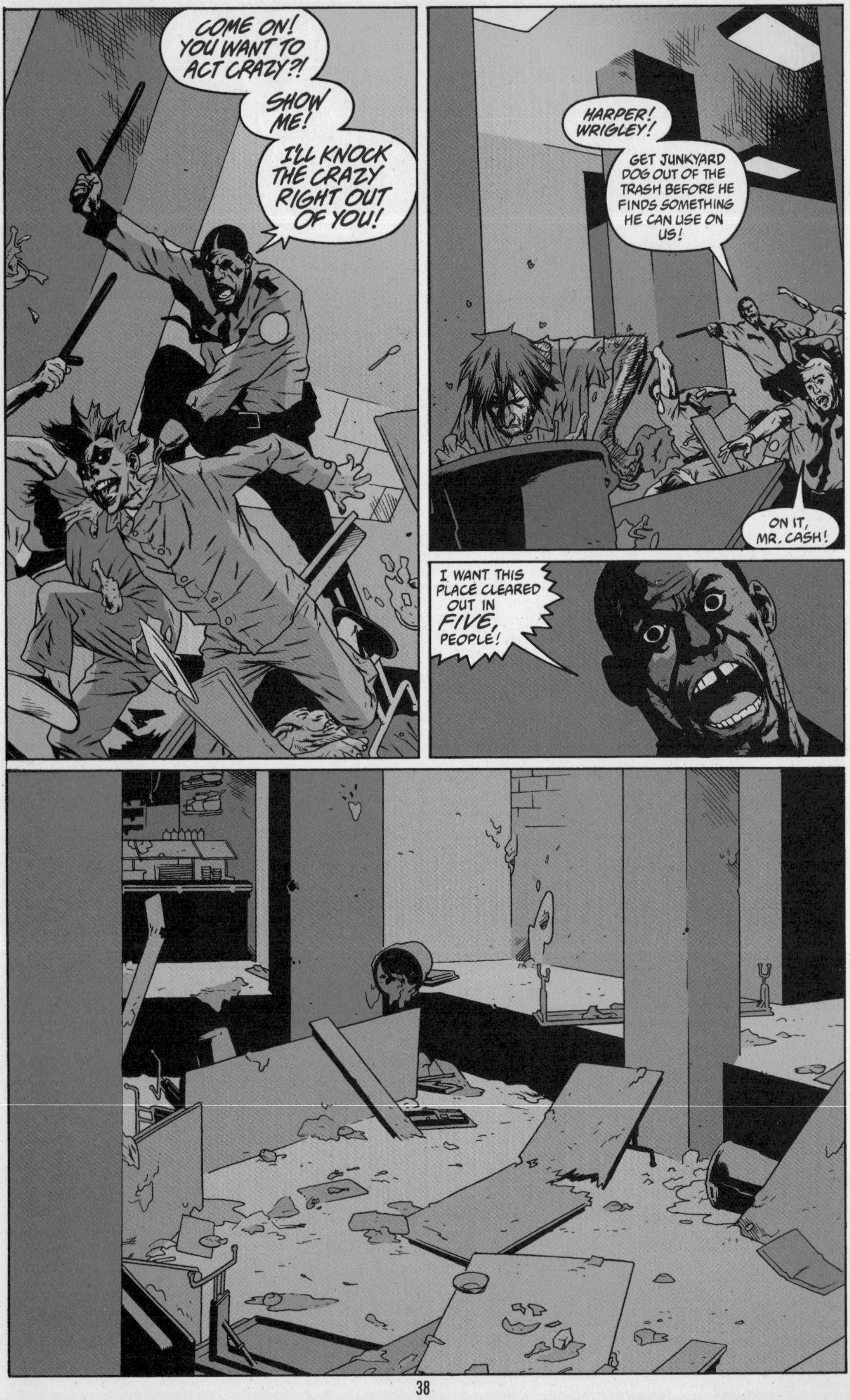
COME ON! YOU WANT TO ACT CRAZY?!
SHOW ME!
I'LL KNOCK THE CRAZY RIGHT OUT OF YOU!
HARPER! WRIGLEY!
GET JUNKYARD DOG OUT OF THE TRASH BEFORE HE FINDS SOMETHING HE CAN USE ON US!
ON IT, MR. CASH!
I WANT THIS PLACE CLEARED OUT IN FIVE, PEOPLE!

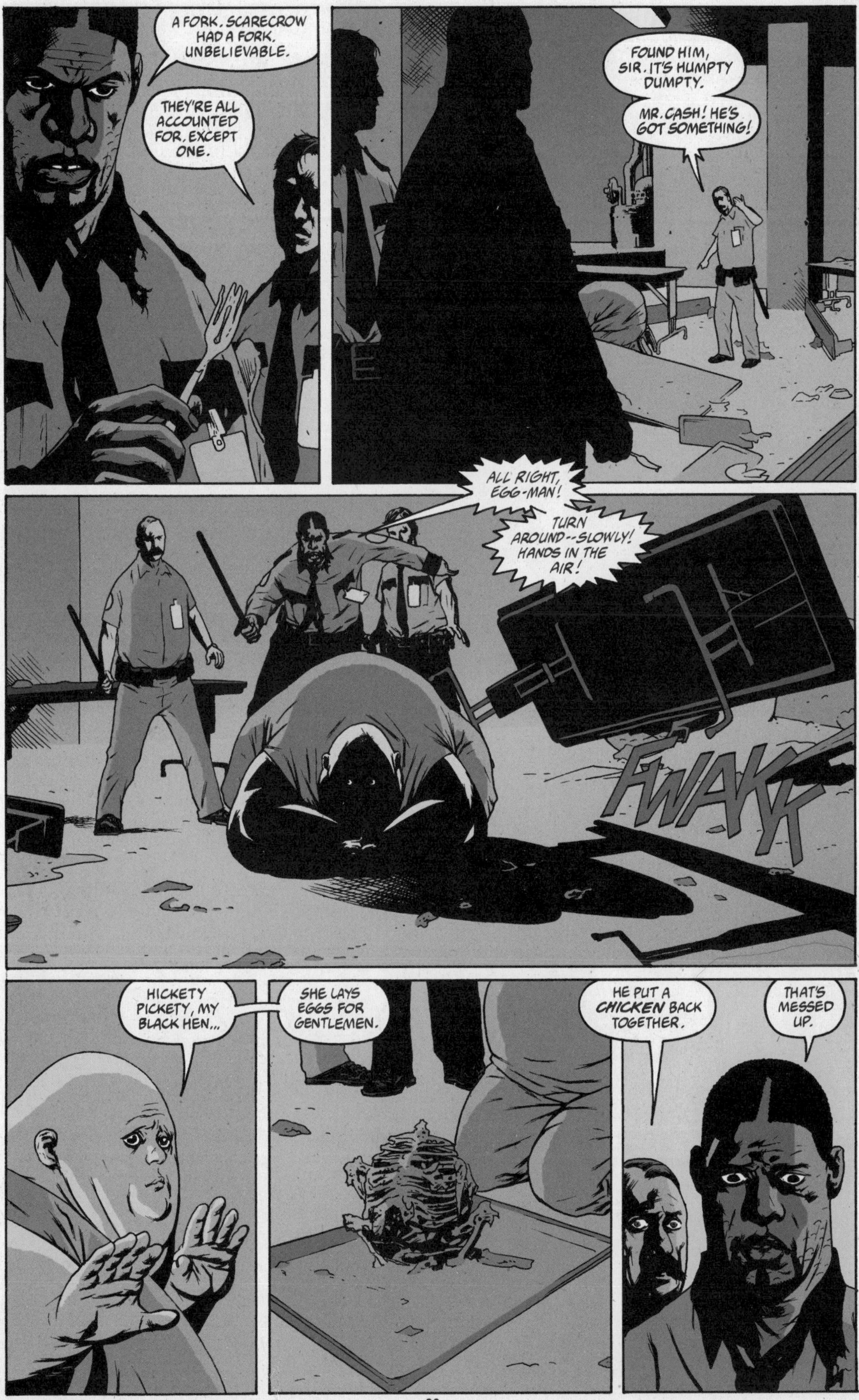
A FORK. SCARECROW HAD A FORK. UNBELIEVABLE.
THEY'RE ALL ACCOUNTED FOR, EXCEPT ONE.
FOUND HIM, SIR. IT'S HUMPTY DUMPTY.
MR. CASH! HE'S GOT SOMETHING!
ALL RIGHT, EGG-MAN!
TURN AROUND--SLOWLY! HANDS IN THE AIR!
FWAKK
HICKETY PICKETY, MY BLACK HEN...
SHE LAYS EGGS FOR GENTLEMEN.
HE PUT A CHICKEN BACK TOGETHER.
THAT'S MESSED UP.

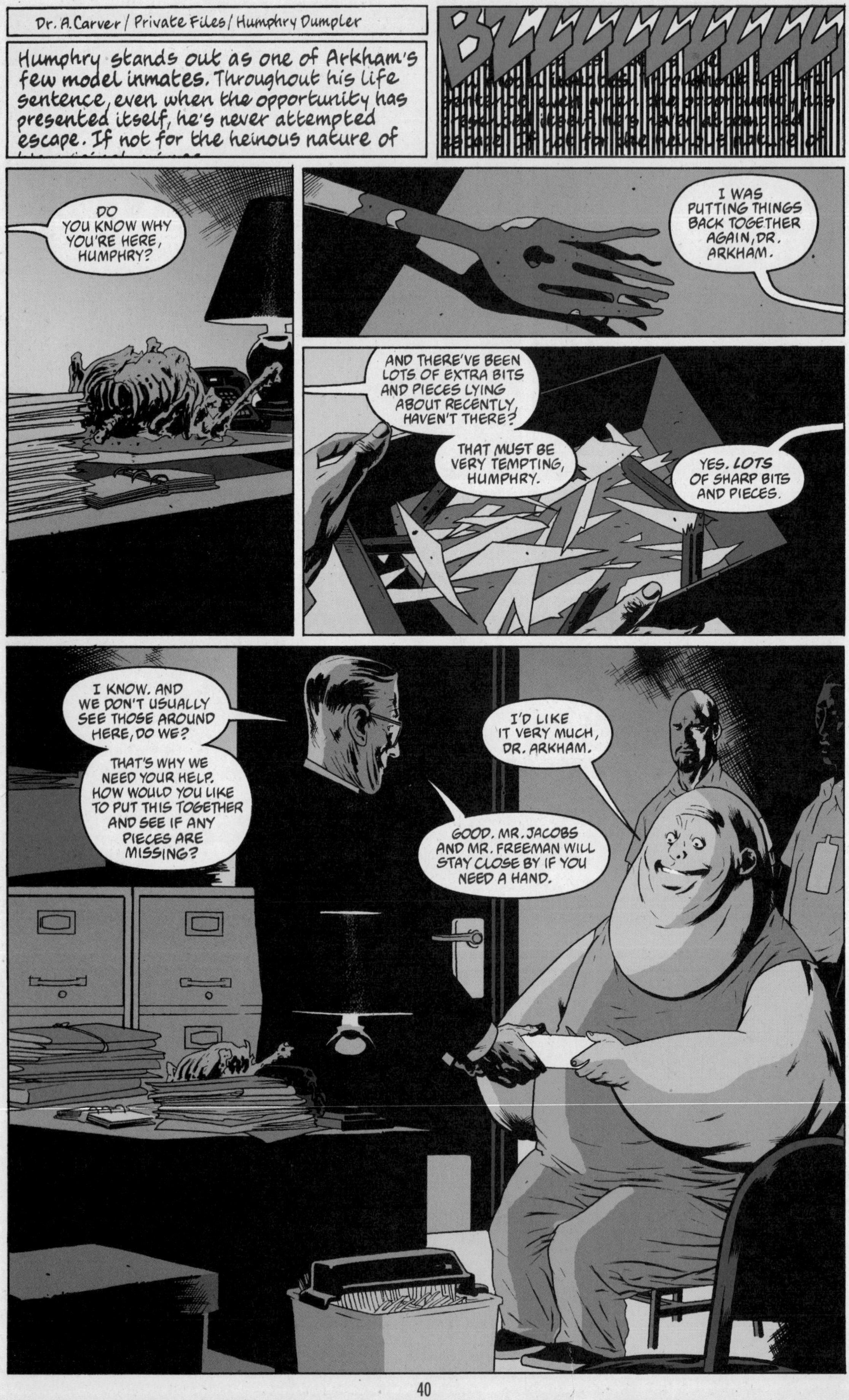

Dr. A.Carver / Private Files / Humphry Dumpler
Humphry stands out as one of Arkham's few model inmates. Throughout his life sentence, even when the opportunity has presented itself, he's never attempted escape. If not for the heinous nature of
BZZZZZZZZZZZ
DO YOU KNOW WHY YOU'RE HERE, HUMPHRY?
I WAS PUTTING THINGS BACK TOGETHER AGAIN, DR. ARKHAM.
AND THERE'VE BEEN LOTS OF EXTRA BITS AND PIECES LYING ABOUT RECENTLY, HAVEN'T THERE?
THAT MUST BE VERY TEMPTING, HUMPHRY.
YES. LOTS OF SHARP BITS AND PIECES.
I KNOW. AND WE DON'T USUALLY SEE THOSE AROUND HERE, DO WE?
THAT'S WHY WE NEED YOUR HELP. HOW WOULD YOU LIKE TO PUT THIS TOGETHER AND SEE IF ANY PIECES ARE MISSING?
I'D LIKE IT VERY MUCH, DR. ARKHAM.
GOOD. MR. JACOBS AND MR. FREEMAN WILL STAY CLOSE BY IF YOU NEED A HAND.

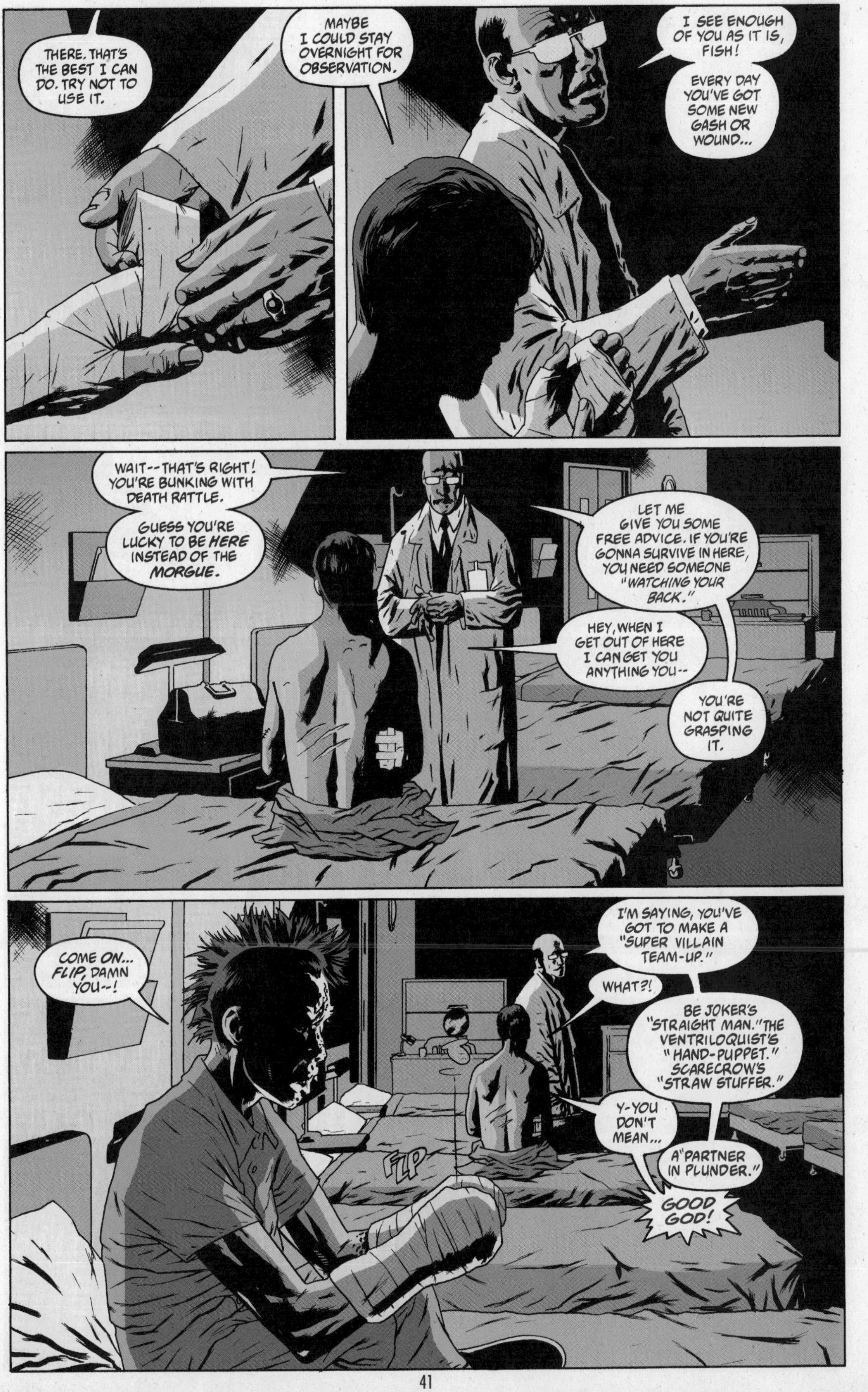

THERE. THAT'S THE BEST I CAN DO. TRY NOT TO USE IT.
MAYBE I COULD STAY OVERNIGHT FOR OBSERVATION.
I SEE ENOUGH OF YOU AS IT IS, FISH!
EVERY DAY YOU'VE GOT SOME NEW GASH OR WOUND...
WAIT--THAT'S RIGHT! YOU'RE BUNKING WITH DEATH RATTLE.
GUESS YOU'RE LUCKY TO BE HERE INSTEAD OF THE MORGUE.
LET ME GIVE YOU SOME FREE ADVICE. IF YOU'RE GONNA SURVIVE IN HERE, YOU NEED SOMEONE "WATCHING YOUR BACK."
HEY, WHEN I GET OUT OF HERE I CAN GET YOU ANYTHING YOU--
YOU'RE NOT QUITE GRASPING IT.
COME ON... FLIP, DAMN YOU--!
I'M SAYING, YOU'VE GOT TO MAKE A "SUPER VILLAIN TEAM-UP."
WHAT?!
BE JOKER'S "STRAIGHT MAN." THE VENTRILOQUIST'S "HAND-PUPPET." SCARECROW'S "STRAW STUFFER."
Y-YOU DON'T MEAN...
A "PARTNER IN PLUNDER."
FLIP
GOOD GOD!

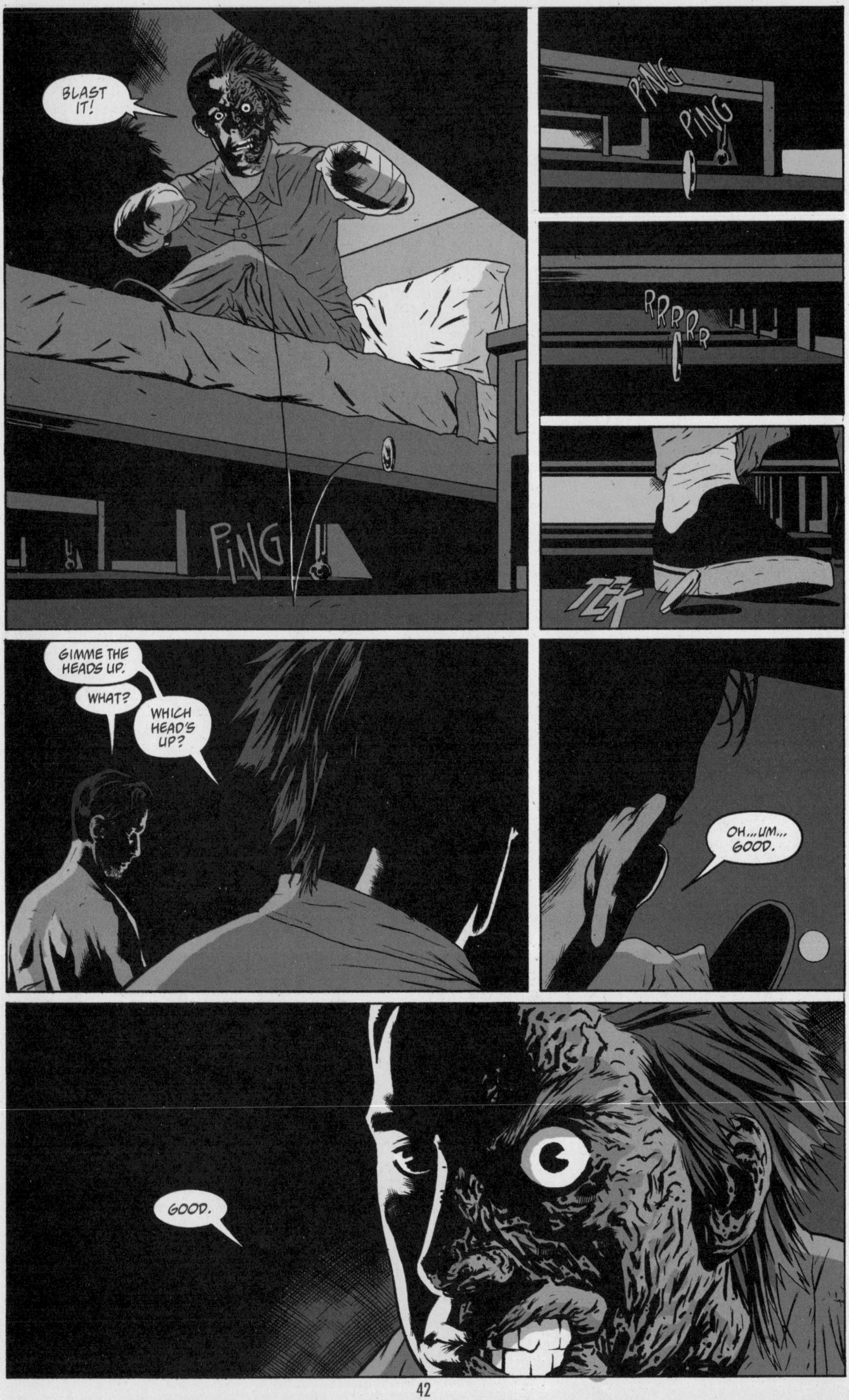
BLAST IT!
PiNG
PiNG
PING
RRRRRR
TEK
GIMME THE HEADS UP.
WHAT?
WHICH HEAD'S UP?
OH...UM... GOOD.
GOOD.

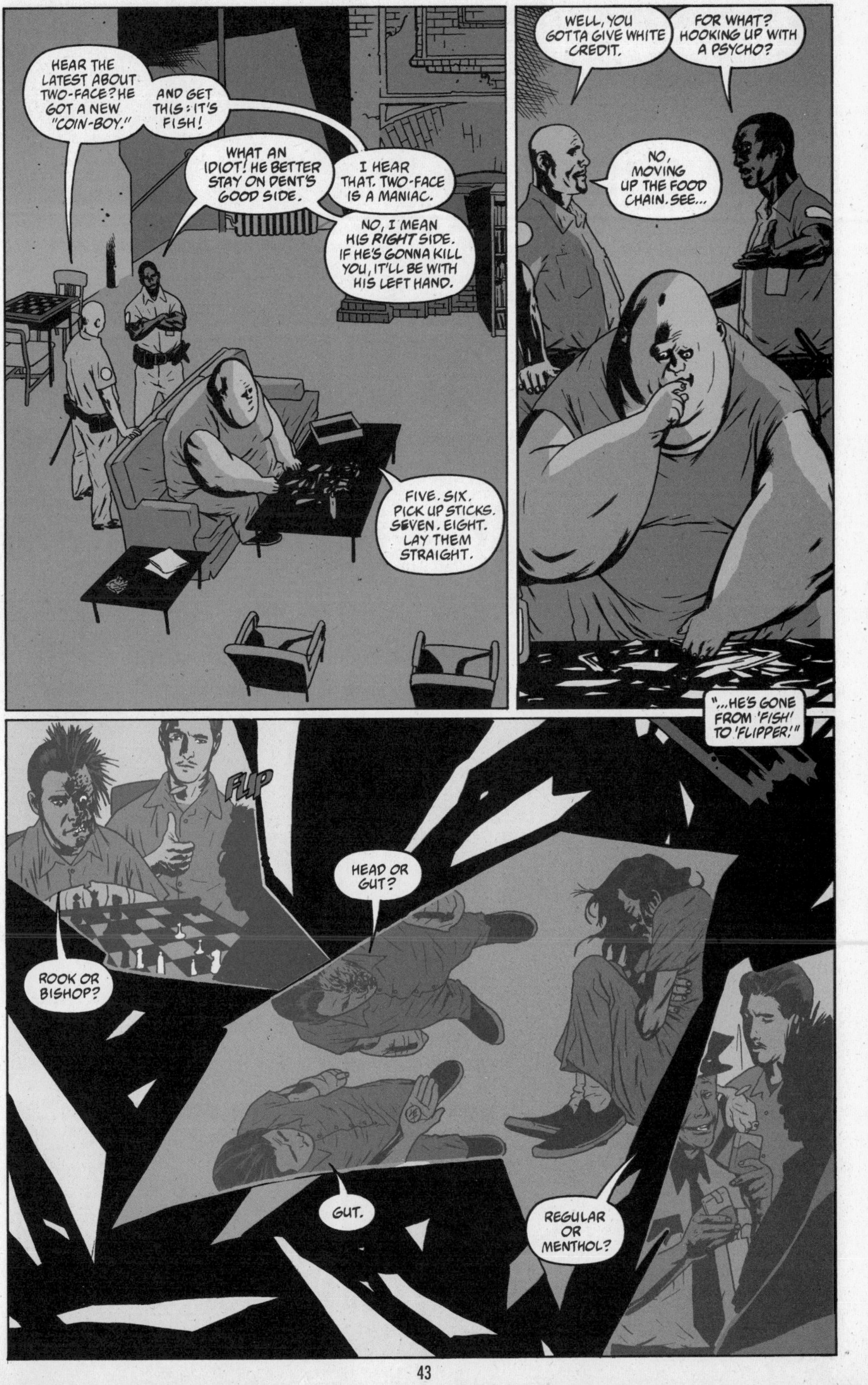
HEAR THE LATEST ABOUT TWO-FACE? HE GOT A NEW "COIN-BOY."
AND GET THIS: IT'S FISH!
WHAT AN IDIOT! HE BETTER STAY ON DENT'S GOOD SIDE.
I HEAR THAT. TWO-FACE IS A MANIAC.
NO, I MEAN HIS RIGHT SIDE. IF HE'S GONNA KILL YOU, IT'LL BE WITH HIS LEFT HAND.
FIVE. SIX. PICK UP STICKS. SEVEN. EIGHT. LAY THEM STRAIGHT.
WELL, YOU GOTTA GIVE WHITE CREDIT.
FOR WHAT? HOOKING UP WITH A PSYCHO?
NO, MOVING UP THE FOOD CHAIN. SEE...
"...HE'S GONE FROM 'FISH' TO 'FLIPPER.'"
FLIP
HEAD OR GUT?
ROOK OR BISHOP?
GUT.
REGULAR OR MENTHOL?

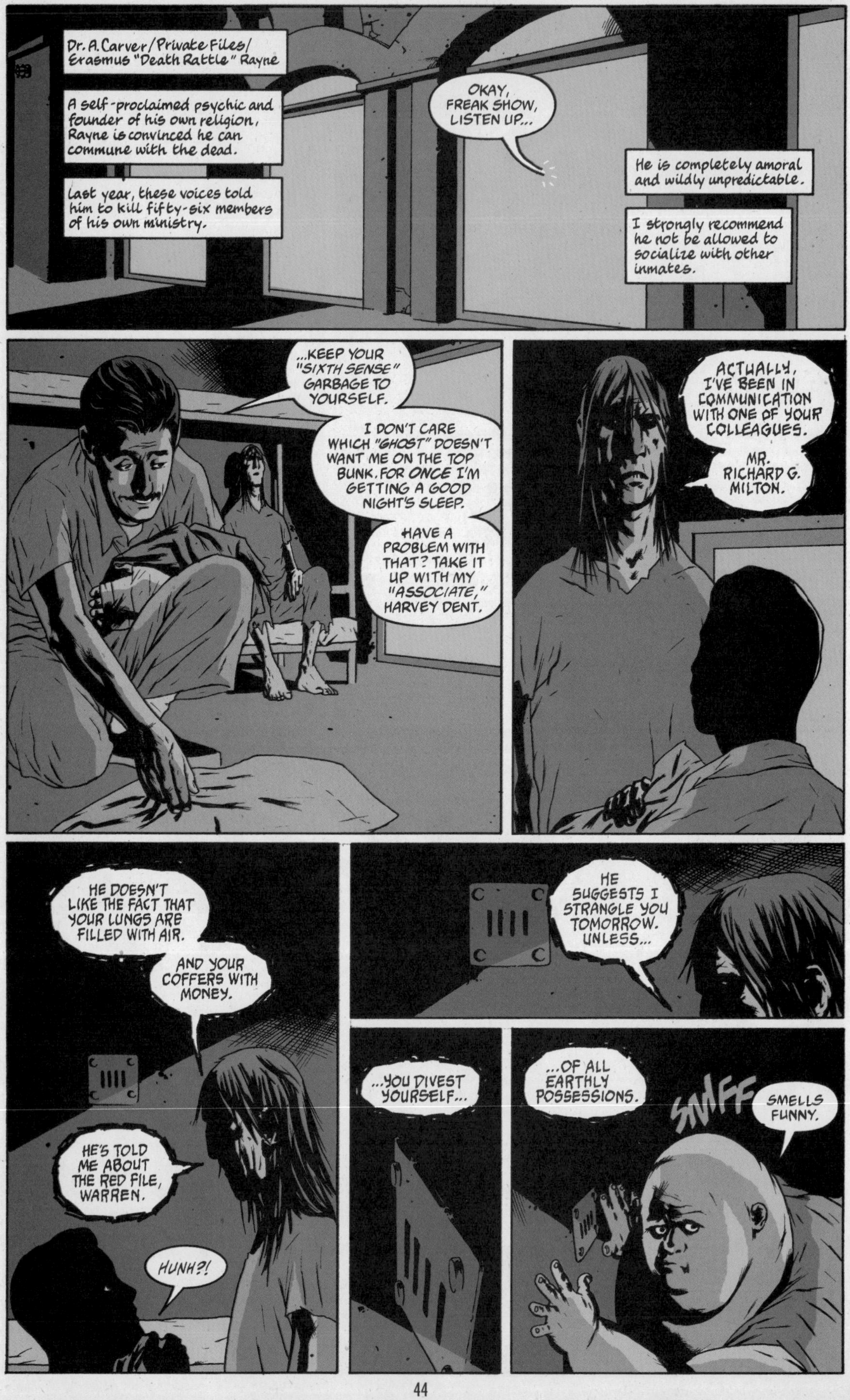
Dr. A. Carver/Private Files/ Erasmus "Death Rattle" Rayne
A self-proclaimed psychic and founder of his own religion, Rayne is convinced he can commune with the dead.
Last year, these voices told him to kill fifty-six members of his own ministry.
OKAY, FREAK SHOW, LISTEN UP...
He is completely amoral and wildly unpredictable.
I strongly recommend he not be allowed to socialize with other inmates.
...KEEP YOUR "SIXTH SENSE" GARBAGE TO YOURSELF.
I DON'T CARE WHICH "GHOST" DOESN'T WANT ME ON THE TOP BUNK. FOR ONCE I'M GETTING A GOOD NIGHT'S SLEEP.
HAVE A PROBLEM WITH THAT? TAKE IT UP WITH MY "ASSOCIATE," HARVEY DENT.
ACTUALLY, I'VE BEEN IN COMMUNICATION WITH ONE OF YOUR COLLEAGUES.
MR. RICHARD G. MILTON.
HE DOESN'T LIKE THE FACT THAT YOUR LUNGS ARE FILLED WITH AIR.
AND YOUR COFFERS WITH MONEY.
HE'S TOLD ME ABOUT THE RED FILE, WARREN.
HUNH?!
HE SUGGESTS I STRANGLE YOU TOMORROW. UNLESS...
...YOU DIVEST YOURSELF...
...OF ALL EARTHLY POSSESSIONS.
SNIFF
SMELLS FUNNY.

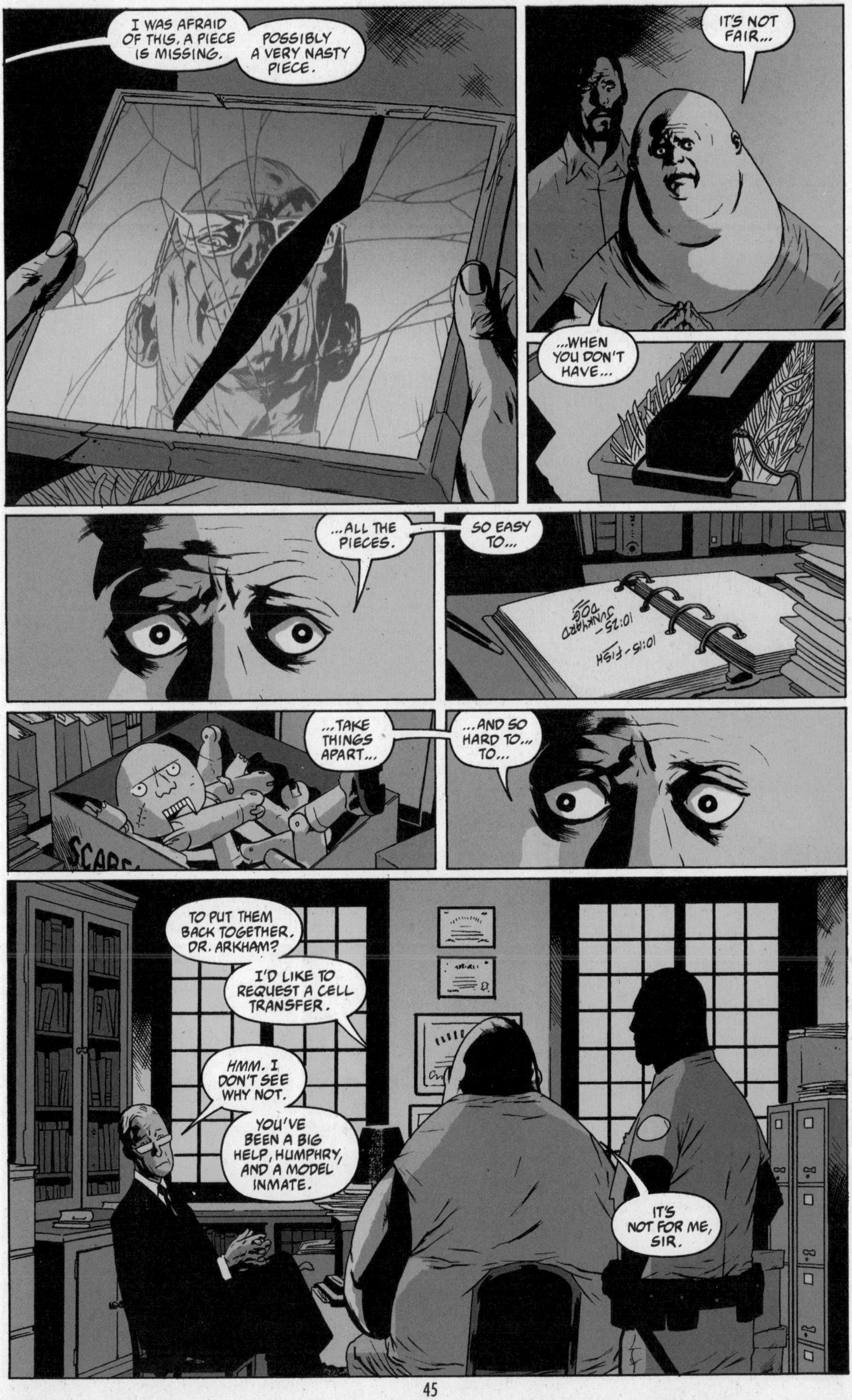
I WAS AFRAID OF THIS. A PIECE IS MISSING.
POSSIBLY A VERY NASTY PIECE.
IT'S NOT FAIR...
...WHEN YOU DON'T HAVE...
...ALL THE PIECES.
SO EASY TO...
10:15 - FISH
10:25 - JUNKYARD DOG
...TAKE THINGS APART...
...AND SO HARD TO... TO...
TO PUT THEM BACK TOGETHER. DR. ARKHAM?
I'D LIKE TO REQUEST A CELL TRANSFER.
HMM. I DON'T SEE WHY NOT.
YOU'VE BEEN A BIG HELP, HUMPHRY, AND A MODEL INMATE.
IT'S NOT FOR ME, SIR.

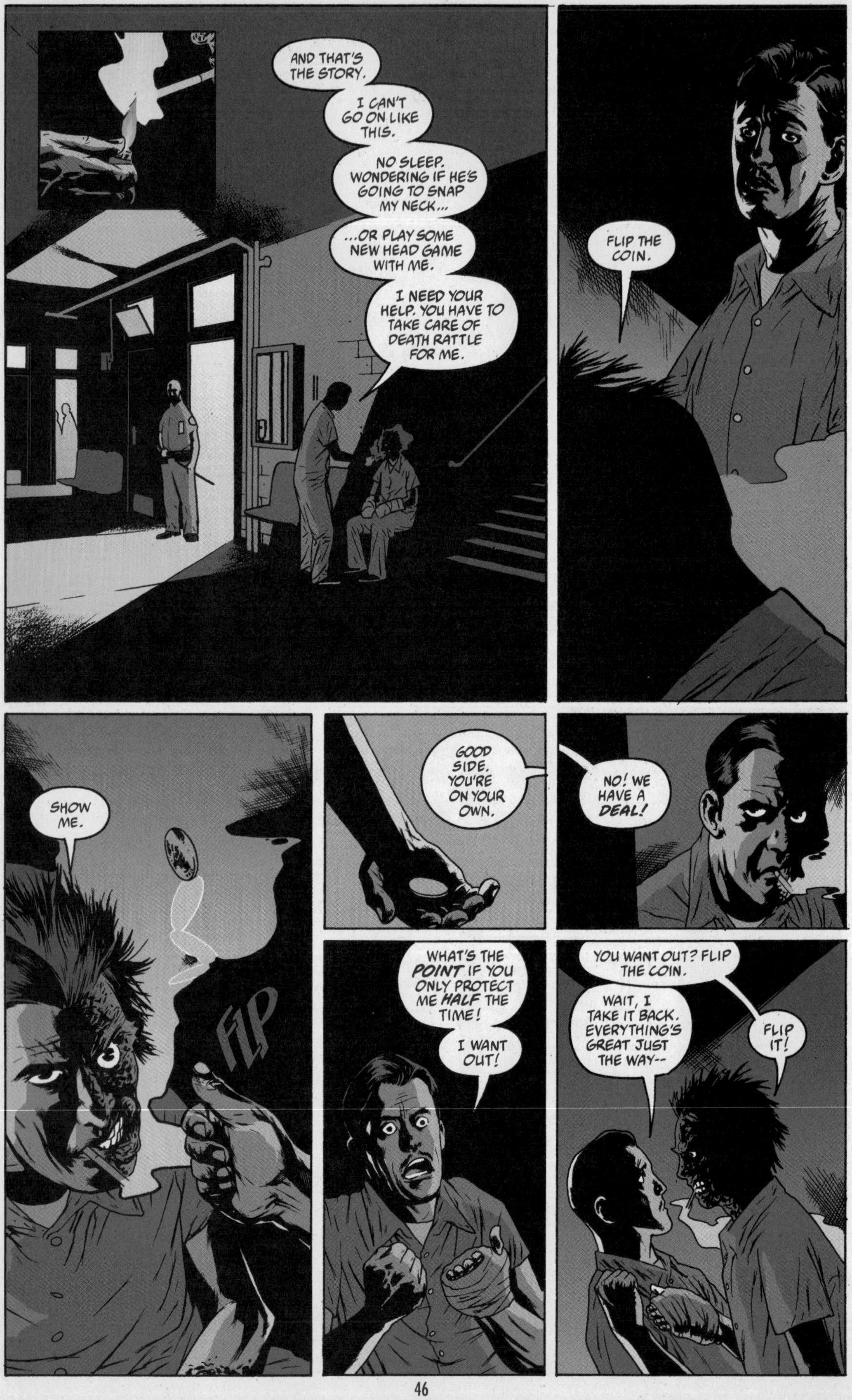
AND THAT'S THE STORY.
I CAN'T GO ON LIKE THIS.
NO SLEEP. WONDERING IF HE'S GOING TO SNAP MY NECK...
...OR PLAY SOME NEW HEAD GAME WITH ME.
I NEED YOUR HELP. YOU HAVE TO TAKE CARE OF DEATH RATTLE FOR ME.
FLIP THE COIN.
SHOW ME.
FLIP
GOOD SIDE. YOU'RE ON YOUR OWN.
NO! WE HAVE A DEAL!
WHAT'S THE POINT IF YOU ONLY PROTECT ME HALF THE TIME!
I WANT OUT!
YOU WANT OUT? FLIP THE COIN.
WAIT, I TAKE IT BACK. EVERYTHING'S GREAT JUST THE WAY--
FLIP IT!

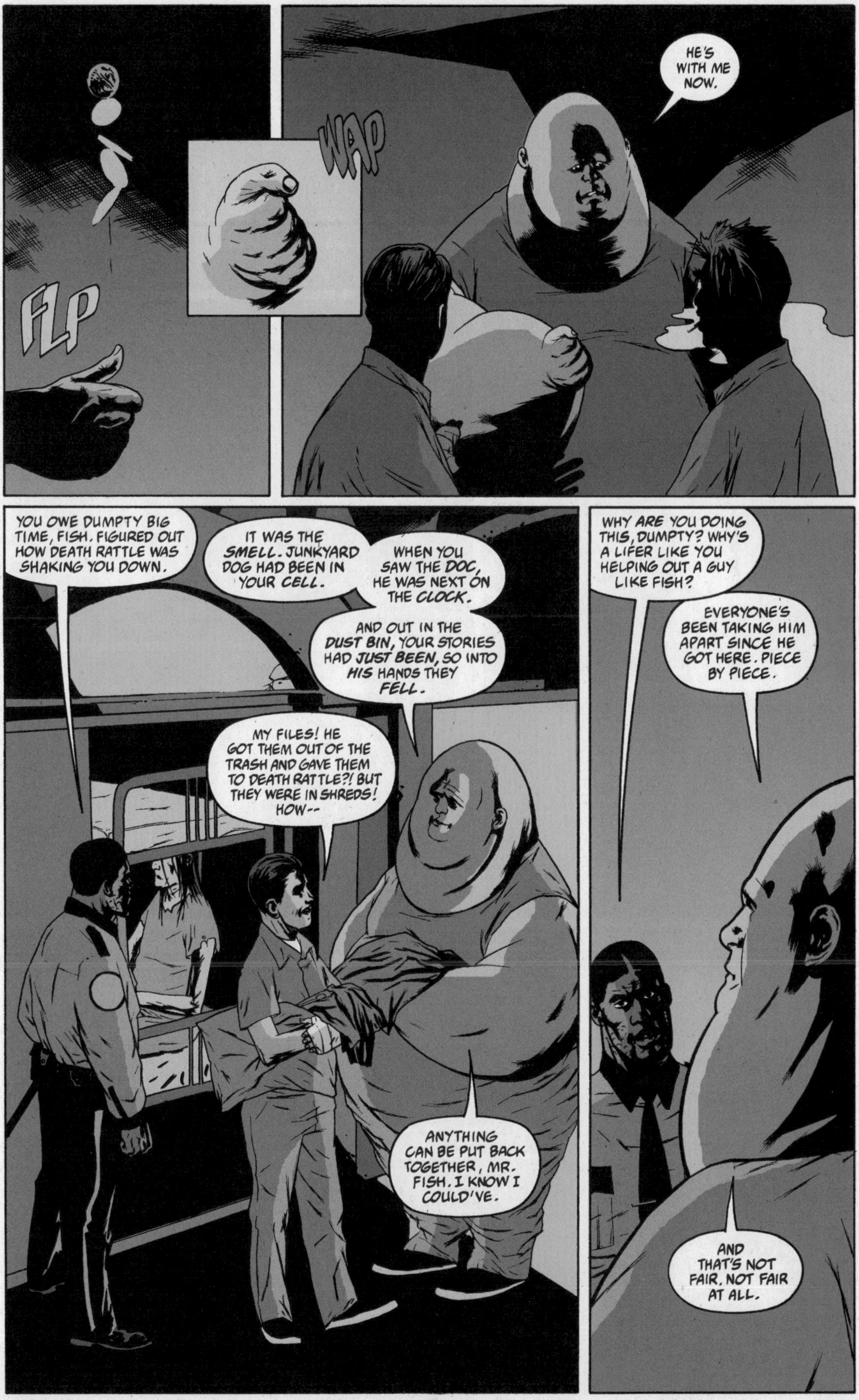
FLP
WAP
HE'S WITH ME NOW.
YOU OWE DUMPTY BIG TIME, FISH. FIGURED OUT HOW DEATH RATTLE WAS SHAKING YOU DOWN.
IT WAS THE SMELL. JUNKYARD DOG HAD BEEN IN YOUR CELL.
WHEN YOU SAW THE DOC, HE WAS NEXT ON THE CLOCK.
AND OUT IN THE DUST BIN, YOUR STORIES HAD JUST BEEN, SO INTO HIS HANDS THEY FELL.
MY FILES! HE GOT THEM OUT OF THE TRASH AND GAVE THEM TO DEATH RATTLE?! BUT THEY WERE IN SHREDS! HOW--
ANYTHING CAN BE PUT BACK TOGETHER, MR. FISH. I KNOW I COULD'VE.
WHY ARE YOU DOING THIS, DUMPTY? WHY'S A LIFER LIKE YOU HELPING OUT A GUY LIKE FISH?
EVERYONE'S BEEN TAKING HIM APART SINCE HE GOT HERE. PIECE BY PIECE.
AND THAT'S NOT FAIR. NOT FAIR AT ALL.

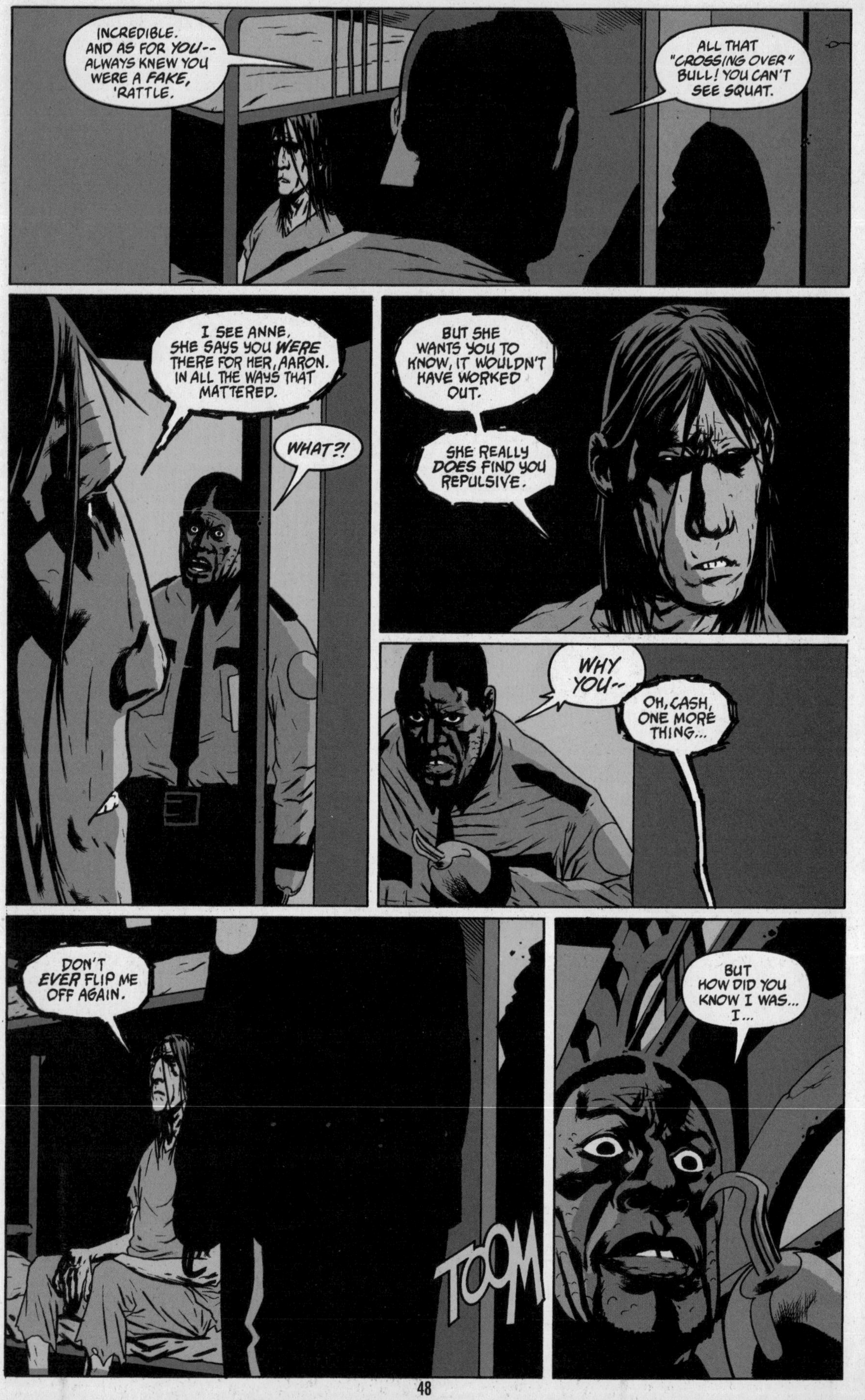

INCREDIBLE. AND AS FOR YOU-- ALWAYS KNEW YOU WERE A FAKE, 'RATTLE.
ALL THAT "CROSSING OVER" BULL! YOU CAN'T SEE SQUAT.
I SEE ANNE, SHE SAYS YOU WERE THERE FOR HER, AARON. IN ALL THE WAYS THAT MATTERED.
WHAT?!
BUT SHE WANTS YOU TO KNOW, IT WOULDN'T HAVE WORKED OUT.
SHE REALLY DOES FIND YOU REPULSIVE.
WHY YOU--
OH, CASH, ONE MORE THING...
DON'T EVER FLIP ME OFF AGAIN.
TOOM
BUT HOW DID YOU KNOW I WAS... I...

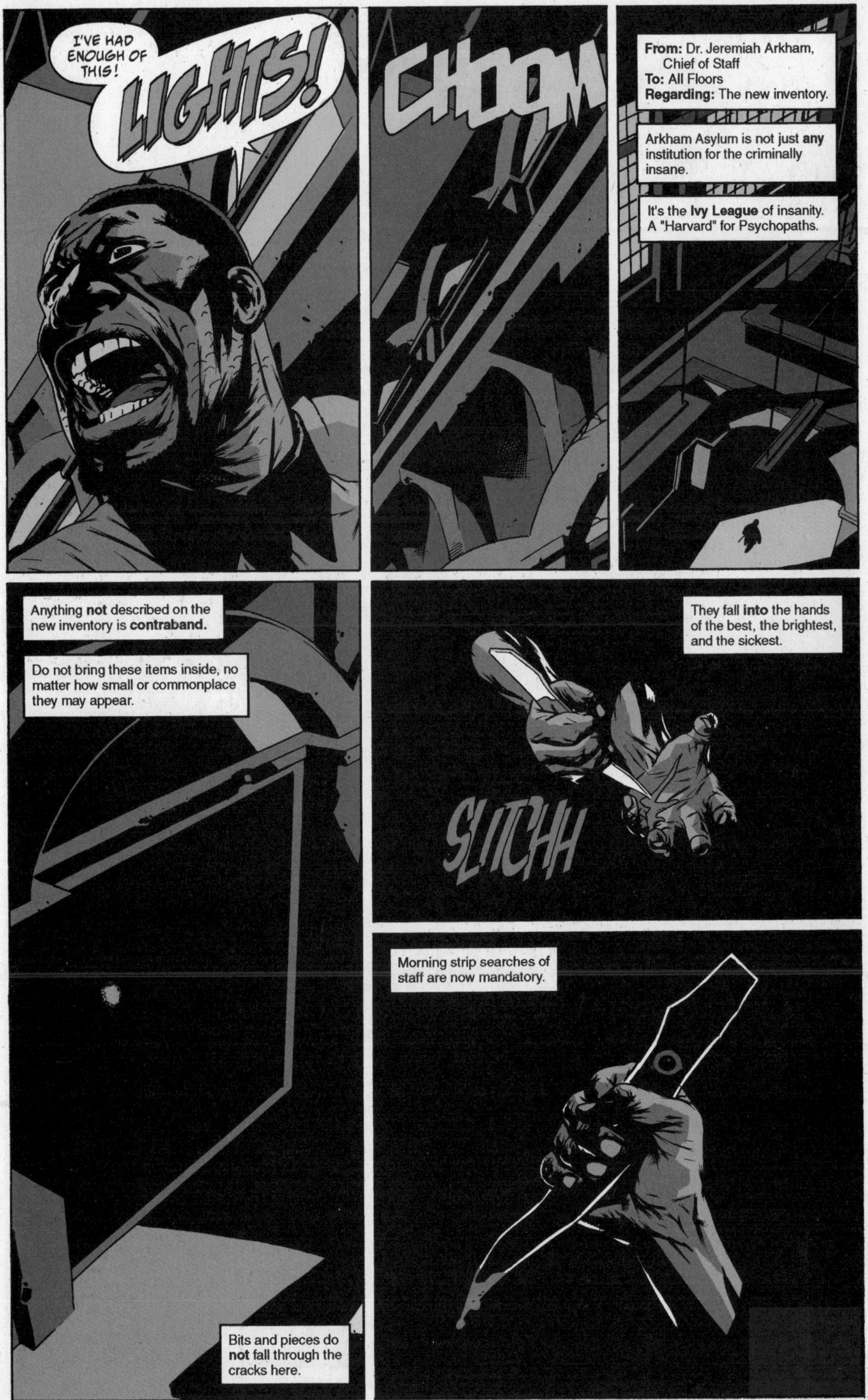
I'VE HAD ENOUGH OF THIS!
LIGHTS!
CHOOM
From: Dr. Jeremiah Arkham, Chief of Staff
To: All Floors
Regarding: The new inventory.
Arkham Asylum is not just any institution for the criminally insane.
It's the Ivy League of insanity. A "Harvard" for Psychopaths.
Anything not described on the new inventory is contraband.
Do not bring these items inside, no matter how small or commonplace they may appear.
Bits and pieces do not fall through the cracks here.
They fall into the hands of the best, the brightest, and the sickest.
SLITCHH
Morning strip searches of staff are now mandatory.

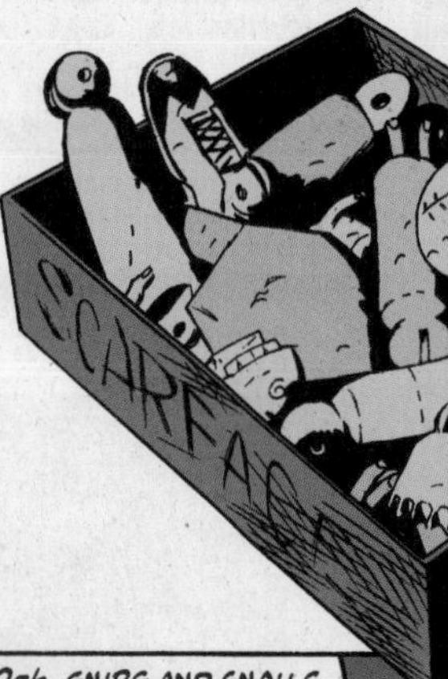
SCARFACE

CHAPTER THREE: Cracked Up

DAN SLOTT writer
RYAN SOOK penciller
JIM ROYAL inker
LEE LOUGHRIDGE colorist
MIKE HEISLER letterer
DAN RASPLER + VALERIE D'ORAZIO editors

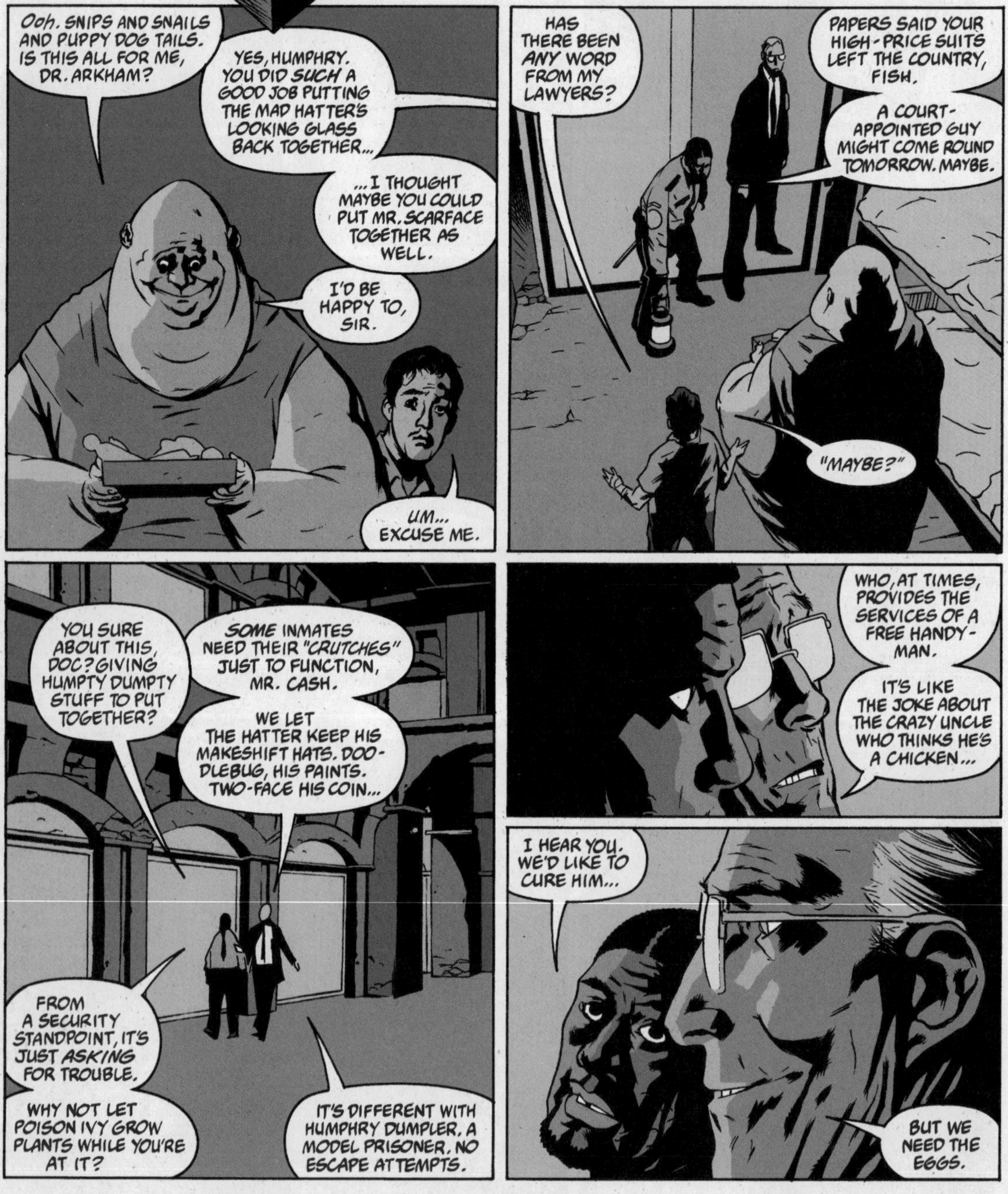
Ooh. SNIPS AND SNAILS AND PUPPY DOG TAILS. IS THIS ALL FOR ME, DR. ARKHAM?
YES, HUMPHRY. YOU DID SUCH A GOOD JOB PUTTING THE MAD HATTER'S LOOKING GLASS BACK TOGETHER...
...I THOUGHT MAYBE YOU COULD PUT MR. SCARFACE TOGETHER AS WELL.
I'D BE HAPPY TO, SIR.
UM... EXCUSE ME.
HAS THERE BEEN ANY WORD FROM MY LAWYERS?
PAPERS SAID YOUR HIGH-PRICE SUITS LEFT THE COUNTRY, FISH.
A COURT-APPOINTED GUY MIGHT COME ROUND TOMORROW. MAYBE.
"MAYBE?"
YOU SURE ABOUT THIS, DOC? GIVING HUMPTY DUMPTY STUFF TO PUT TOGETHER?
SOME INMATES NEED THEIR "CRUTCHES" JUST TO FUNCTION, MR. CASH.
WE LET THE HATTER KEEP HIS MAKESHIFT HATS. DOODLEBUG, HIS PAINTS. TWO-FACE HIS COIN...
FROM A SECURITY STANDPOINT, IT'S JUST ASKING FOR TROUBLE.
WHY NOT LET POISON IVY GROW PLANTS WHILE YOU'RE AT IT?
IT'S DIFFERENT WITH HUMPHRY DUMPLER, A MODEL PRISONER, NO ESCAPE ATTEMPTS.
WHO, AT TIMES, PROVIDES THE SERVICES OF A FREE HANDY-MAN.
IT'S LIKE THE JOKE ABOUT THE CRAZY UNCLE WHO THINKS HE'S A CHICKEN...
I HEAR YOU. WE'D LIKE TO CURE HIM...
BUT WE NEED THE EGGS.

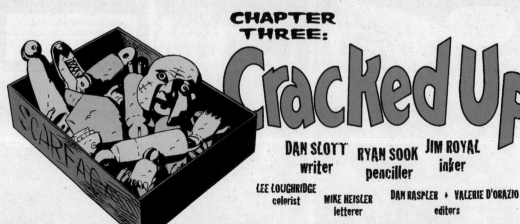

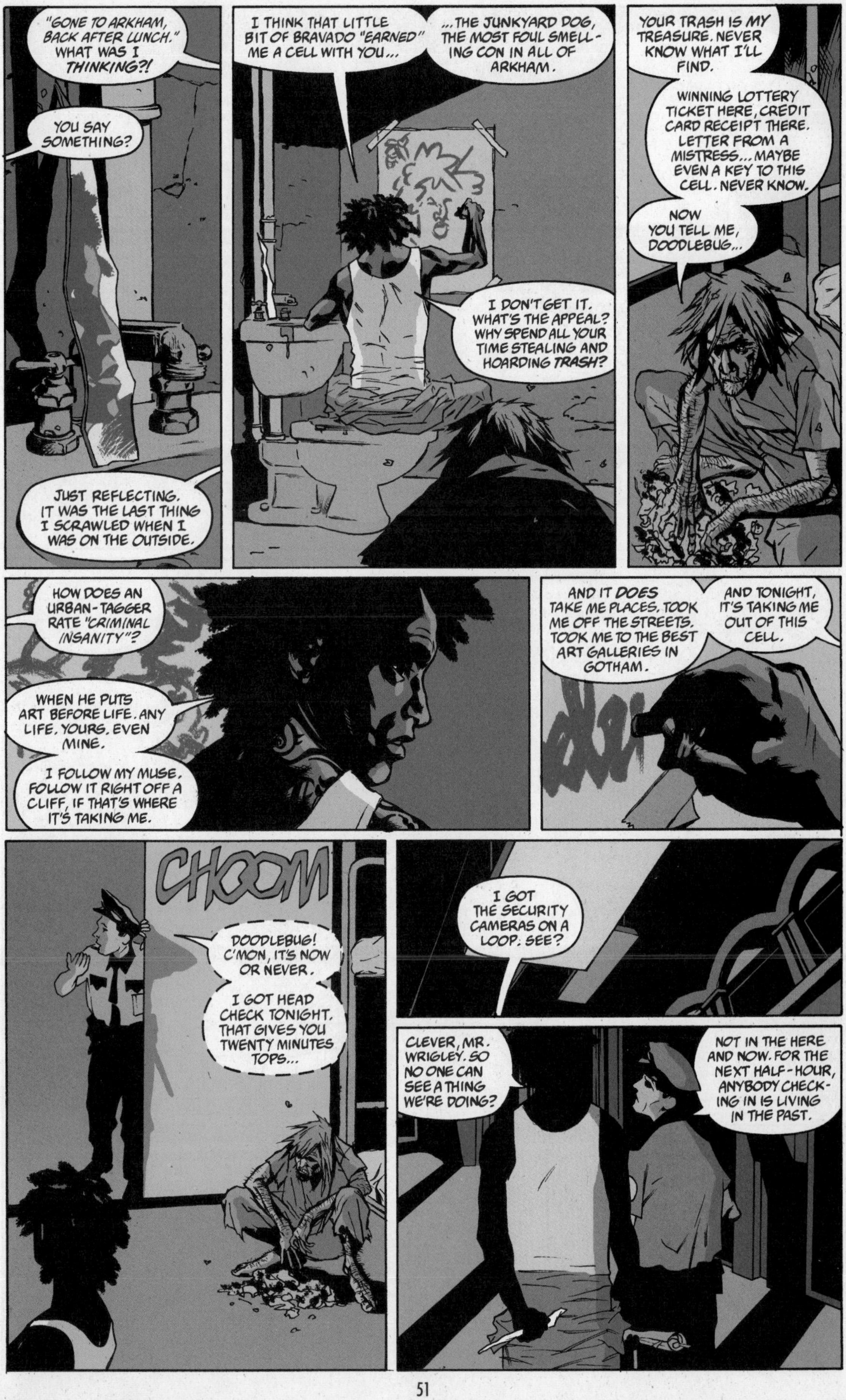
"GONE TO ARKHAM, BACK AFTER LUNCH." WHAT WAS I THINKING?!
YOU SAY SOMETHING?
JUST REFLECTING. IT WAS THE LAST THING I SCRAWLED WHEN I WAS ON THE OUTSIDE.
I THINK THAT LITTLE BIT OF BRAVADO "EARNED" ME A CELL WITH YOU...
...THE JUNKYARD DOG, THE MOST FOUL SMELLING CON IN ALL OF ARKHAM.
I DON'T GET IT. WHAT'S THE APPEAL? WHY SPEND ALL YOUR TIME STEALING AND HOARDING TRASH?
YOUR TRASH IS MY TREASURE. NEVER KNOW WHAT I'LL FIND.
WINNING LOTTERY TICKET HERE, CREDIT CARD RECEIPT THERE. LETTER FROM A MISTRESS... MAYBE EVEN A KEY TO THIS CELL. NEVER KNOW.
NOW YOU TELL ME, DOODLEBUG...
HOW DOES AN URBAN-TAGGER RATE "CRIMINAL INSANITY"?
WHEN HE PUTS ART BEFORE LIFE. ANY LIFE. YOURS. EVEN MINE.
I FOLLOW MY MUSE. FOLLOW IT RIGHT OFF A CLIFF, IF THAT'S WHERE IT'S TAKING ME.
AND IT DOES TAKE ME PLACES. TOOK ME OFF THE STREETS. TOOK ME TO THE BEST ART GALLERIES IN GOTHAM.
AND TONIGHT, IT'S TAKING ME OUT OF THIS CELL.
CHOOM
DOODLEBUG! C'MON, IT'S NOW OR NEVER.
I GOT HEAD CHECK TONIGHT. THAT GIVES YOU TWENTY MINUTES TOPS...
I GOT THE SECURITY CAMERAS ON A LOOP. SEE?
CLEVER, MR. WRIGLEY. SO NO ONE CAN SEE A THING WE'RE DOING?
NOT IN THE HERE AND NOW. FOR THE NEXT HALF-HOUR, ANYBODY CHECKING IN IS LIVING IN THE PAST.

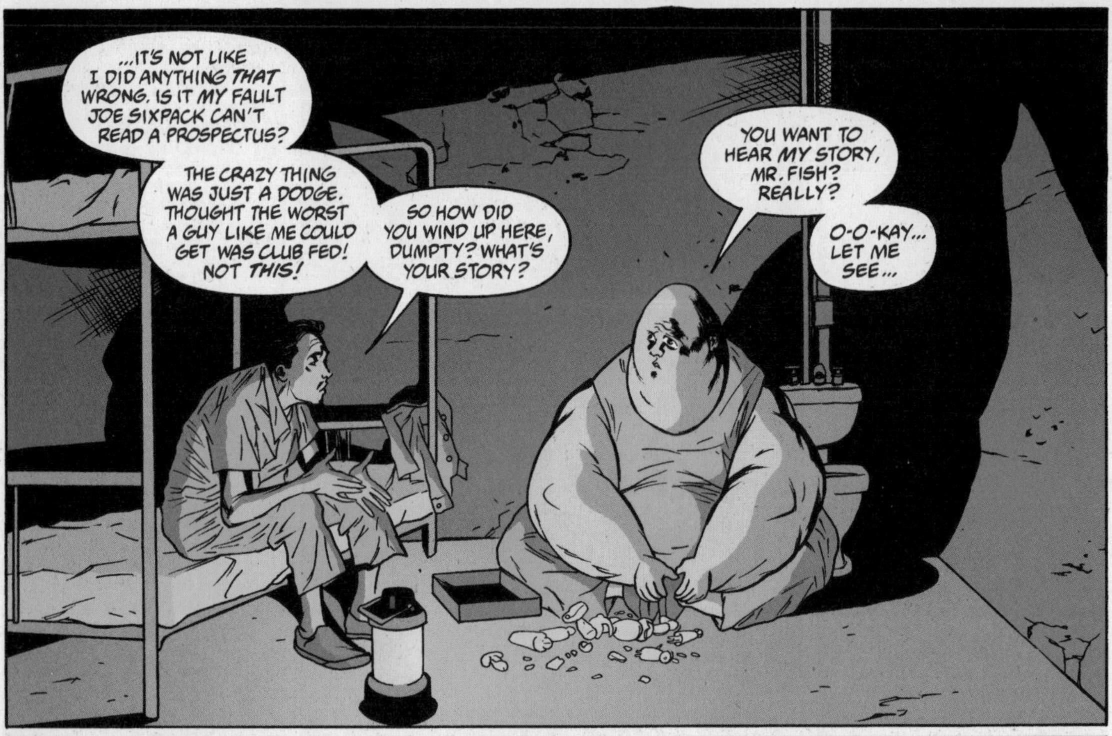
...IT'S NOT LIKE I DID ANYTHING THAT WRONG. IS IT MY FAULT JOE SIXPACK CAN'T READ A PROSPECTUS?
THE CRAZY THING WAS JUST A DODGE. THOUGHT THE WORST A GUY LIKE ME COULD GET WAS CLUB FED! NOT THIS!
SO HOW DID YOU WIND UP HERE, DUMPTY? WHAT'S YOUR STORY?
YOU WANT TO HEAR MY STORY, MR. FISH? REALLY?
O-O-KAY... LET ME SEE...

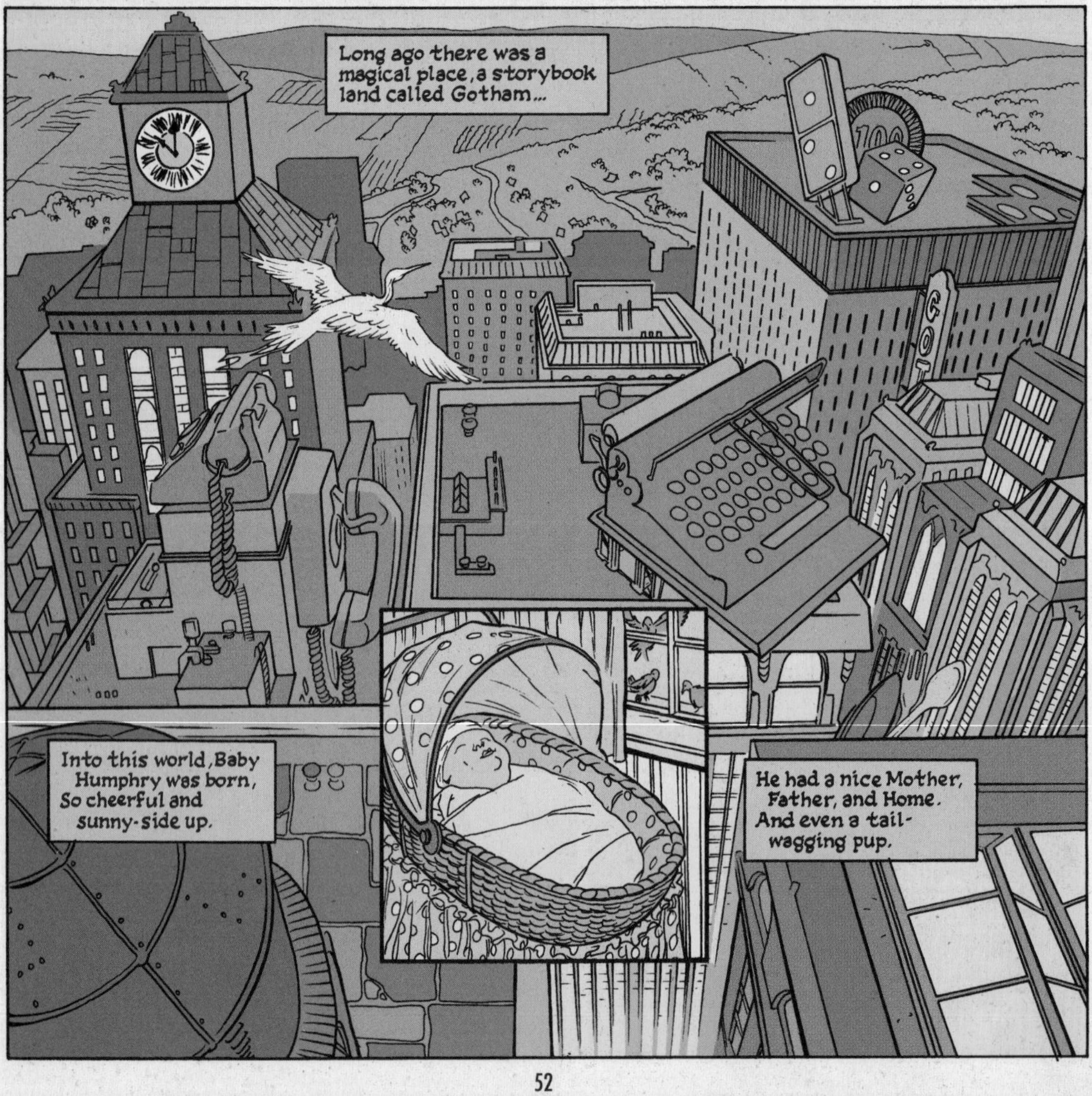
Long ago there was a magical place, a storybook land called Gotham...
Into this world, Baby Humphry was born, So cheerful and sunny-side up.
He had a nice Mother, Father, and Home. And even a tail-wagging pup.

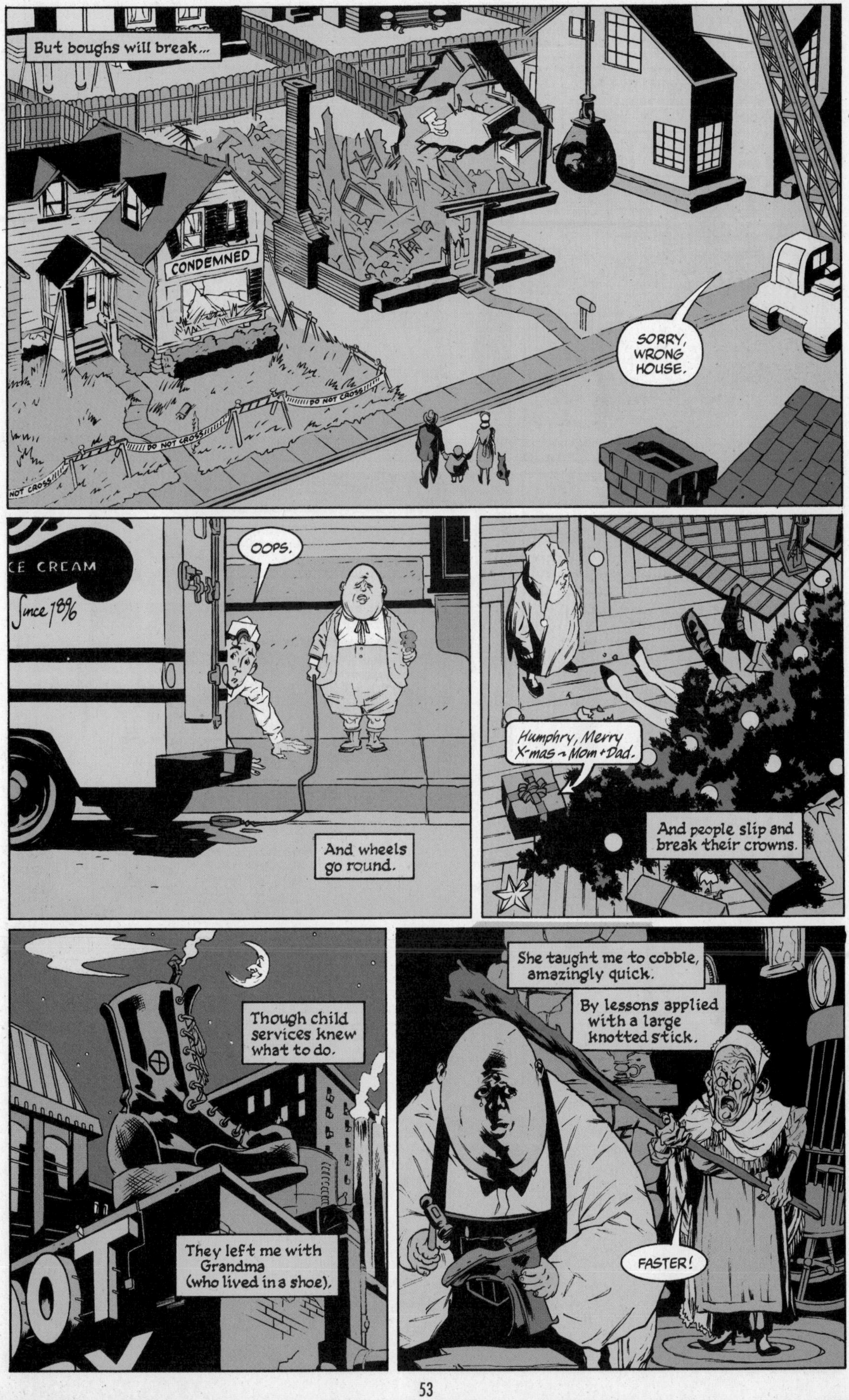
But boughs will break...
CONDEMNED
DO NOT CROSS
DO NOT CROSS
DO NOT CROSS
NOT CROSS
SORRY, WRONG HOUSE.
CE CREAM
Since 1896
OOPS.
And wheels go round.
Humphry, Merry X-mas ~ Mom + Dad.
And people slip and break their crowns.
Though child services knew what to do.
They left me with Grandma (who lived in a shoe).
She taught me to cobble, amazingly quick.
By lessons applied with a large knotted stick.
FASTER!

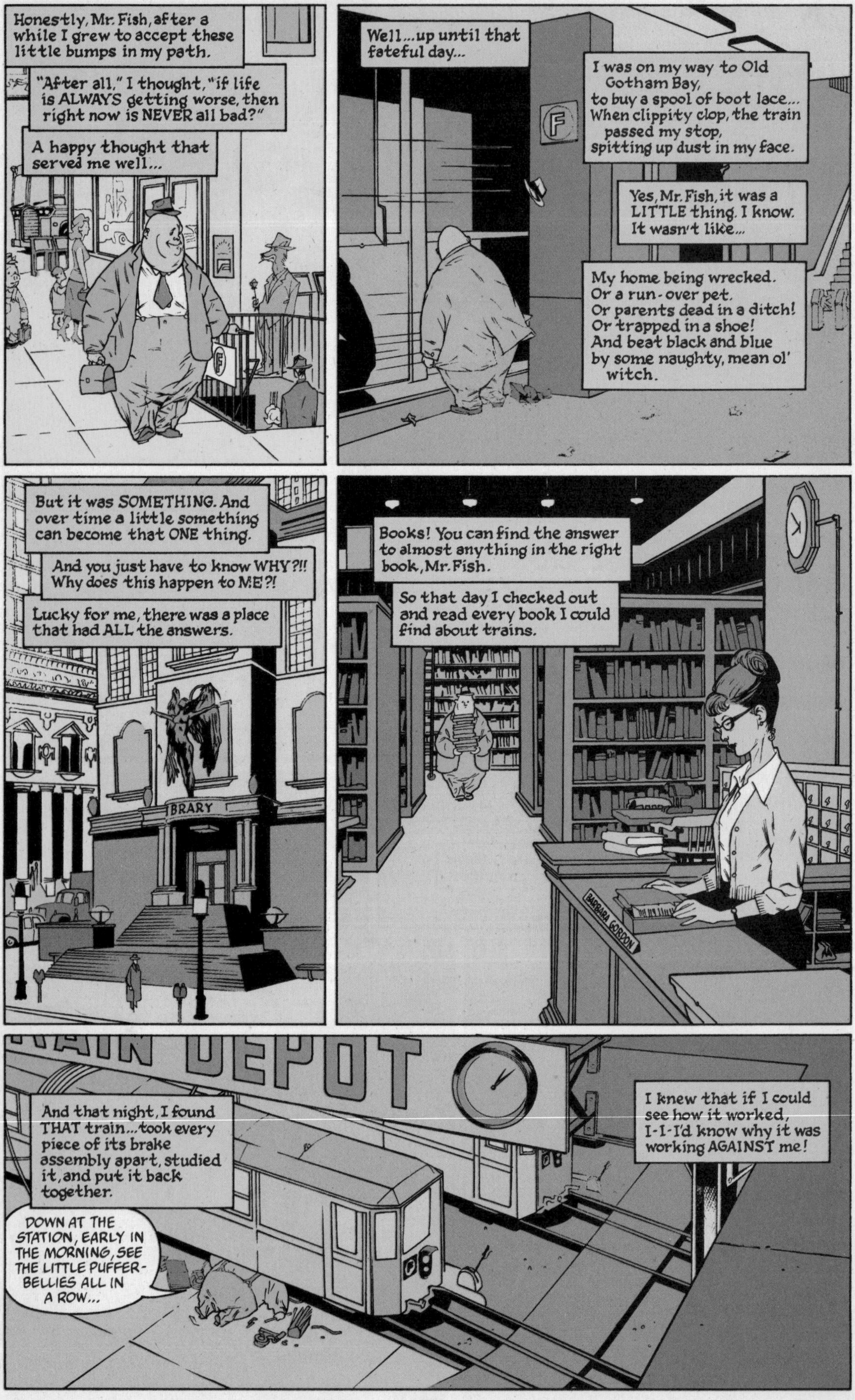
Honestly, Mr. Fish, after a while I grew to accept these little bumps in my path.
"After all," I thought, "if life is ALWAYS getting worse, then right now is NEVER all bad?"
A happy thought that served me well...
Well... up until that fateful day...
I was on my way to Old Gotham Bay,
to buy a spool of boot lace...
When clippity clop, the train passed my stop,
spitting up dust in my face.
Yes, Mr. Fish, it was a LITTLE thing. I know.
It wasn't like...
My home being wrecked.
Or a run-over pet.
Or parents dead in a ditch!
Or trapped in a shoe!
And beat black and blue
by some naughty, mean ol' witch.
But it was SOMETHING. And over time a little something can become that ONE thing.
And you just have to know WHY?!! Why does this happen to ME?!
Lucky for me, there was a place that had ALL the answers.
BRARY
Books! You can find the answer to almost anything in the right book, Mr. Fish.
So that day I checked out and read every book I could find about trains.
BARBARA GORDON
DEPOT
And that night, I found THAT train... took every piece of its brake assembly apart, studied it, and put it back together.
DOWN AT THE STATION, EARLY IN THE MORNING, SEE THE LITTLE PUFFER-BELLIES ALL IN A ROW...
I knew that if I could see how it worked, I-I-I'd know why it was working AGAINST me!

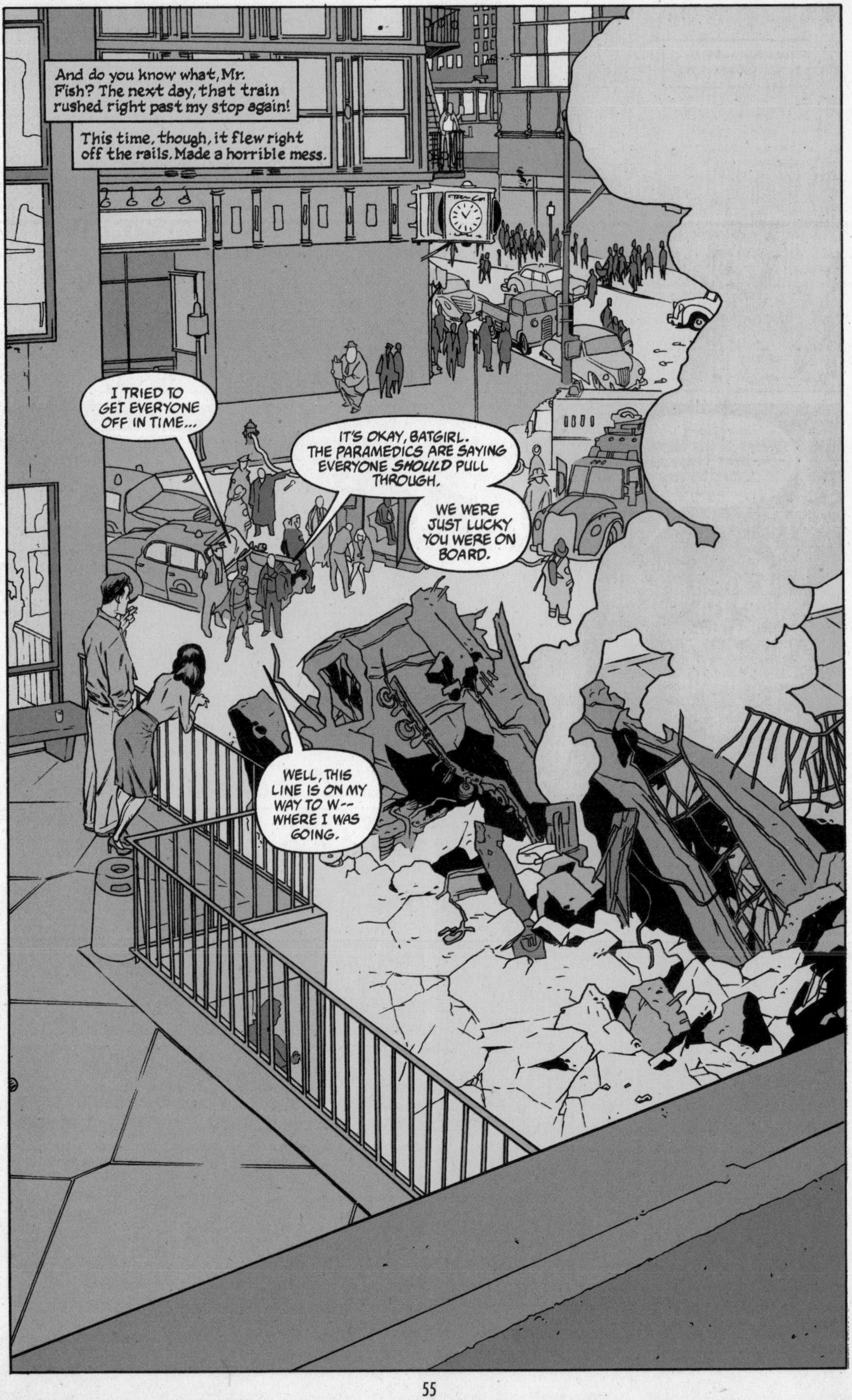
And do you know what, Mr. Fish? The next day, that train rushed right past my stop again!
This time, though, it flew right off the rails. Made a horrible mess.
I TRIED TO GET EVERYONE OFF IN TIME...
IT'S OKAY, BATGIRL. THE PARAMEDICS ARE SAYING EVERYONE *SHOULD* PULL THROUGH.
WE WERE JUST LUCKY YOU WERE ON BOARD.
WELL, THIS LINE IS ON MY WAY TO W-- WHERE I WAS GOING.

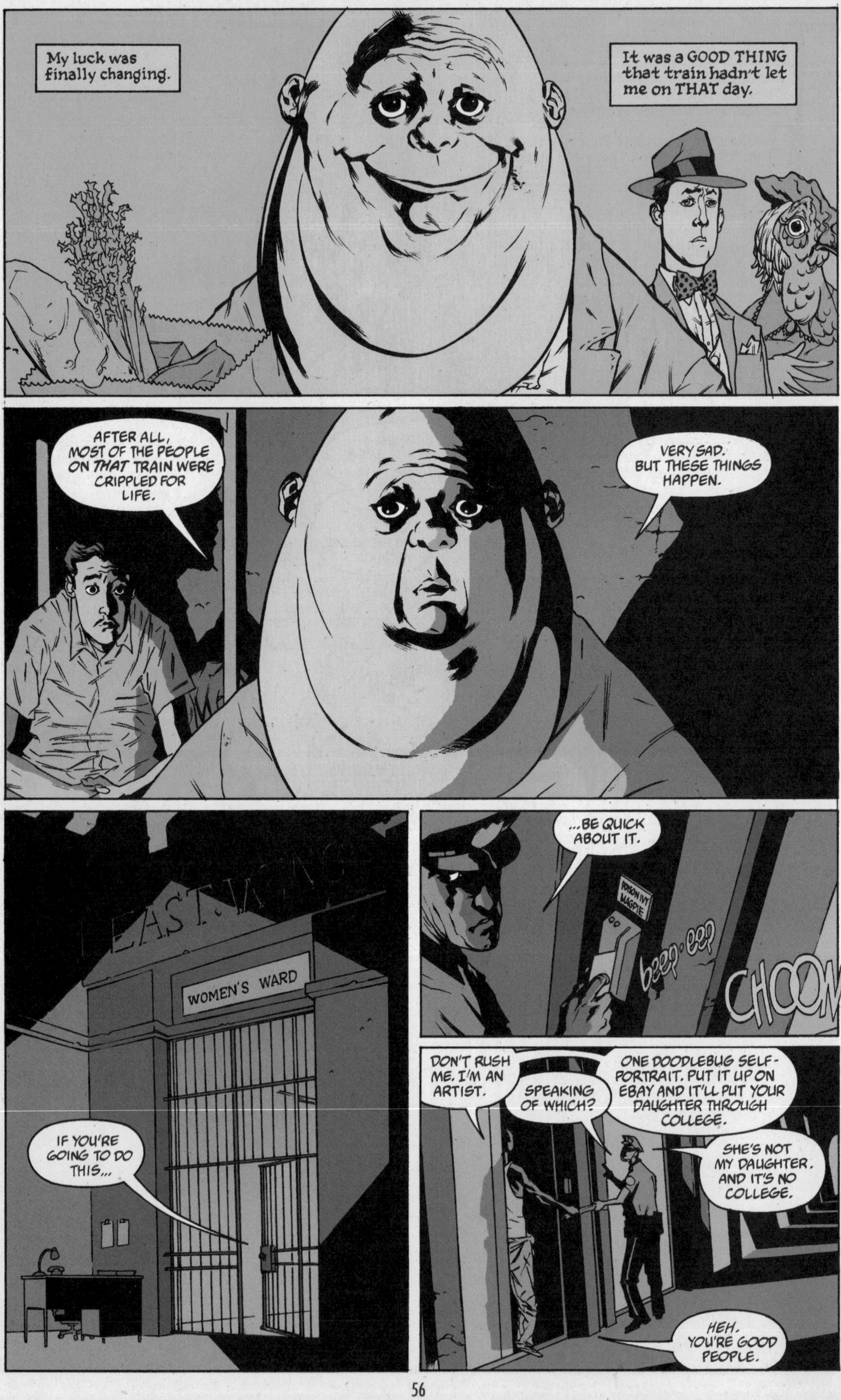
My luck was finally changing.
It was a GOOD THING that train hadn't let me on THAT day.
AFTER ALL, MOST OF THE PEOPLE ON *THAT* TRAIN WERE CRIPPLED FOR LIFE.
VERY SAD. BUT THESE THINGS HAPPEN.
EAST WING
WOMEN'S WARD
IF YOU'RE GOING TO DO THIS...
...BE QUICK ABOUT IT.
POISON IVY MAGPIE
beep-eep
CHOOM
DON'T RUSH ME. I'M AN ARTIST.
SPEAKING OF WHICH?
ONE DOODLEBUG SELF-PORTRAIT. PUT IT UP ON EBAY AND IT'LL PUT YOUR DAUGHTER THROUGH COLLEGE.
SHE'S NOT MY DAUGHTER. AND IT'S NO COLLEGE.
HEH. YOU'RE GOOD PEOPLE.

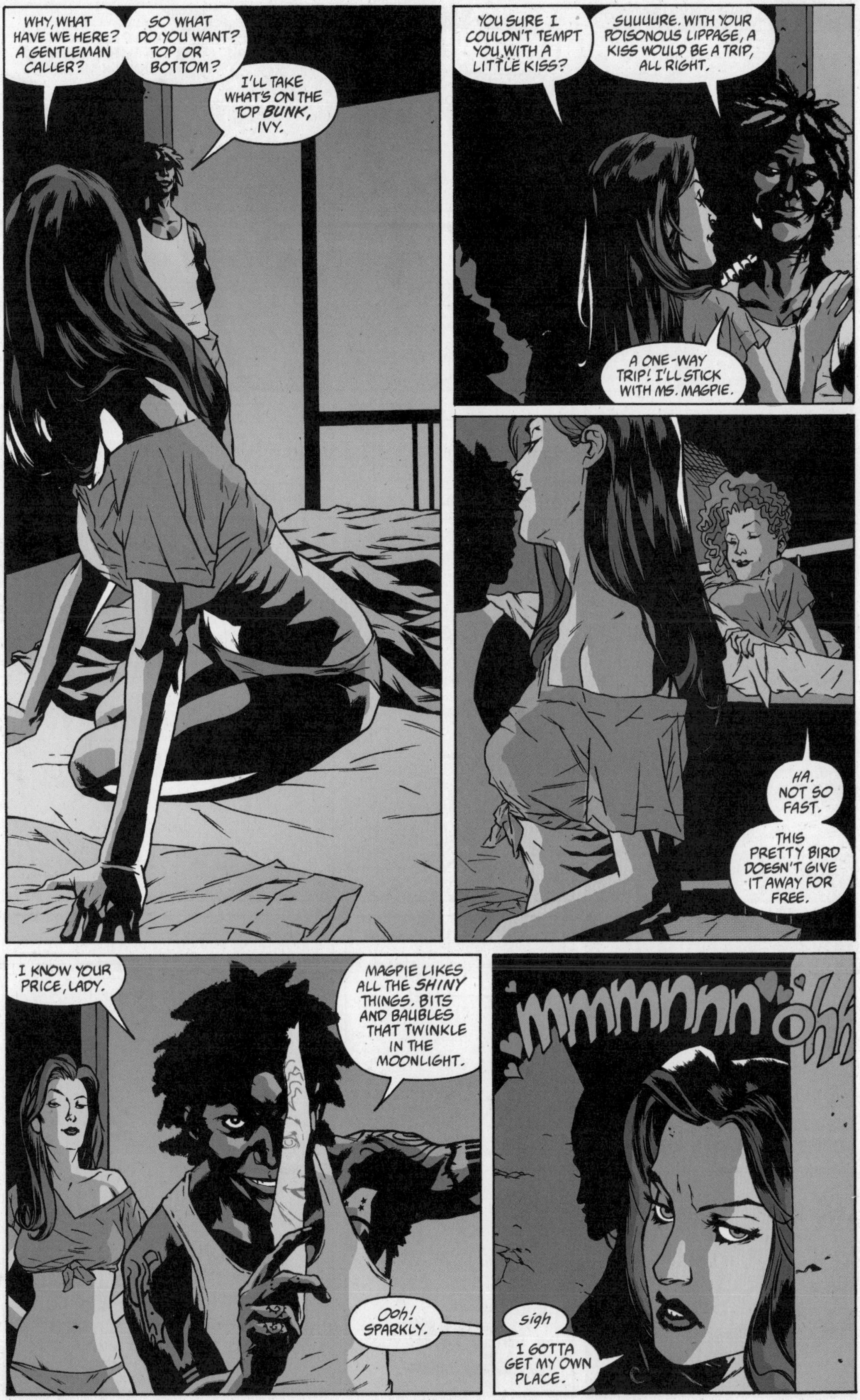
WHY, WHAT HAVE WE HERE? A GENTLEMAN CALLER?
SO WHAT DO YOU WANT? TOP OR BOTTOM?
I'LL TAKE WHAT'S ON THE TOP BUNK, IVY.
YOU SURE I COULDN'T TEMPT YOU WITH A LITTLE KISS?
SUUUURE. WITH YOUR POISONOUS LIPPAGE, A KISS WOULD BE A TRIP, ALL RIGHT.
A ONE-WAY TRIP! I'LL STICK WITH MS. MAGPIE.
HA. NOT SO FAST.
THIS PRETTY BIRD DOESN'T GIVE IT AWAY FOR FREE.
I KNOW YOUR PRICE, LADY.
MAGPIE LIKES ALL THE SHINY THINGS. BITS AND BAUBLES THAT TWINKLE IN THE MOONLIGHT.
Ooh! SPARKLY.
mmmnnn ohh
sigh
I GOTTA GET MY OWN PLACE.

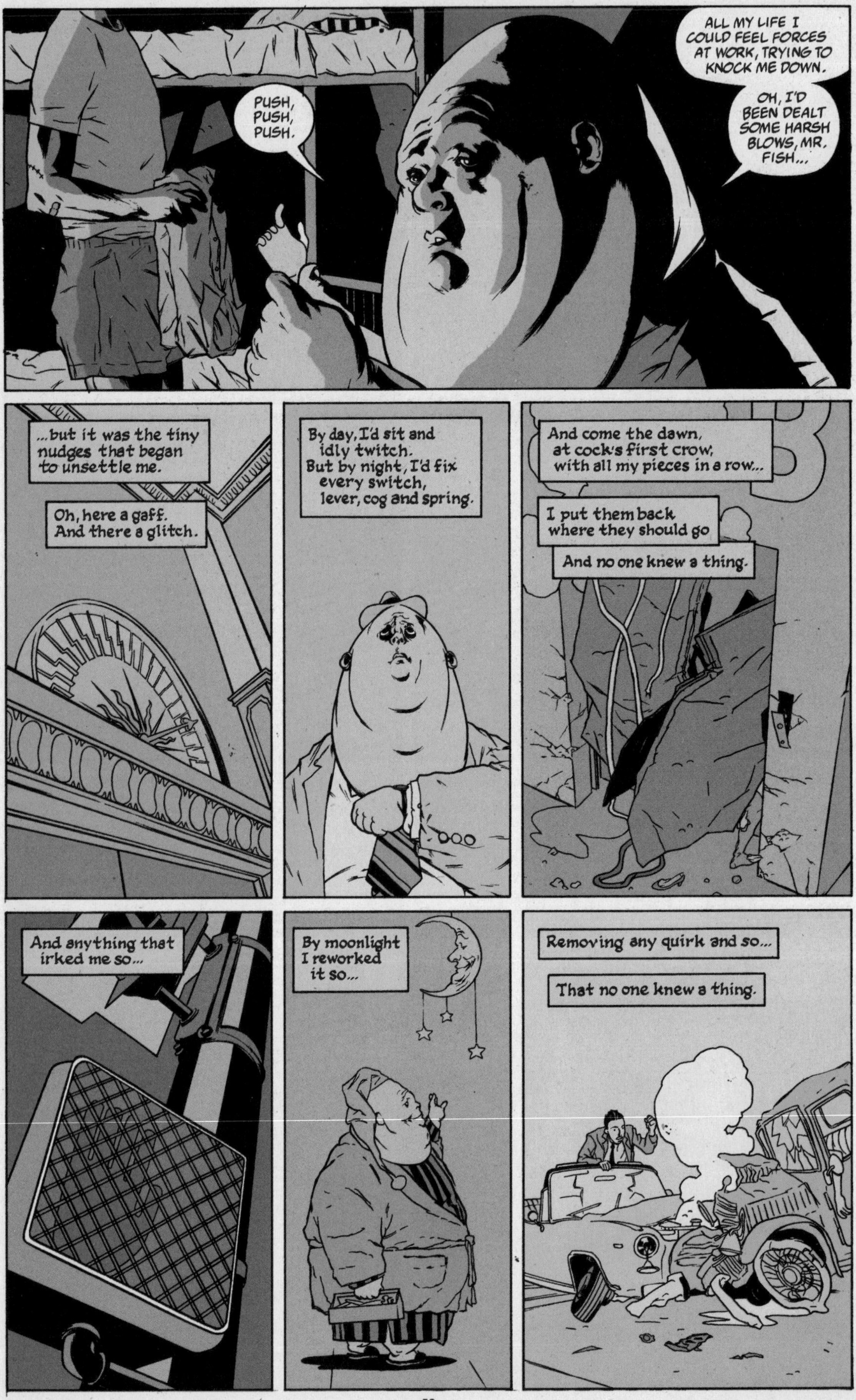

ALL MY LIFE I COULD FEEL FORCES AT WORK, TRYING TO KNOCK ME DOWN.
PUSH, PUSH, PUSH.
OH, I'D BEEN DEALT SOME HARSH BLOWS, MR. FISH...
...but it was the tiny nudges that began to unsettle me.
Oh, here a gaff. And there a glitch.
By day, I'd sit and idly twitch. But by night, I'd fix every switch, lever, cog and spring.
And come the dawn, at cock's first crow, with all my pieces in a row...
I put them back where they should go
And no one knew a thing.
And anything that irked me so...
By moonlight I reworked it so...
Removing any quirk and so...
That no one knew a thing.

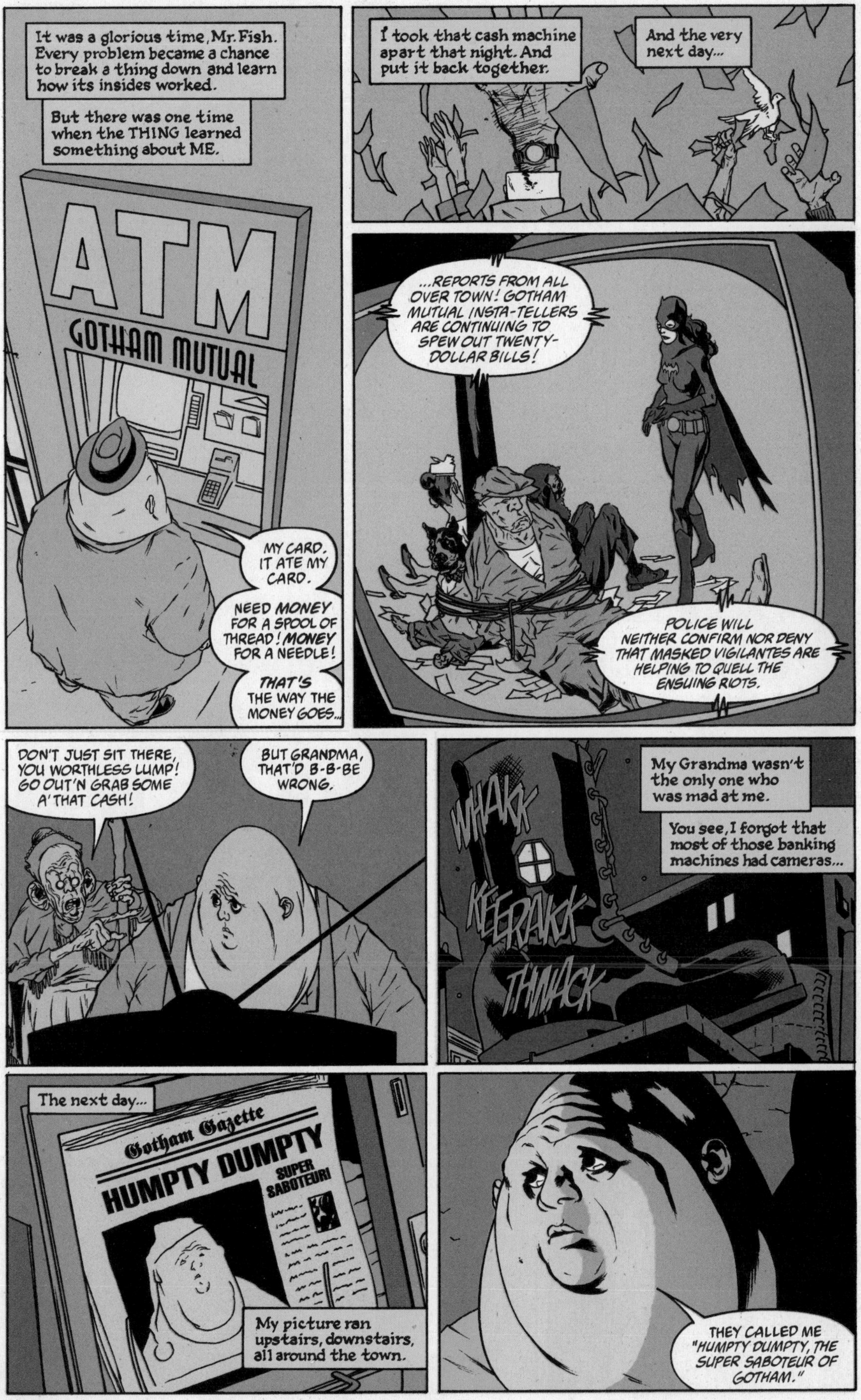

It was a glorious time, Mr. Fish. Every problem became a chance to break a thing down and learn how its insides worked.
But there was one time when the THING learned something about ME.
ATM
GOTHAM MUTUAL
MY CARD. IT ATE MY CARD.
NEED MONEY FOR A SPOOL OF THREAD! MONEY FOR A NEEDLE!
THAT'S THE WAY THE MONEY GOES...
I took that cash machine apart that night. And put it back together.
And the very next day...
...REPORTS FROM ALL OVER TOWN! GOTHAM MUTUAL INSTA-TELLERS ARE CONTINUING TO SPEW OUT TWENTY-DOLLAR BILLS!
POLICE WILL NEITHER CONFIRM NOR DENY THAT MASKED VIGILANTES ARE HELPING TO QUELL THE ENSUING RIOTS.
DON'T JUST SIT THERE, YOU WORTHLESS LUMP! GO OUT'N GRAB SOME A' THAT CASH!
BUT GRANDMA, THAT'D B-B-BE WRONG.
My Grandma wasn't the only one who was mad at me.
You see, I forgot that most of those banking machines had cameras...
WHAKK
KEERAKK
THWACK
The next day...
Gotham Gazette
HUMPTY DUMPTY
SUPER SABOTEUR!
My picture ran upstairs, downstairs, all around the town.
THEY CALLED ME "HUMPTY DUMPTY, THE SUPER SABOTEUR OF GOTHAM."

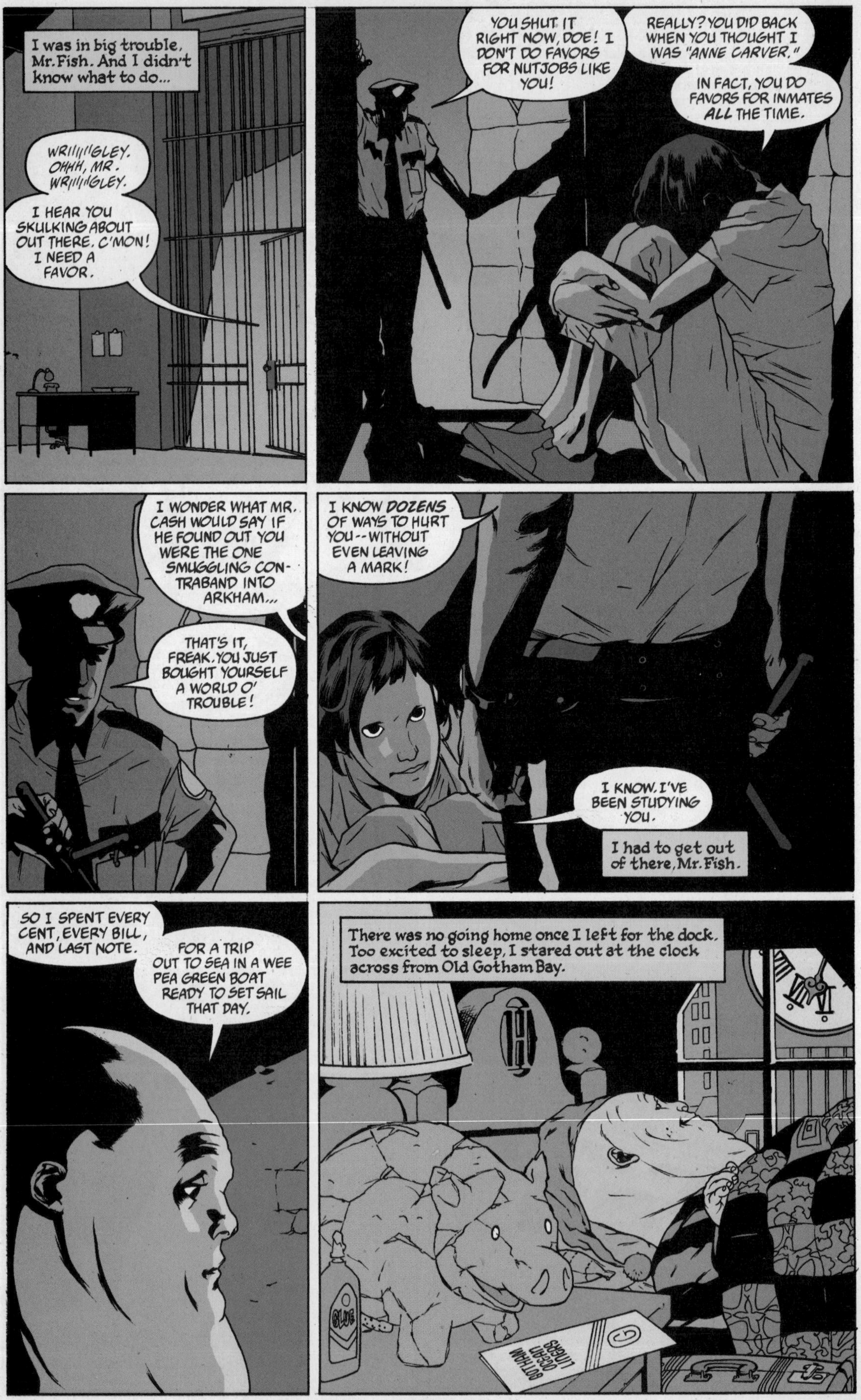
I was in big trouble, Mr. Fish. And I didn't know what to do...
WRI///I'GLEY. OHHH, MR. WRI///I'GLEY.
I HEAR YOU SKULKING ABOUT OUT THERE. C'MON! I NEED A FAVOR.
YOU SHUT IT RIGHT NOW, DOE! I DON'T DO FAVORS FOR NUTJOBS LIKE YOU!
REALLY? YOU DID BACK WHEN YOU THOUGHT I WAS "ANNE CARVER."
IN FACT, YOU DO FAVORS FOR INMATES ALL THE TIME.
I WONDER WHAT MR. CASH WOULD SAY IF HE FOUND OUT YOU WERE THE ONE SMUGGLING CONTRABAND INTO ARKHAM...
THAT'S IT, FREAK. YOU JUST BOUGHT YOURSELF A WORLD O' TROUBLE!
I KNOW DOZENS OF WAYS TO HURT YOU--WITHOUT EVEN LEAVING A MARK!
I KNOW. I'VE BEEN STUDYING YOU.
I had to get out of there, Mr. Fish.
SO I SPENT EVERY CENT, EVERY BILL, AND LAST NOTE.
FOR A TRIP OUT TO SEA IN A WEE PEA GREEN BOAT READY TO SET SAIL THAT DAY.
There was no going home once I left for the dock. Too excited to sleep, I stared out at the clock across from Old Gotham Bay.
GLUE

There were no fond farewells as I went to the pier.
I was ready to go, but to my greatest fear
my wee ship had sailed away.

That rotten clock tower
was off by an hour.
I would have to set it right!

Climbing up to the gears
I held back all my tears
And wound the works good and tight...

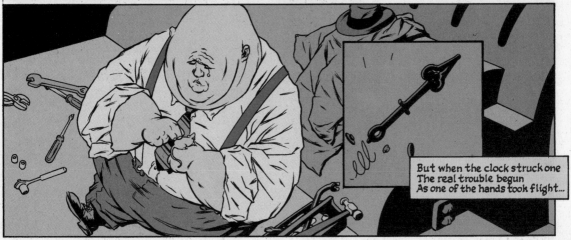

But when the clock struck one
The real trouble begun
As one of the hands took flight...

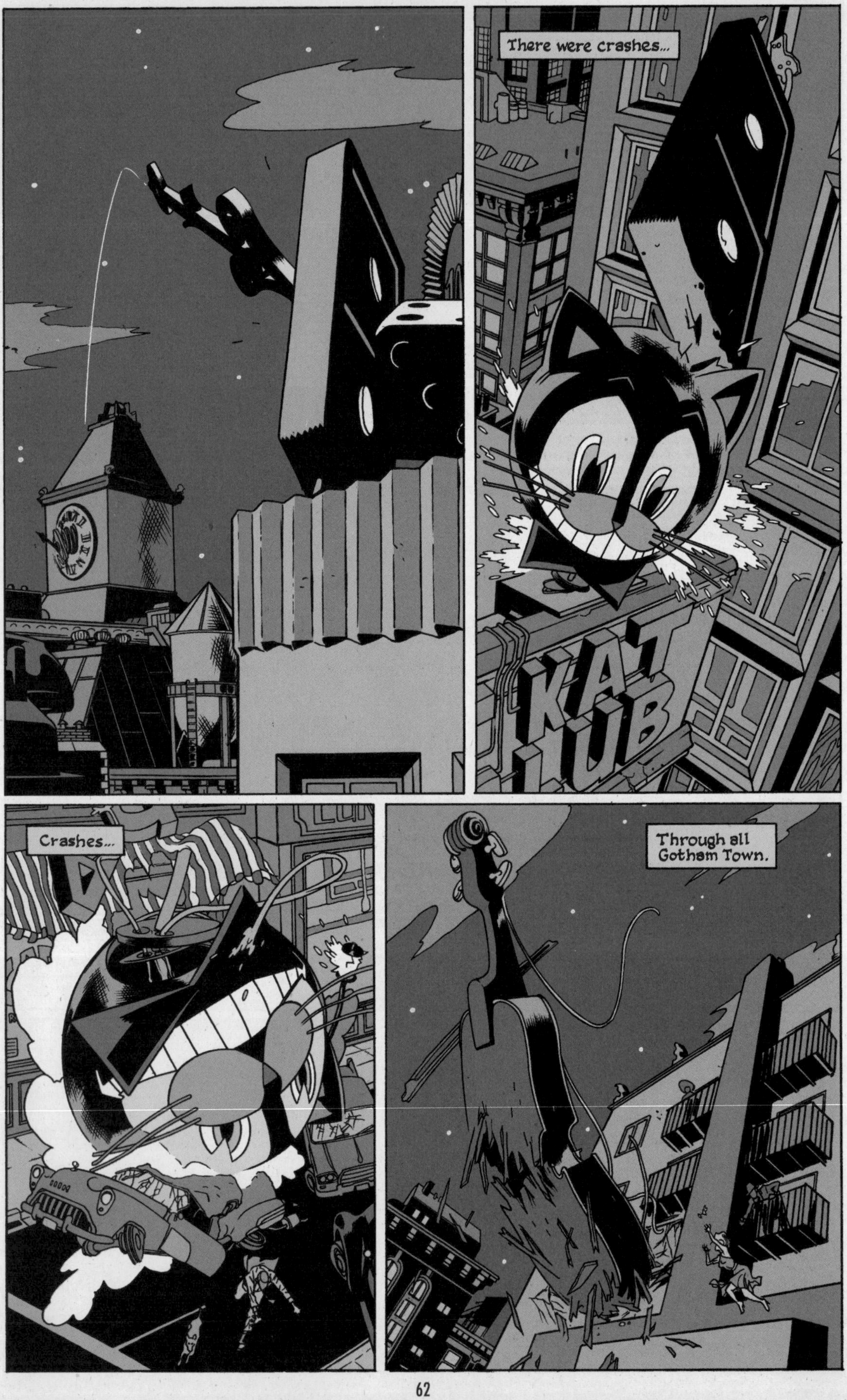
There were crashes...
KAT
Crashes...
Through all
Gotham Town.

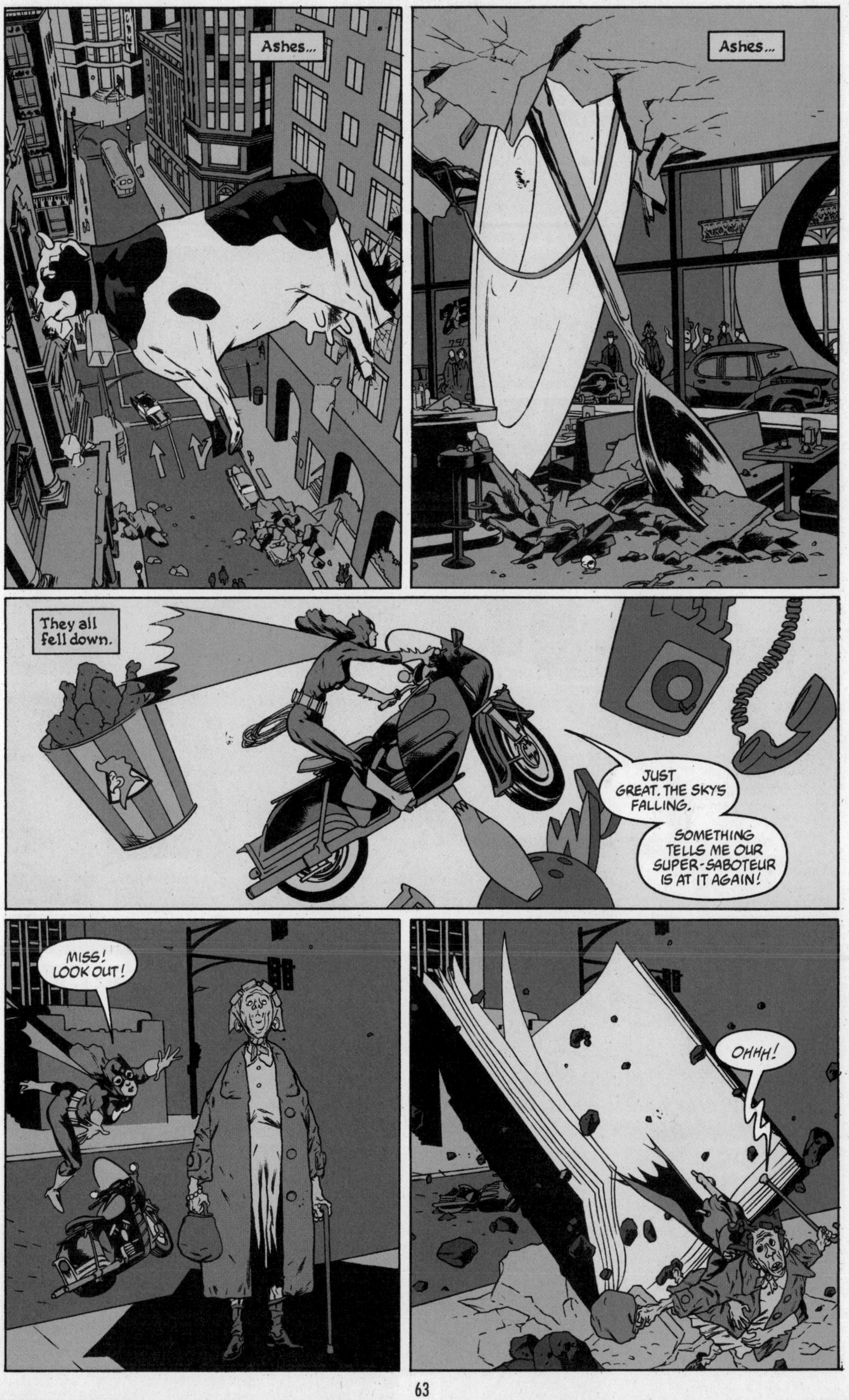

Ashes...
Ashes...
They all fell down.
JUST GREAT. THE SKY'S FALLING.
SOMETHING TELLS ME OUR SUPER-SABOTEUR IS AT IT AGAIN!
MISS! LOOK OUT!
OHHH!

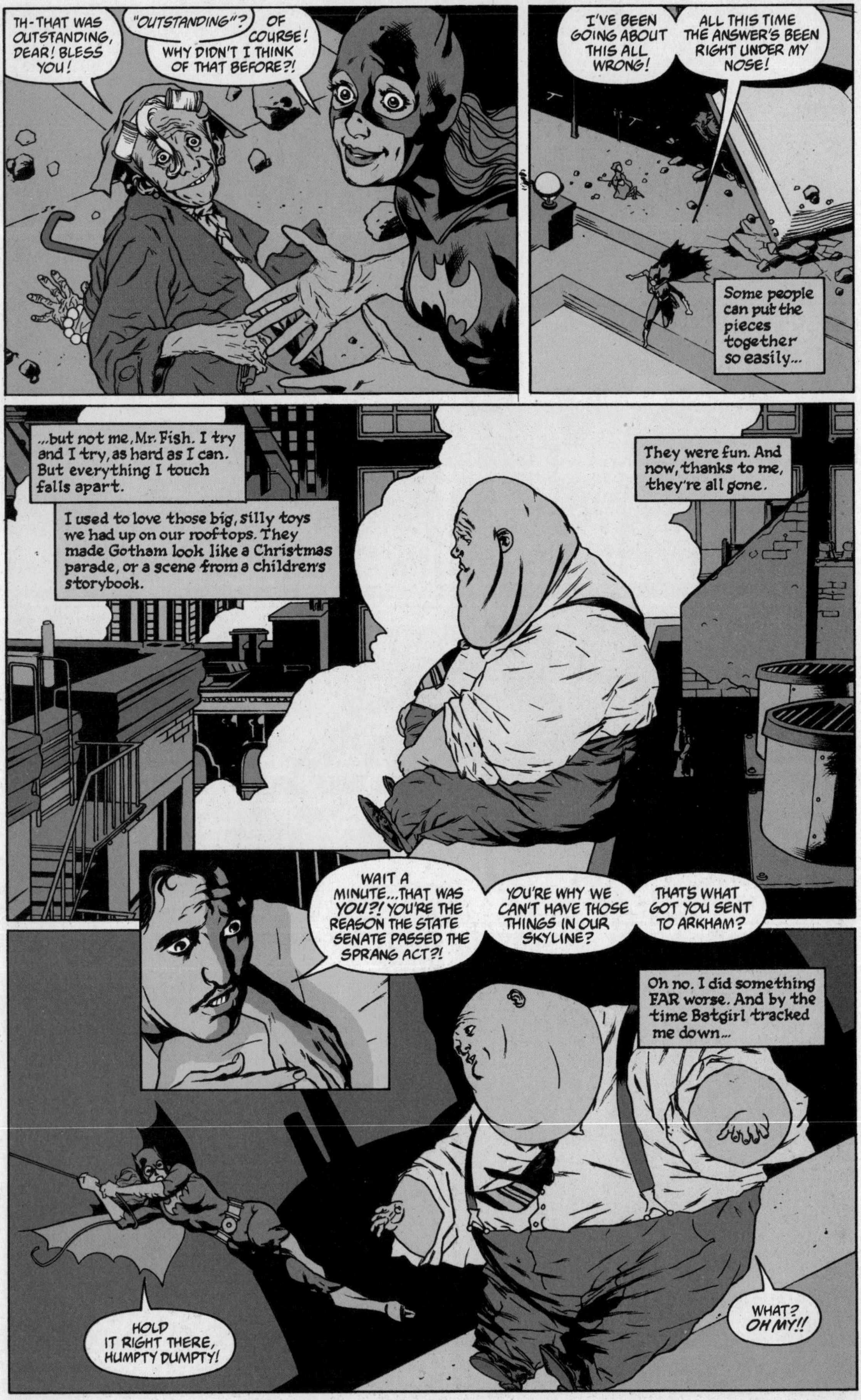
TH-THAT WAS OUTSTANDING, DEAR! BLESS YOU!
"OUTSTANDING"? OF COURSE! WHY DIDN'T I THINK OF THAT BEFORE?!
I'VE BEEN GOING ABOUT THIS ALL WRONG!
ALL THIS TIME THE ANSWER'S BEEN RIGHT UNDER MY NOSE!
Some people can put the pieces together so easily...
...but not me, Mr. Fish. I try and I try, as hard as I can. But everything I touch falls apart.
I used to love those big, silly toys we had up on our rooftops. They made Gotham look like a Christmas parade, or a scene from a children's storybook.
They were fun. And now, thanks to me, they're all gone.
WAIT A MINUTE...THAT WAS YOU?! YOU'RE THE REASON THE STATE SENATE PASSED THE SPRANG ACT?!
YOU'RE WHY WE CAN'T HAVE THOSE THINGS IN OUR SKYLINE?
THAT'S WHAT GOT YOU SENT TO ARKHAM?
Oh no. I did something FAR worse. And by the time Batgirl tracked me down...
HOLD IT RIGHT THERE, HUMPTY DUMPTY!
WHAT? OH MY!!

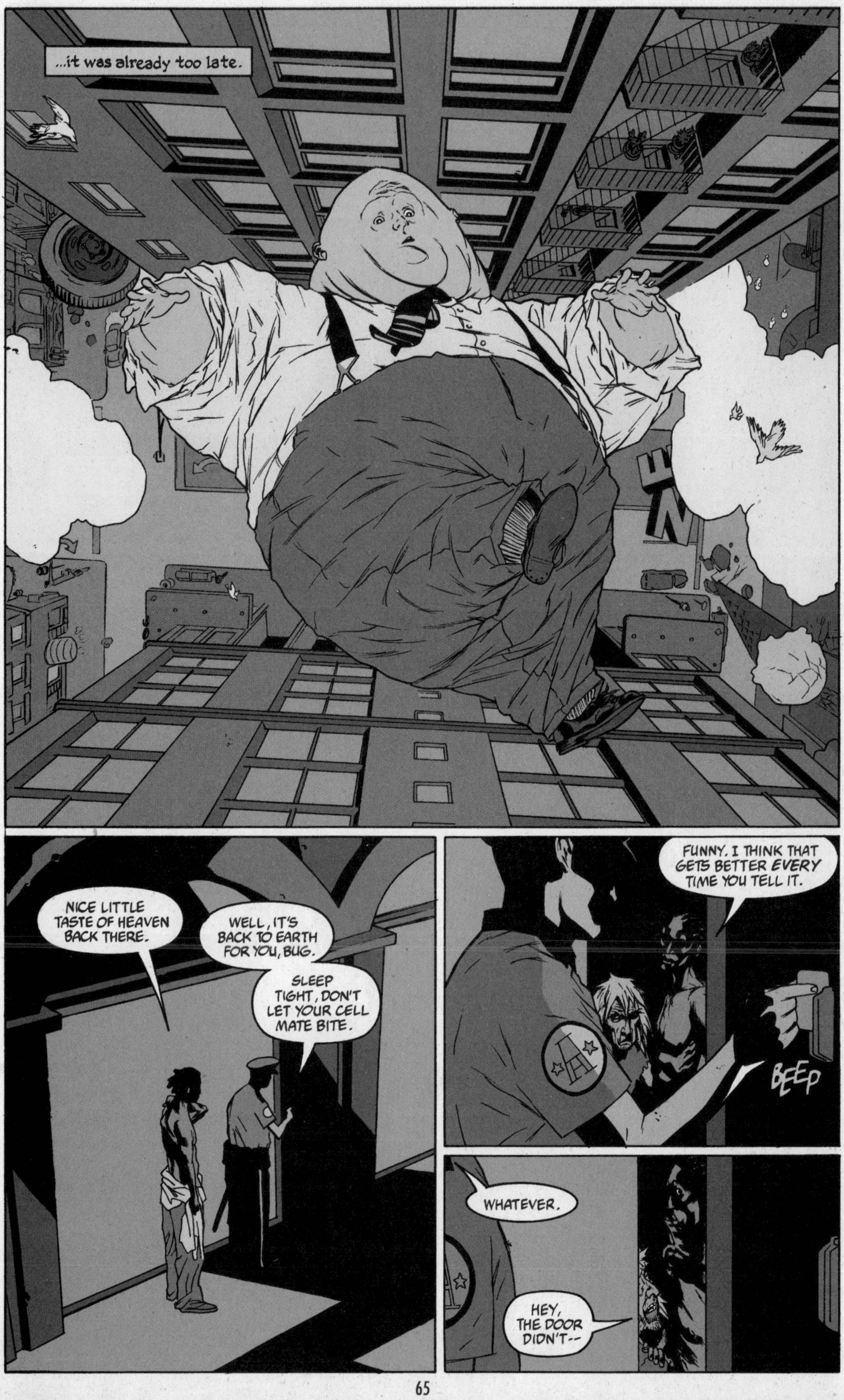
...it was already too late.
NICE LITTLE TASTE OF HEAVEN BACK THERE.
WELL, IT'S BACK TO EARTH FOR YOU, BUG.
SLEEP TIGHT, DON'T LET YOUR CELL MATE BITE.
FUNNY. I THINK THAT GETS BETTER EVERY TIME YOU TELL IT.
BEEP
WHATEVER.
HEY, THE DOOR DIDN'T--

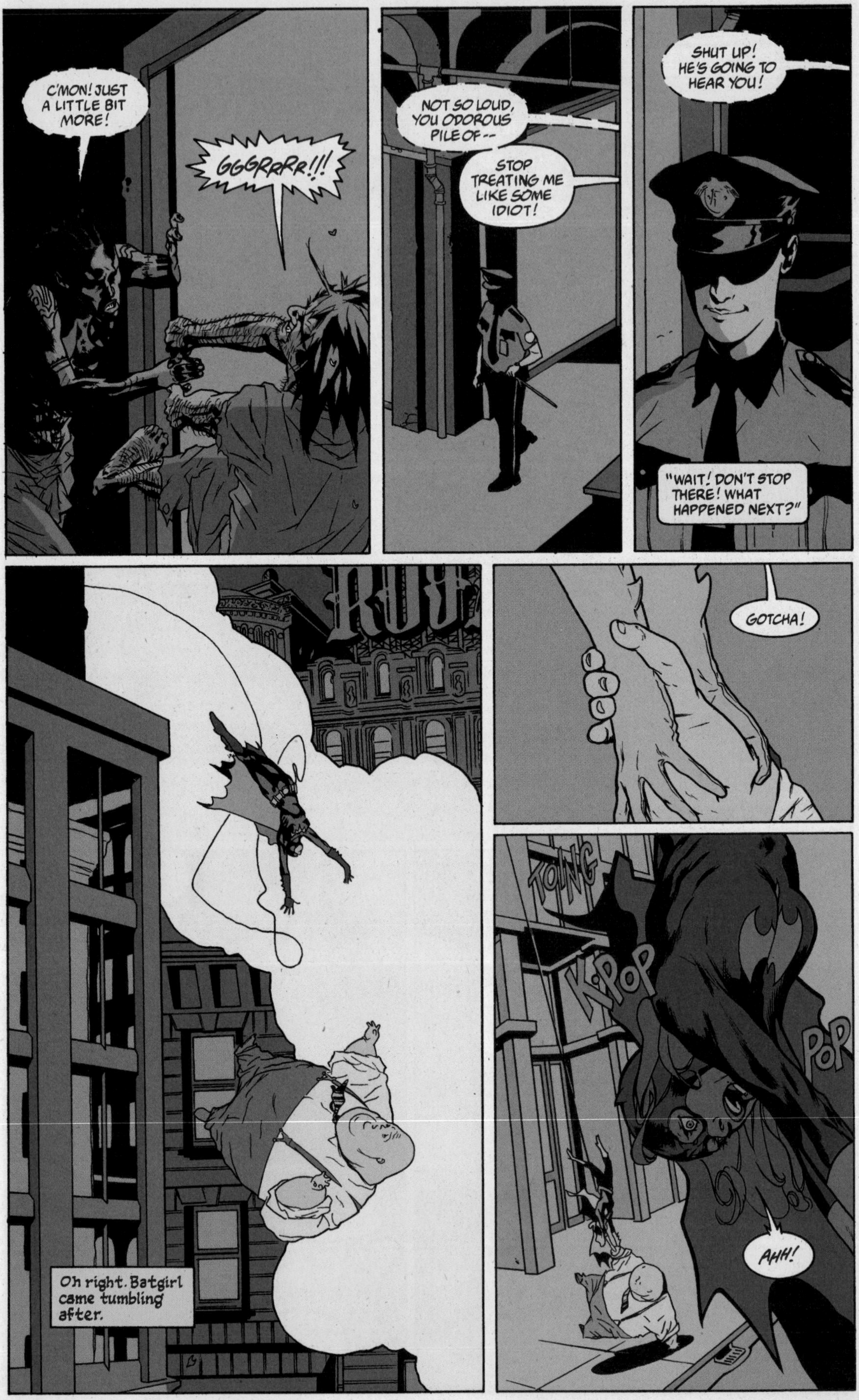
C'MON! JUST A LITTLE BIT MORE!
GGGRRRR!!!
NOT SO LOUD, YOU ODOROUS PILE OF --
STOP TREATING ME LIKE SOME IDIOT!
SHUT UP! HE'S GOING TO HEAR YOU!
"WAIT! DON'T STOP THERE! WHAT HAPPENED NEXT?"
Oh right. Batgirl came tumbling after.
GOTCHA!
KOING
K-POP
POP
AHH!

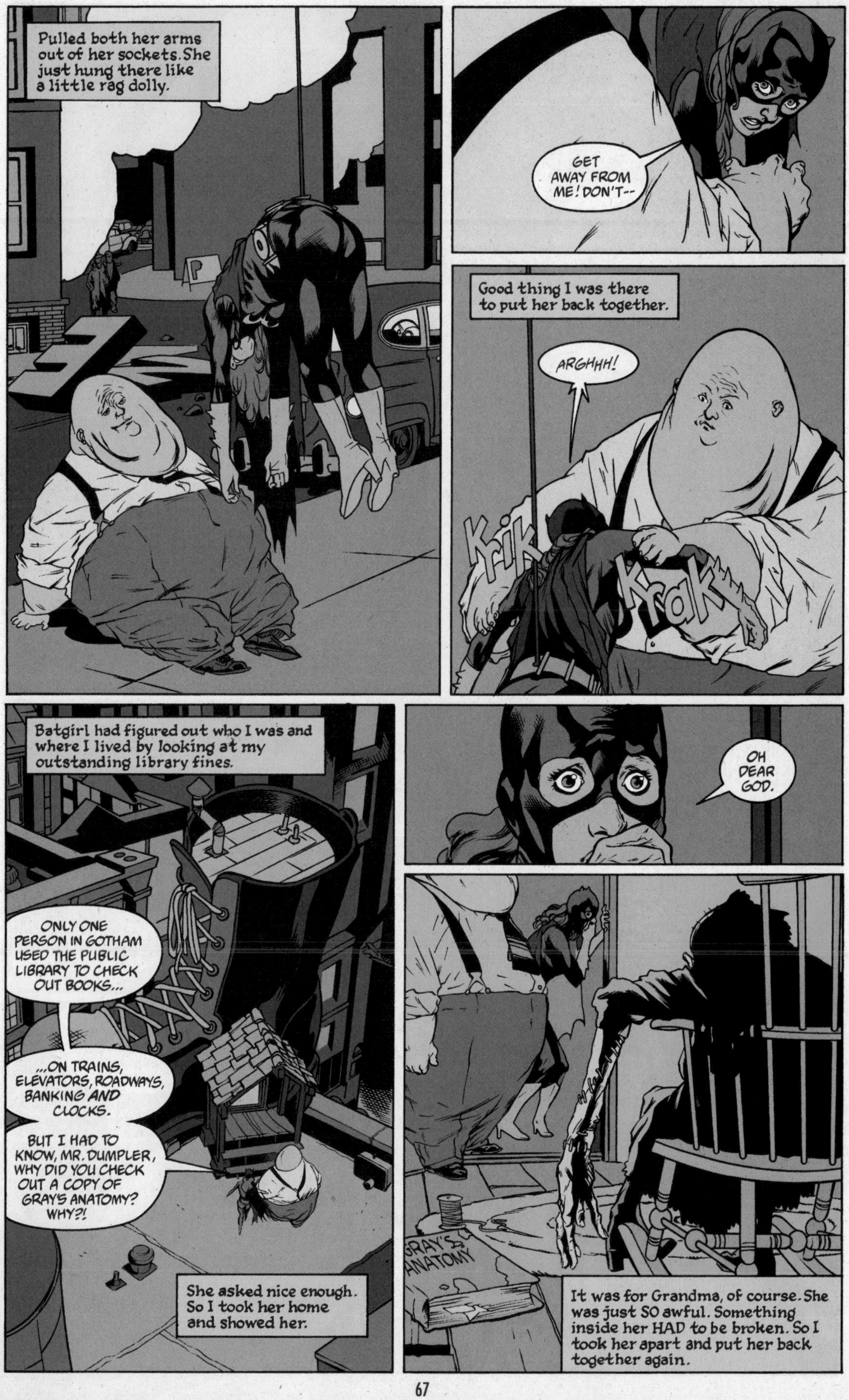
Pulled both her arms out of her sockets. She just hung there like a little rag dolly.
GET AWAY FROM ME! DON'T--
Good thing I was there to put her back together.
ARGHHH!
Krik
Krak
Batgirl had figured out who I was and where I lived by looking at my outstanding library fines.
ONLY ONE PERSON IN GOTHAM USED THE PUBLIC LIBRARY TO CHECK OUT BOOKS...
...ON TRAINS, ELEVATORS, ROADWAYS, BANKING AND CLOCKS.
BUT I HAD TO KNOW, MR. DUMPLER, WHY DID YOU CHECK OUT A COPY OF GRAY'S ANATOMY? WHY?!
She asked nice enough. So I took her home and showed her.
OH DEAR GOD.
GRAY'S ANATOMY
It was for Grandma, of course. She was just SO awful. Something inside her HAD to be broken. So I took her apart and put her back together again.

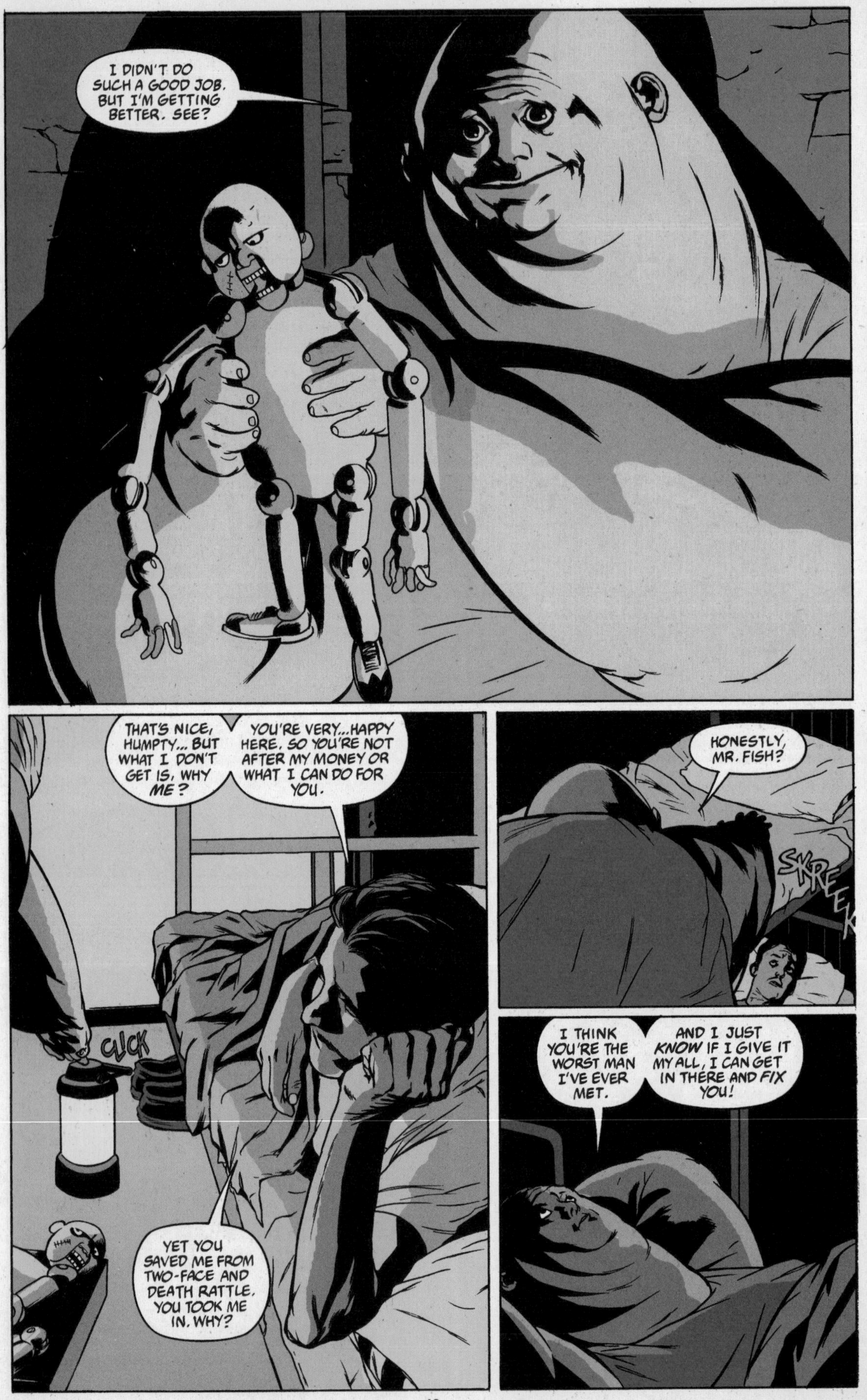
I DIDN'T DO SUCH A GOOD JOB. BUT I'M GETTING BETTER. SEE?
THAT'S NICE, HUMPTY... BUT WHAT I DON'T GET IS, WHY *ME*?
YOU'RE VERY... HAPPY HERE. SO YOU'RE NOT AFTER MY MONEY OR WHAT I CAN DO FOR YOU.
CLICK
YET YOU SAVED ME FROM TWO-FACE AND DEATH RATTLE. YOU TOOK ME IN. WHY?
HONESTLY, MR. FISH?
SKREEEK
I THINK YOU'RE THE WORST MAN I'VE EVER MET.
AND I JUST *KNOW* IF I GIVE IT MY ALL, I CAN GET IN THERE AND *FIX* YOU!

GOOD NIGHT, MR. FISH.

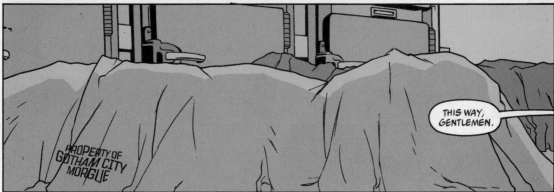

THIS WAY, GENTLEMEN.

PROPERTY OF GOTHAM CITY MORGUE

I WANT TO WARN YOU, THIS ISN'T GOING TO BE PRETTY.

DON'T WORRY, DOC. I BEEN ON THE FORCE OVER TWENTY YEARS.

HAD A CASE ONCE, GUY HACKED UP HIS GRAND-MOTHER AND SEWED HER BACK UP WITH SHOELACES.

AIN'T NOTHIN' IN THIS TOWN I HAVEN'T SEEN!

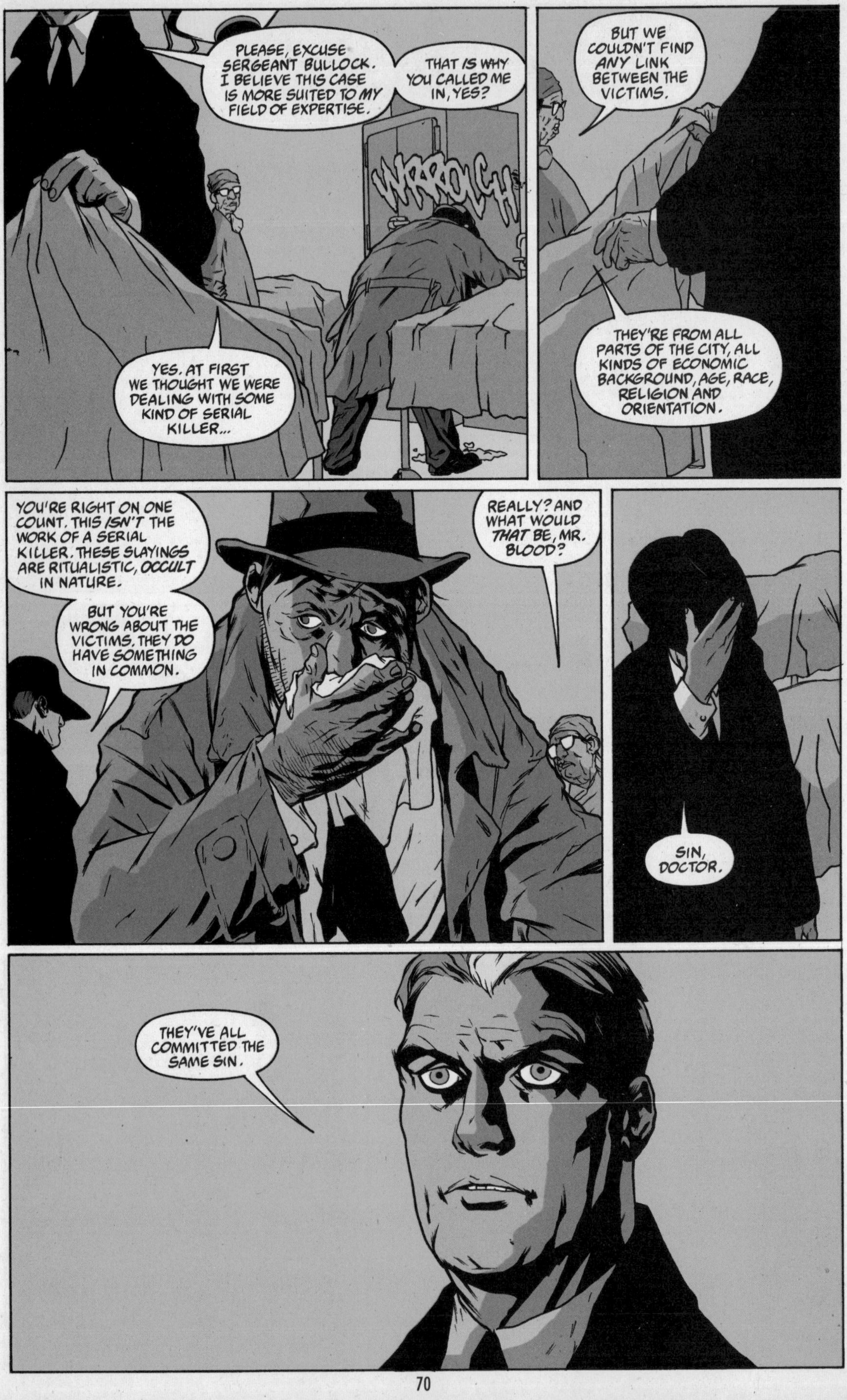
PLEASE, EXCUSE SERGEANT BULLOCK. I BELIEVE THIS CASE IS MORE SUITED TO MY FIELD OF EXPERTISE.
THAT IS WHY YOU CALLED ME IN, YES?
WRROLCH
YES. AT FIRST WE THOUGHT WE WERE DEALING WITH SOME KIND OF SERIAL KILLER...
BUT WE COULDN'T FIND ANY LINK BETWEEN THE VICTIMS.
THEY'RE FROM ALL PARTS OF THE CITY, ALL KINDS OF ECONOMIC BACKGROUND, AGE, RACE, RELIGION AND ORIENTATION.
YOU'RE RIGHT ON ONE COUNT. THIS ISN'T THE WORK OF A SERIAL KILLER. THESE SLAYINGS ARE RITUALISTIC, OCCULT IN NATURE.
BUT YOU'RE WRONG ABOUT THE VICTIMS. THEY DO HAVE SOMETHING IN COMMON.
REALLY? AND WHAT WOULD THAT BE, MR. BLOOD?
SIN, DOCTOR.
THEY'VE ALL COMMITTED THE SAME SIN.

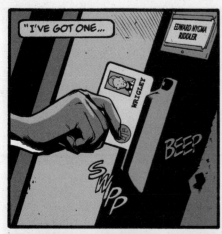

"I'VE GOT ONE...
EDWARD NYGMA RIDDLER
WRIGLEY
BEEP
SWPP
BEEP
?
"...MICHAEL JACKSON."
BEEP
"MICHAEL JACKSON?!"
O FRABJOUS DAY!
"YEAH. THINK ABOUT IT.
BEEP
"DID ALL THAT SURGERY TO HIS FACE. SURROUNDS HIMSELF WITH WEIRD ANIMALS. SOMETIMES WEARS A MASK."
"WHAT WOULD YOU CALL HIM?"
"POP KING. OKAY, YOUR TURN."
"THE ROCK."
"HERE WE GO AGAIN! LOOK, NOBODY FROM THE WWE..."
CALLOOH! CALLAY!
...IT'S TOO OBVIOUS!
MONITOR 1
LIKE YOUR GUY COULD TAKE BATMAN? COME ON...
MONITOR 2

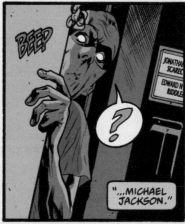

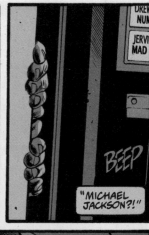

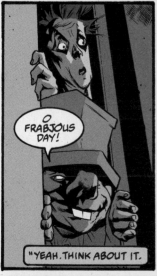

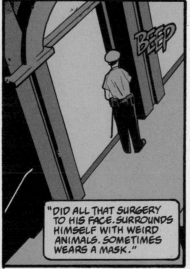

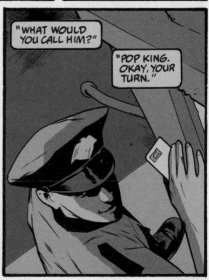

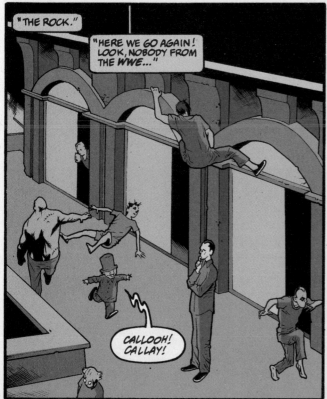

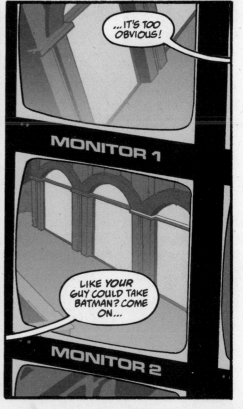

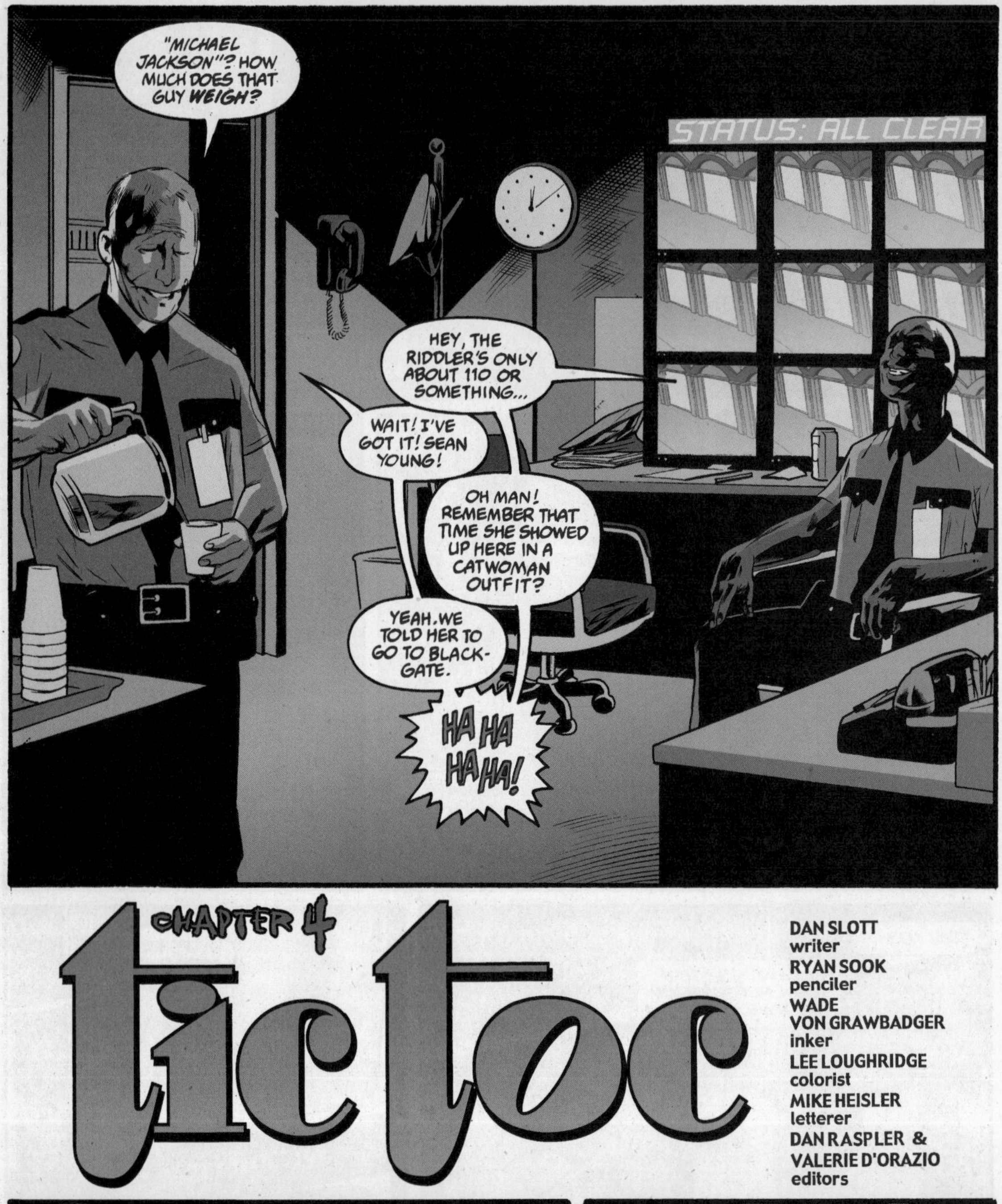
STATUS: ALL CLEAR
"MICHAEL JACKSON"? HOW MUCH DOES THAT GUY WEIGH?
HEY, THE RIDDLER'S ONLY ABOUT 110 OR SOMETHING...
WAIT! I'VE GOT IT! SEAN YOUNG!
OH MAN! REMEMBER THAT TIME SHE SHOWED UP HERE IN A CATWOMAN OUTFIT?
YEAH. WE TOLD HER TO GO TO BLACK-GATE.
HA HA HA HA!

CHAPTER 4

tic toc

DAN SLOTT
writer
RYAN SOOK
penciler
WADE VON GRAWBADGER
inker
LEE LOUGHRIDGE
colorist
MIKE HEISLER
letterer
DAN RASPLER & VALERIE D'ORAZIO
editors

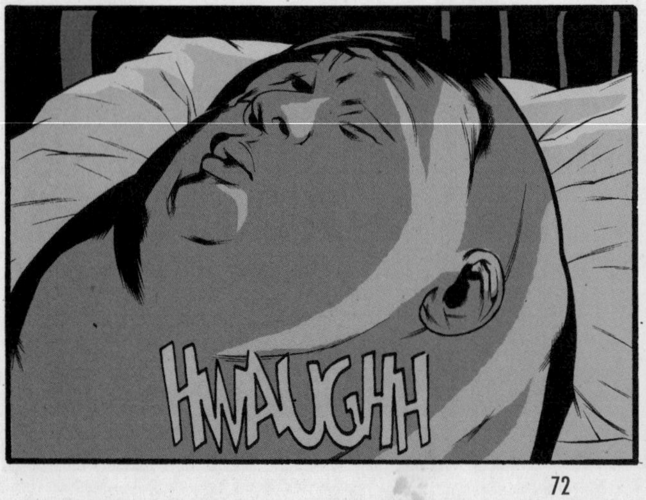
HWAUGHH

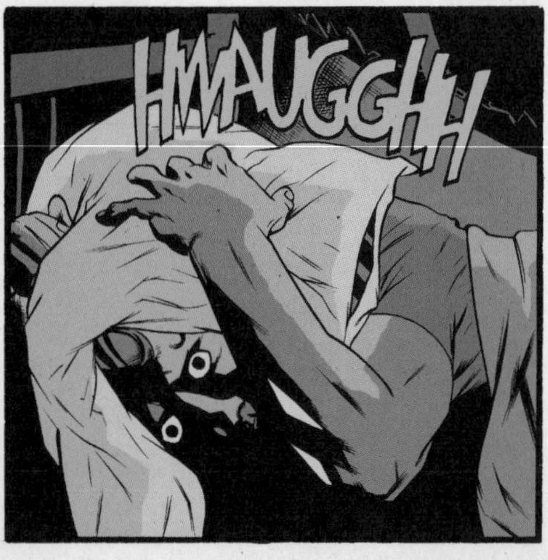
HWAUGGHH

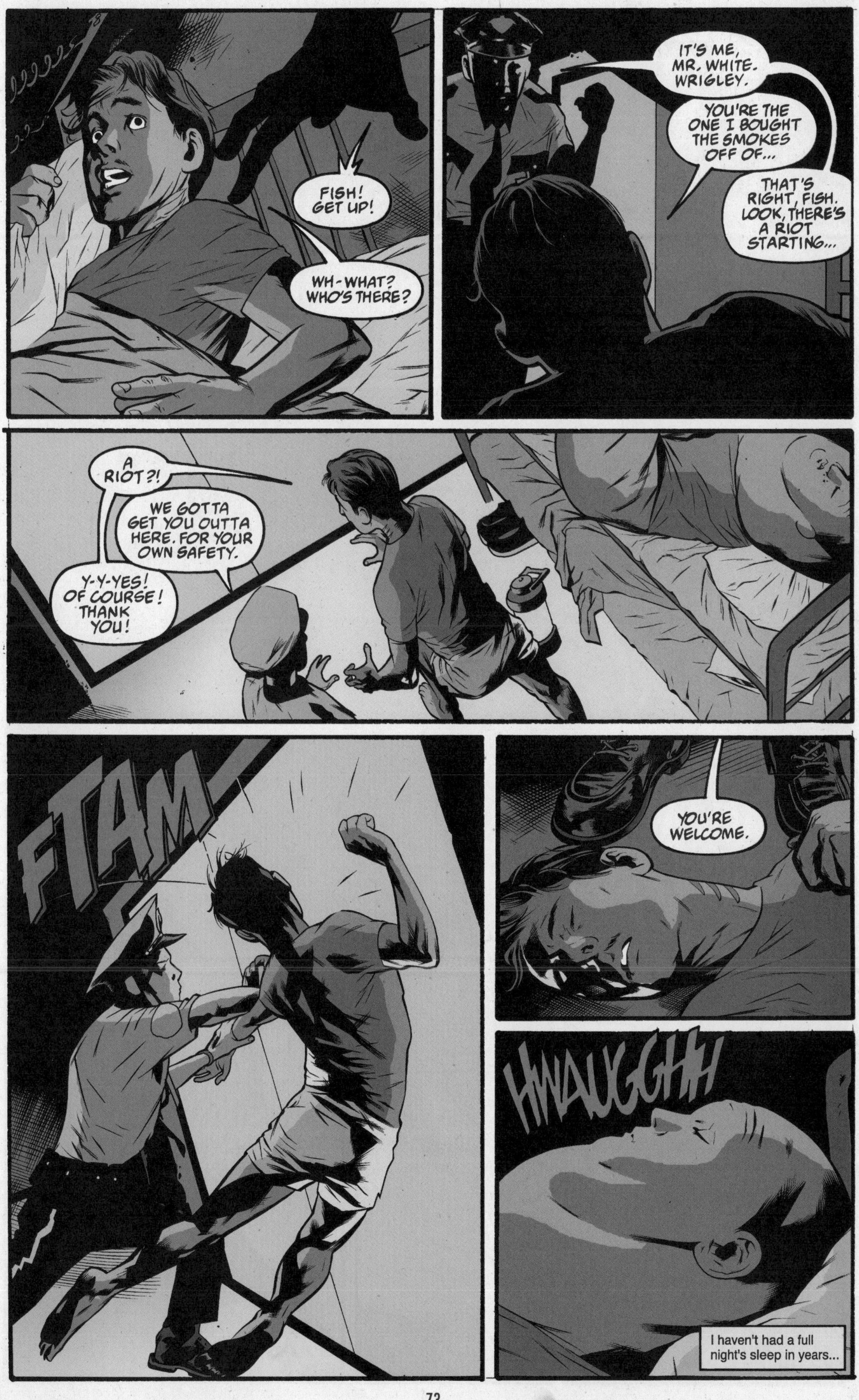
FISH! GET UP!
WH-WHAT? WHO'S THERE?
IT'S ME, MR. WHITE. WRIGLEY.
YOU'RE THE ONE I BOUGHT THE SMOKES OFF OF...
THAT'S RIGHT, FISH. LOOK, THERE'S A RIOT STARTING...
A RIOT?!
WE GOTTA GET YOU OUTTA HERE. FOR YOUR OWN SAFETY.
Y-Y-YES! OF COURSE! THANK YOU!
FTAM
YOU'RE WELCOME.
HWAUGGHH
I haven't had a full night's sleep in years...

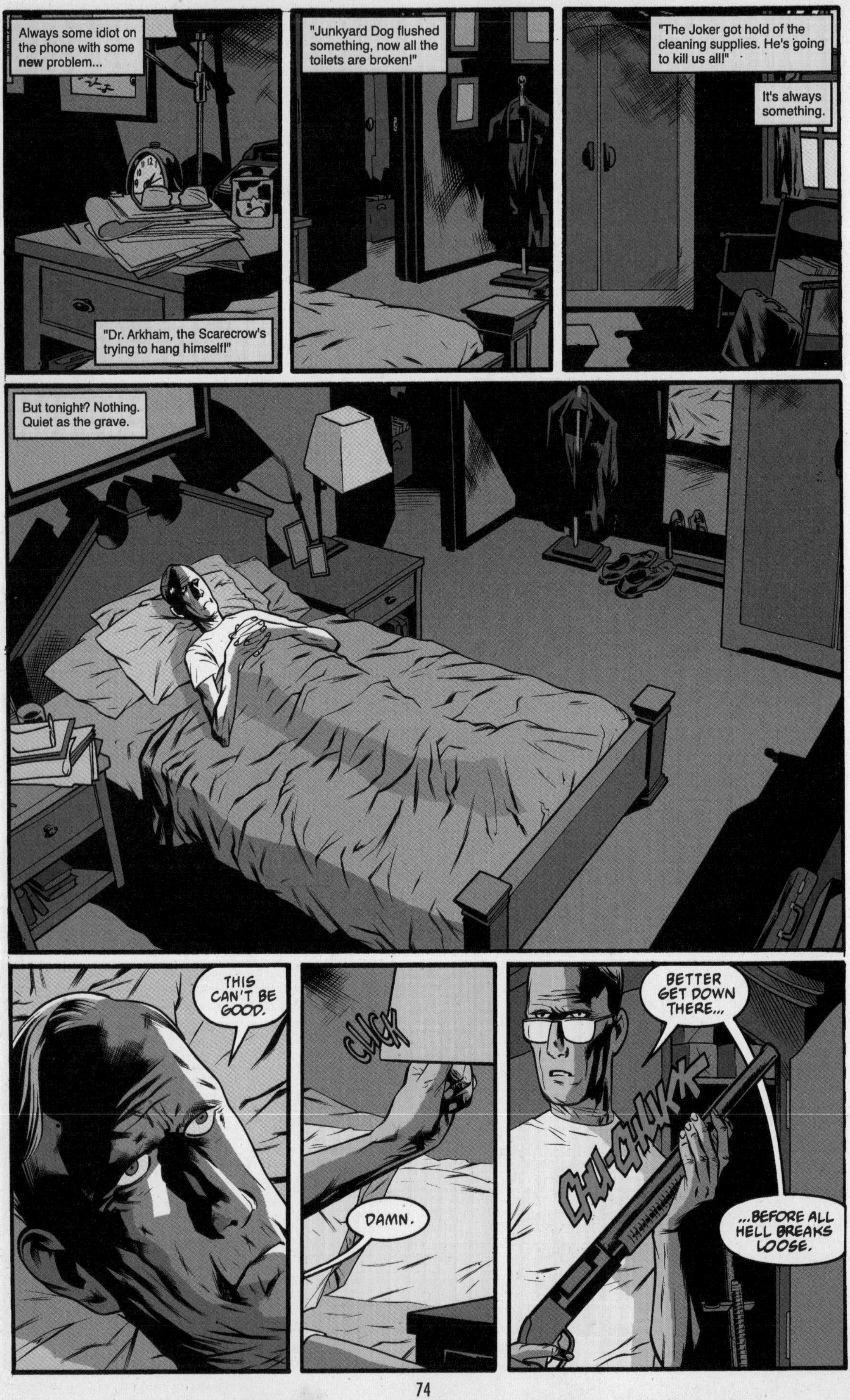
Always some idiot on the phone with some **new** problem...
"Dr. Arkham, the Scarecrow's trying to hang himself!"
"Junkyard Dog flushed something, now all the toilets are broken!"
"The Joker got hold of the cleaning supplies. He's going to kill us all!"
It's always something.
But tonight? Nothing. Quiet as the grave.
THIS CAN'T BE GOOD.
CLICK
DAMN.
BETTER GET DOWN THERE...
CHU-CHUKK
...BEFORE ALL HELL BREAKS LOOSE.

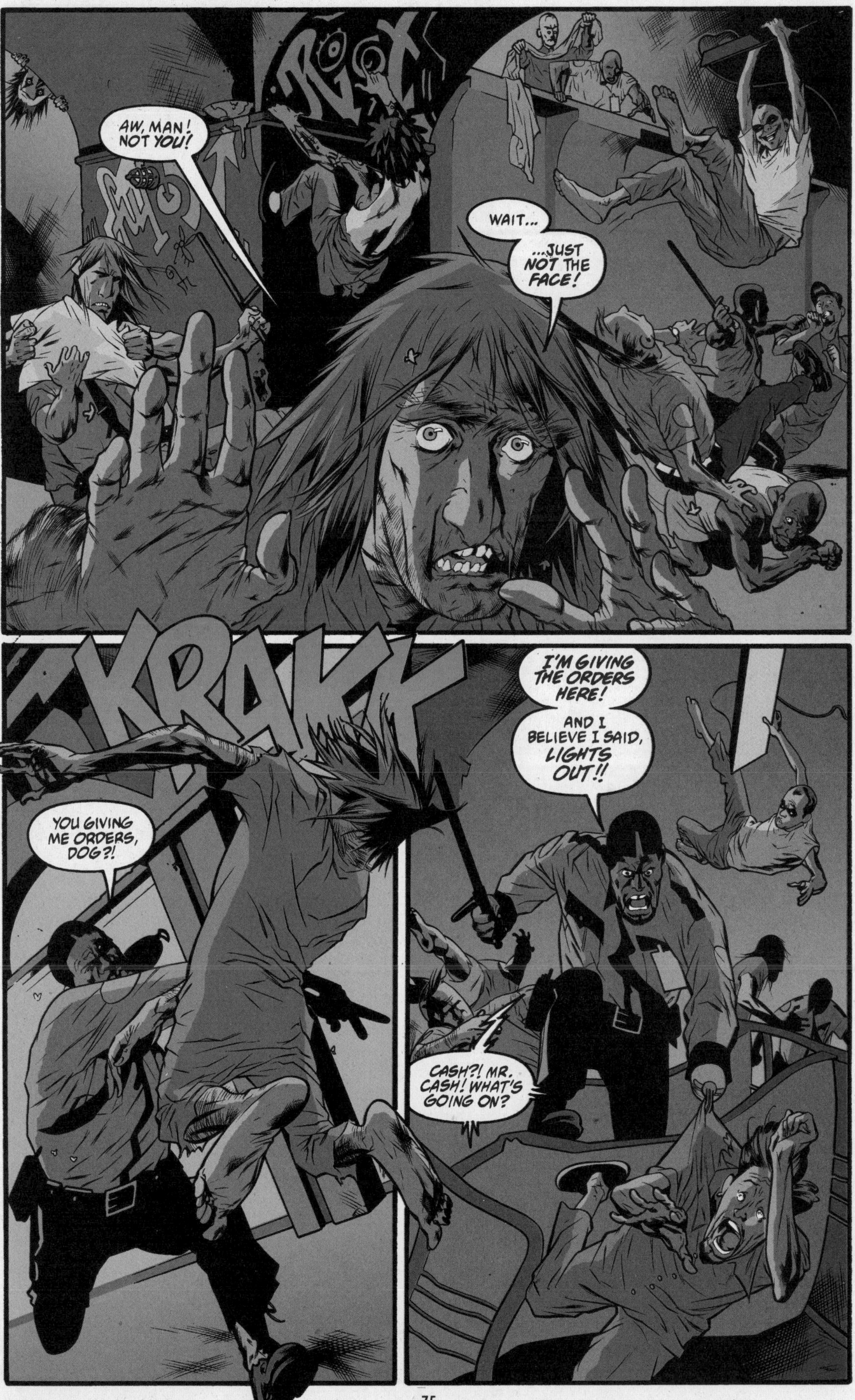
AW, MAN! NOT YOU!
WAIT...
...JUST NOT THE FACE!
KRAKK
I'M GIVING THE ORDERS HERE!
AND I BELIEVE I SAID, LIGHTS OUT!!
YOU GIVING ME ORDERS, DOG?!
CASH?! MR. CASH! WHAT'S GOING ON?

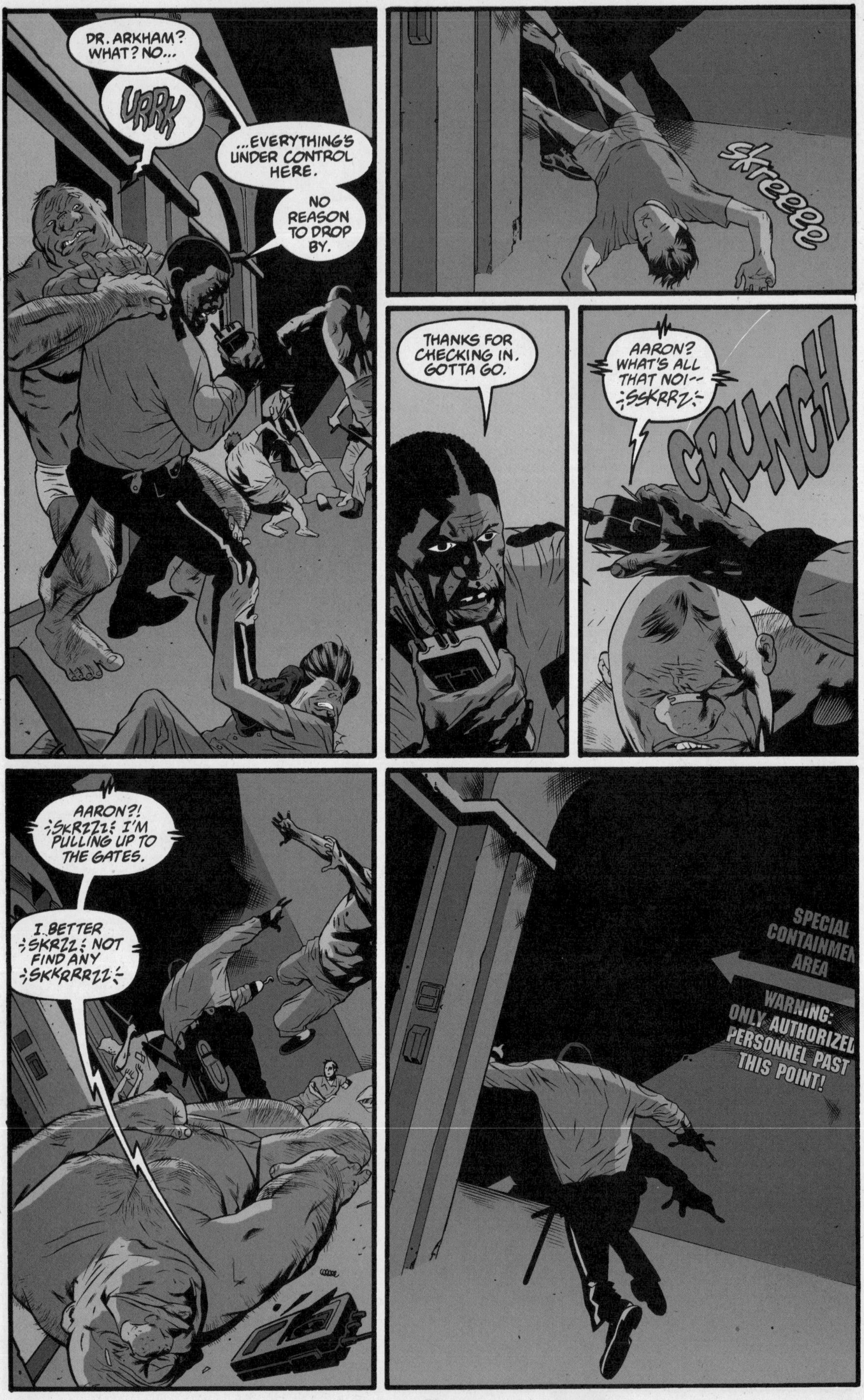
DR. ARKHAM? WHAT? NO...
URRK
...EVERYTHING'S UNDER CONTROL HERE.
NO REASON TO DROP BY.
SKREEEEE
THANKS FOR CHECKING IN. GOTTA GO.
AARON? WHAT'S ALL THAT NOI-- SSKRRZ
CRUNCH
AARON?! SKRZZZ I'M PULLING UP TO THE GATES.
I BETTER SKRZZZ NOT FIND ANY SKKRRRZZZ
SPECIAL CONTAINMEN AREA
WARNING: ONLY AUTHORIZED PERSONNEL PAST THIS POINT!

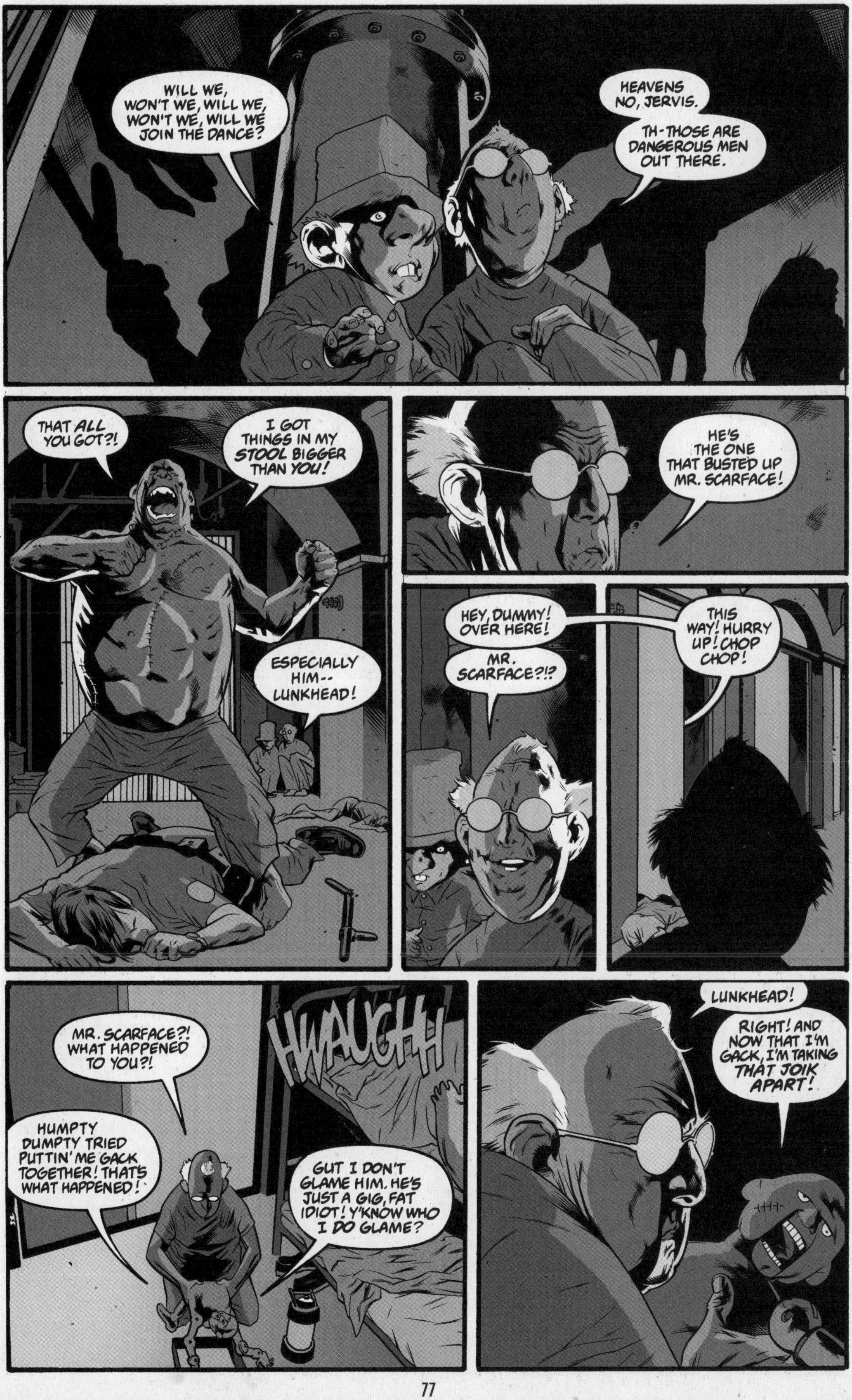

WILL WE, WON'T WE, WILL WE, WON'T WE, WILL WE JOIN THE DANCE?
HEAVENS NO, JERVIS.
TH-THOSE ARE DANGEROUS MEN OUT THERE.
THAT ALL YOU GOT?!
I GOT THINGS IN MY STOOL BIGGER THAN YOU!
ESPECIALLY HIM-- LUNKHEAD!
HE'S THE ONE THAT BUSTED UP MR. SCARFACE!
HEY, DUMMY! OVER HERE!
MR. SCARFACE?!?
THIS WAY! HURRY UP! CHOP CHOP!
HWAUGHH
MR. SCARFACE?! WHAT HAPPENED TO YOU?!
HUMPTY DUMPTY TRIED PUTTIN' ME GACK TOGETHER! THAT'S WHAT HAPPENED!
GUT I DON'T GLAME HIM. HE'S JUST A GIG, FAT IDIOT! Y'KNOW WHO I DO GLAME?
LUNKHEAD!
RIGHT! AND NOW THAT I'M GACK, I'M TAKING THAT JOIK APART!

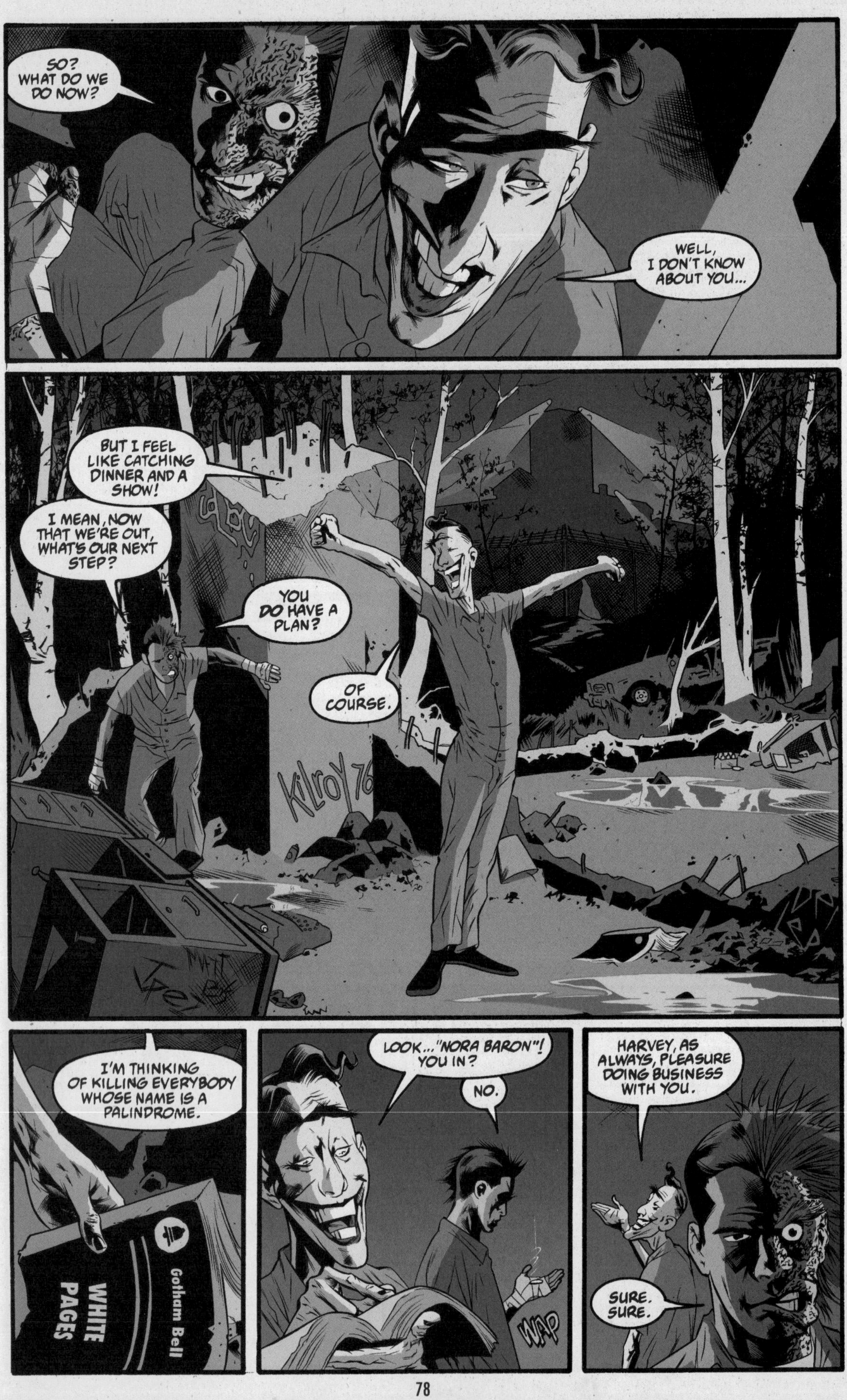
SO? WHAT DO WE DO NOW?
WELL, I DON'T KNOW ABOUT YOU...
BUT I FEEL LIKE CATCHING DINNER AND A SHOW!
I MEAN, NOW THAT WE'RE OUT, WHAT'S OUR NEXT STEP?
YOU DO HAVE A PLAN?
OF COURSE.
KILROY 76
I'M THINKING OF KILLING EVERYBODY WHOSE NAME IS A PALINDROME.
Gotham Bell
WHITE PAGES
LOOK..."NORA BARON"! YOU IN?
NO.
WAP
HARVEY, AS ALWAYS, PLEASURE DOING BUSINESS WITH YOU.
SURE. SURE.

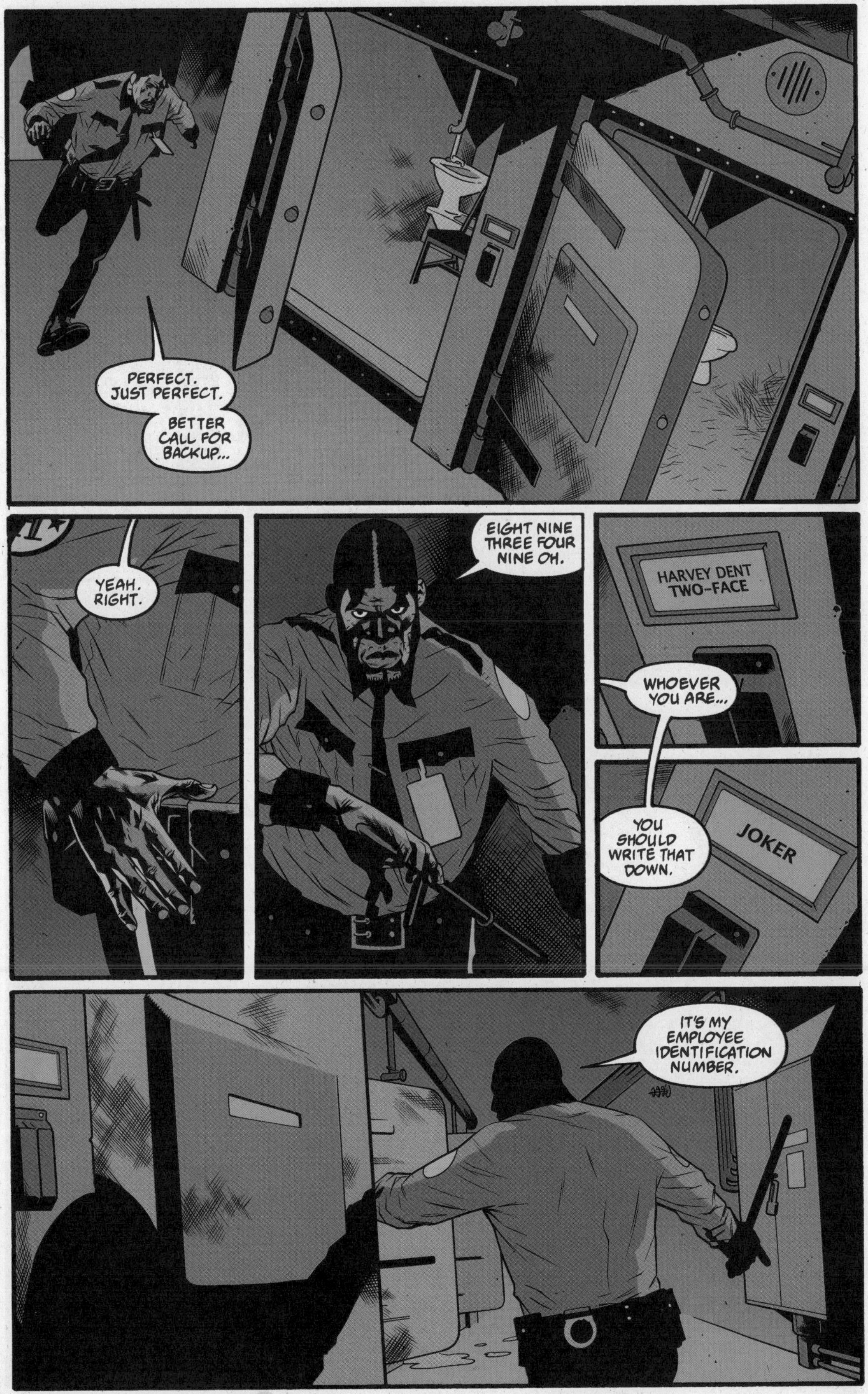
PERFECT. JUST PERFECT.
BETTER CALL FOR BACKUP...
YEAH. RIGHT.
EIGHT NINE THREE FOUR NINE OH.
HARVEY DENT TWO-FACE
WHOEVER YOU ARE...
JOKER
YOU SHOULD WRITE THAT DOWN.
IT'S MY EMPLOYEE IDENTIFICATION NUMBER.

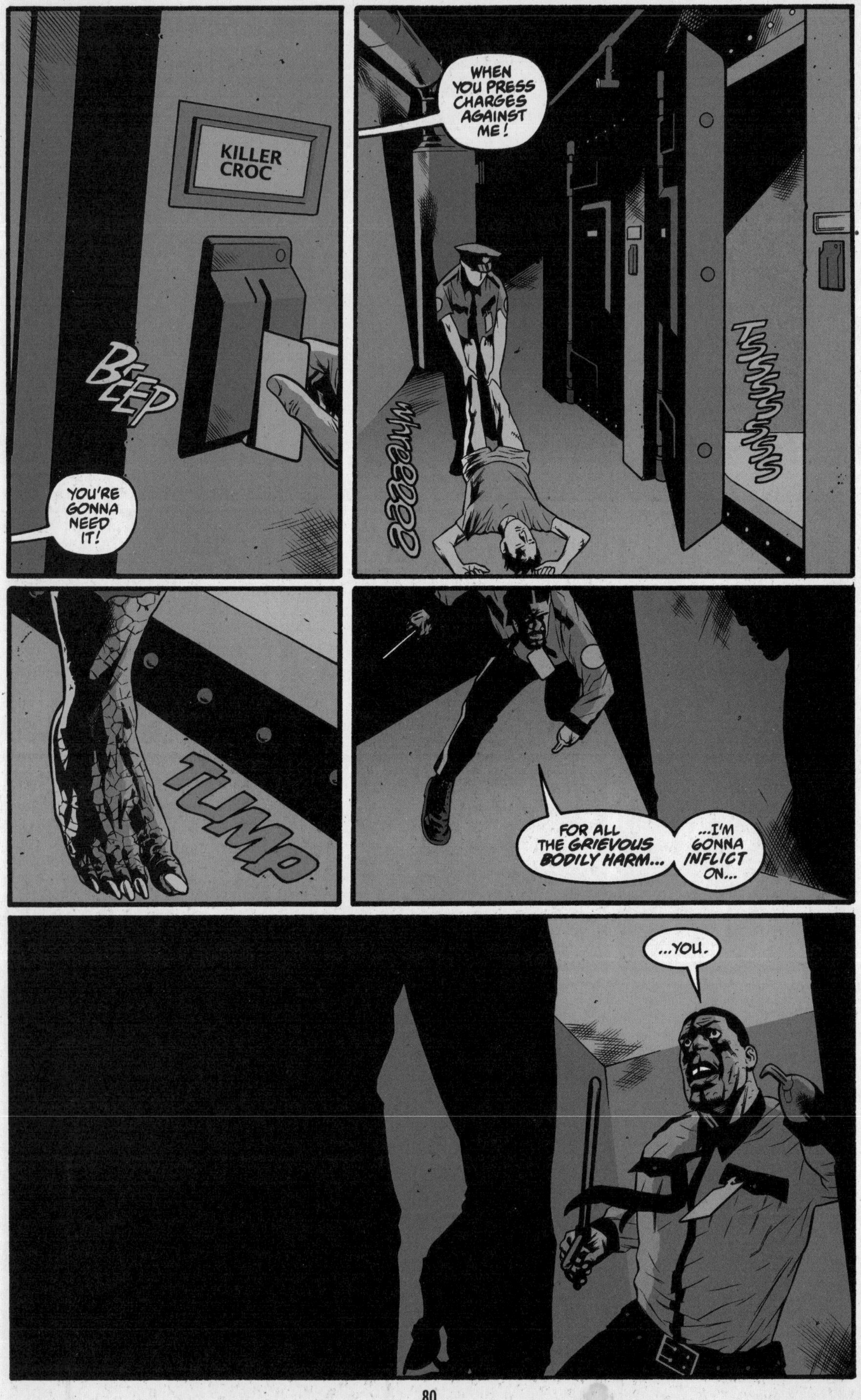
KILLER CROC
BEEEP
YOU'RE GONNA NEED IT!
WHEN YOU PRESS CHARGES AGAINST ME!
WHREEEEE
TSSSSSSSS
TUMP
FOR ALL THE GRIEVOUS BODILY HARM...
...I'M GONNA INFLICT ON...
...YOU.

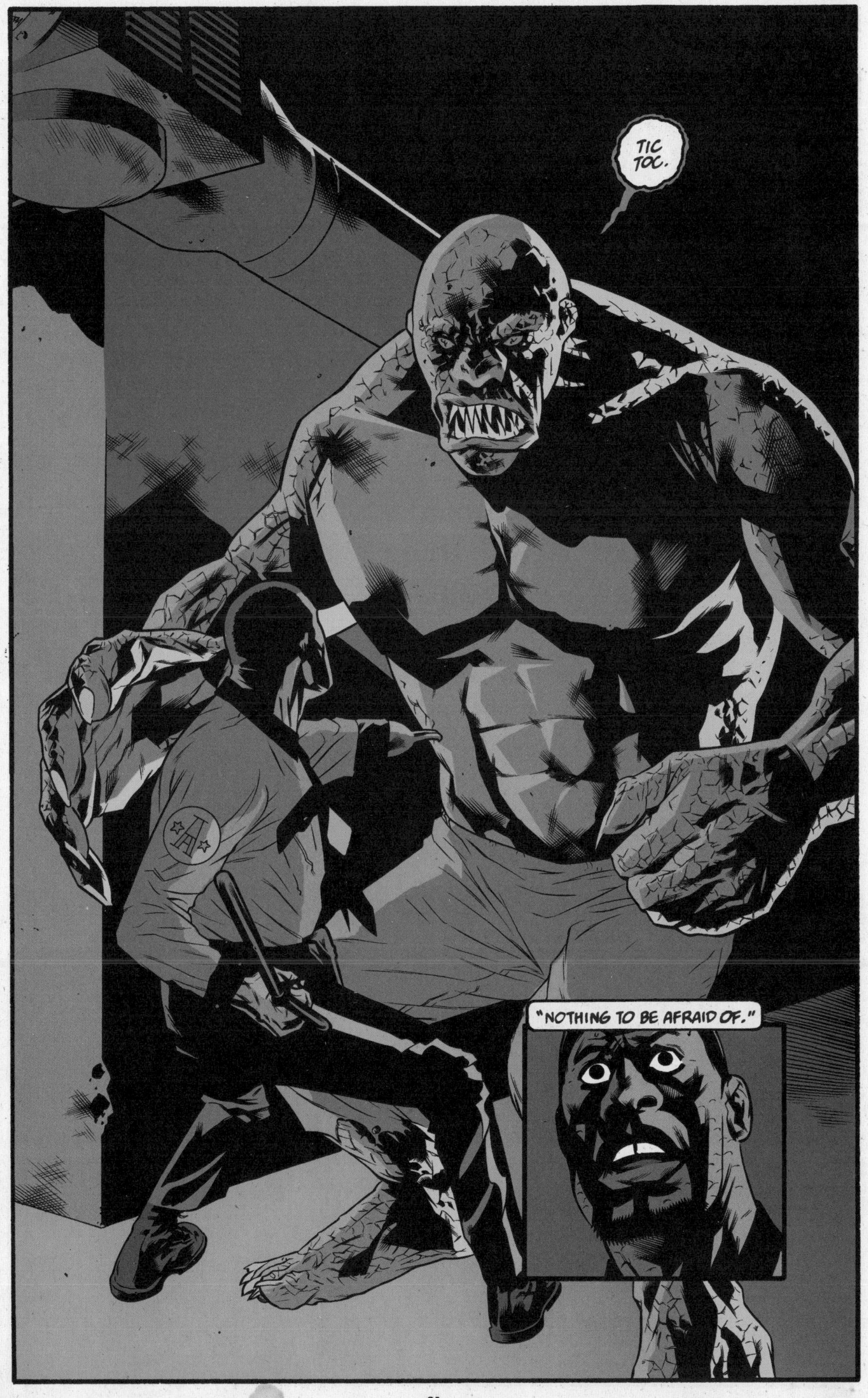
TIC TOC.
"NOTHING TO BE AFRAID OF."

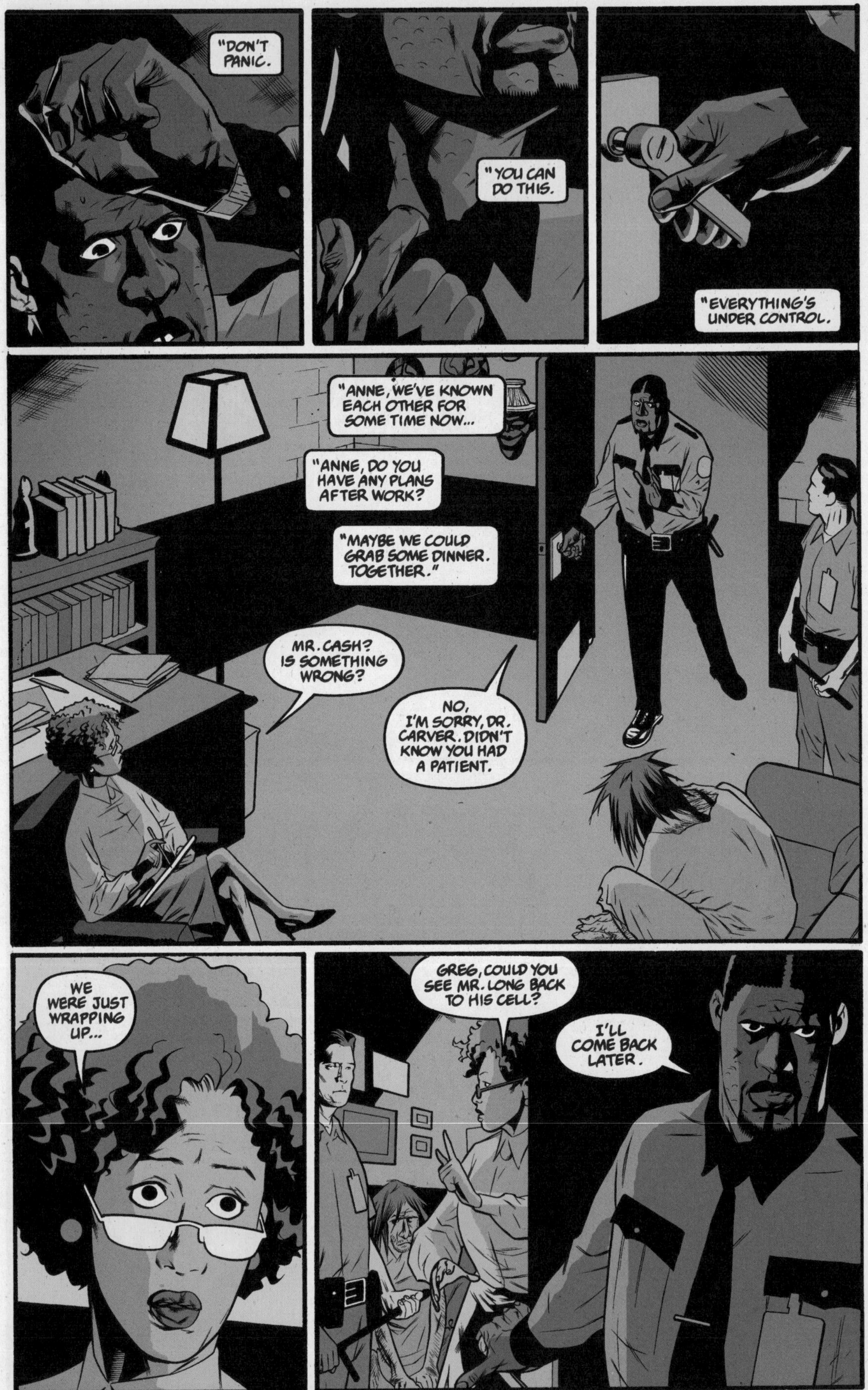
"DON'T PANIC.
"YOU CAN DO THIS.
"EVERYTHING'S UNDER CONTROL.
"ANNE, WE'VE KNOWN EACH OTHER FOR SOME TIME NOW...
"ANNE, DO YOU HAVE ANY PLANS AFTER WORK?
"MAYBE WE COULD GRAB SOME DINNER. TOGETHER."
MR. CASH? IS SOMETHING WRONG?
NO, I'M SORRY, DR. CARVER. DIDN'T KNOW YOU HAD A PATIENT.
WE WERE JUST WRAPPING UP...
GREG, COULD YOU SEE MR. LONG BACK TO HIS CELL?
I'LL COME BACK LATER.

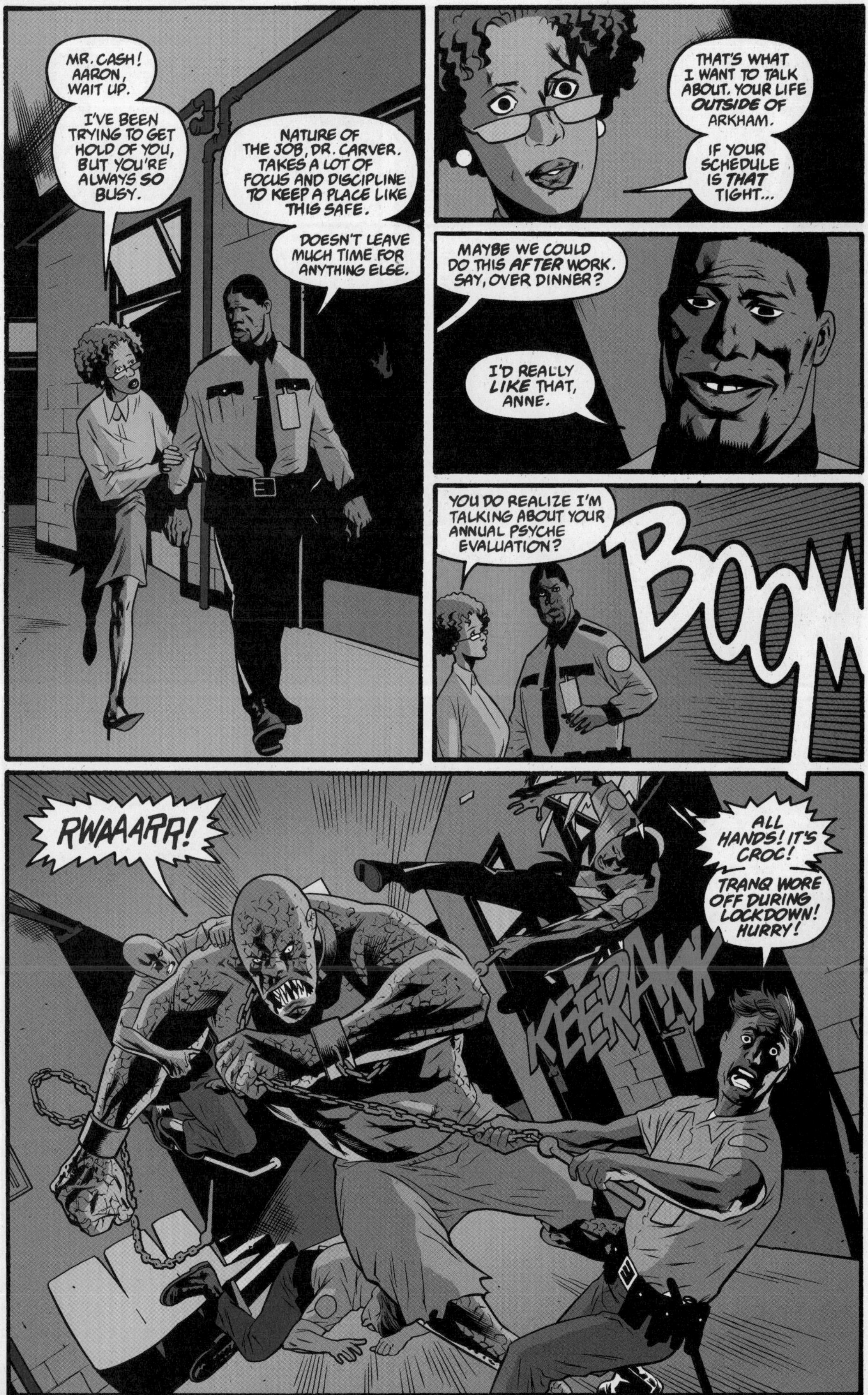
MR. CASH! AARON, WAIT UP.
I'VE BEEN TRYING TO GET HOLD OF YOU, BUT YOU'RE ALWAYS SO BUSY.
NATURE OF THE JOB, DR. CARVER. TAKES A LOT OF FOCUS AND DISCIPLINE TO KEEP A PLACE LIKE THIS SAFE.
DOESN'T LEAVE MUCH TIME FOR ANYTHING ELSE.
THAT'S WHAT I WANT TO TALK ABOUT. YOUR LIFE OUTSIDE OF ARKHAM.
IF YOUR SCHEDULE IS THAT TIGHT...
MAYBE WE COULD DO THIS AFTER WORK. SAY, OVER DINNER?
I'D REALLY LIKE THAT, ANNE.
YOU DO REALIZE I'M TALKING ABOUT YOUR ANNUAL PSYCHE EVALUATION?
BOOM
RWAAARR!
ALL HANDS! IT'S CROC!
TRANQ WORE OFF DURING LOCKDOWN! HURRY!
KEERAKK

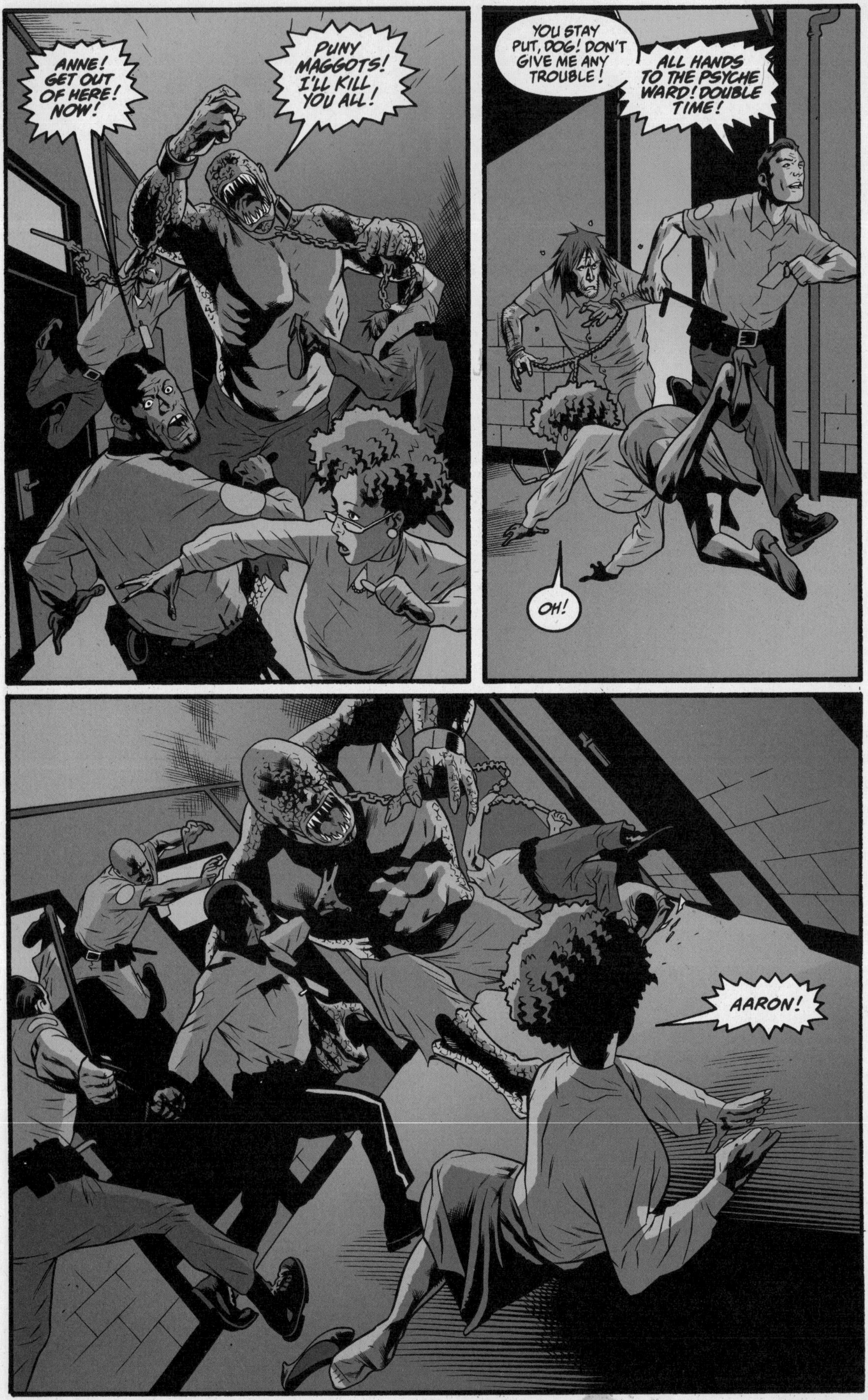

ANNE! GET OUT OF HERE! NOW!
PUNY MAGGOTS! I'LL KILL YOU ALL!
YOU STAY PUT, DOG! DON'T GIVE ME ANY TROUBLE!
ALL HANDS TO THE PSYCHE WARD! DOUBLE TIME!
OH!
AARON!

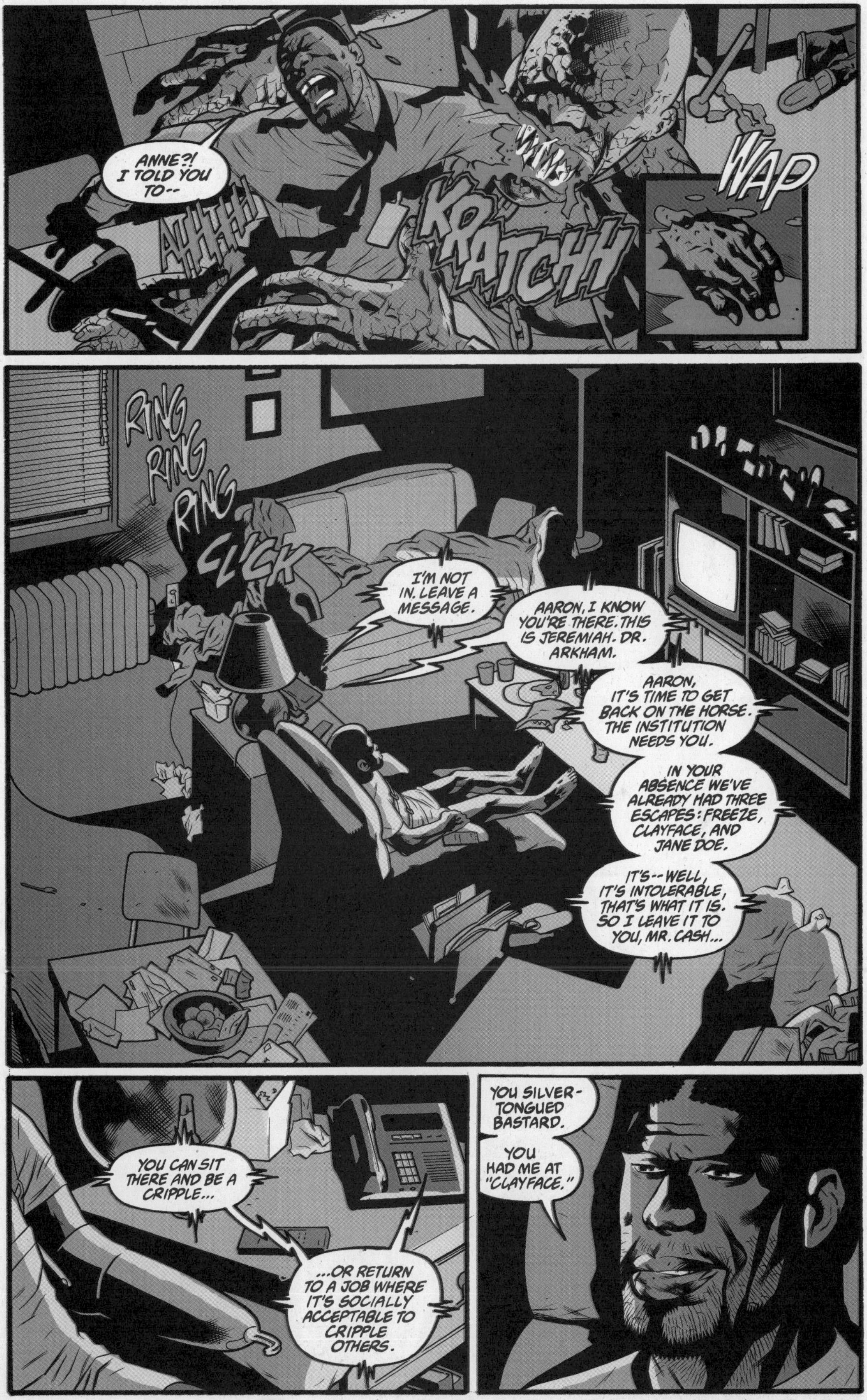
ANNE?! I TOLD YOU TO--
AHHHH
KRATCHH
WAP
RING RING RING
CLICK
I'M NOT IN. LEAVE A MESSAGE.
AARON, I KNOW YOU'RE THERE. THIS IS JEREMIAH. DR. ARKHAM.
AARON, IT'S TIME TO GET BACK ON THE HORSE. THE INSTITUTION NEEDS YOU.
IN YOUR ABSENCE WE'VE ALREADY HAD THREE ESCAPES: FREEZE, CLAYFACE, AND JANE DOE.
IT'S--WELL, IT'S INTOLERABLE, THAT'S WHAT IT IS. SO I LEAVE IT TO YOU, MR. CASH...
YOU CAN SIT THERE AND BE A CRIPPLE...
...OR RETURN TO A JOB WHERE IT'S SOCIALLY ACCEPTABLE TO CRIPPLE OTHERS.
YOU SILVER-TONGUED BASTARD.
YOU HAD ME AT "CLAYFACE."

AKK HIKK

Y'KNOW, NYGMA, YOU'RE RIGHT. I DON'T KNOW THE ANSWER TO YOUR LITTLE RIDDLE.

SO LET ME GIVE YOU ONE OF MINE.

"WHAT INMATE IS GOING TO BE MISSING MOST OF HIS TEETH IF HE DOESN'T DO HIS WORK DETAIL?"

MR. CASH! COME IN! CODE RED! PICK UP!

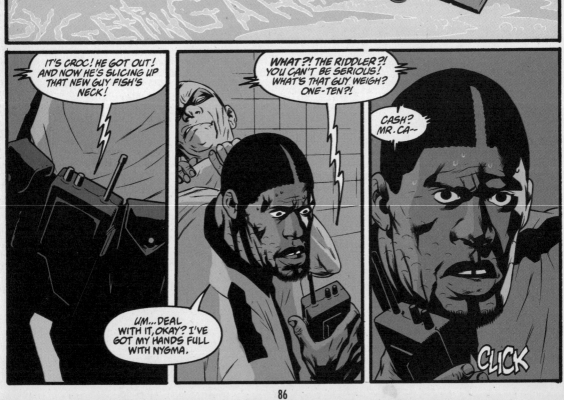

IT'S CROC! HE GOT OUT! AND NOW HE'S SLICING UP THAT NEW GUY FISH'S NECK!

WHAT?! THE RIDDLER?! YOU CAN'T BE SERIOUS! WHAT'S THAT GUY WEIGH? ONE-TEN?!

CASH? MR. CA--

UM...DEAL WITH IT, OKAY? I'VE GOT MY HANDS FULL WITH NYGMA.

CLICK

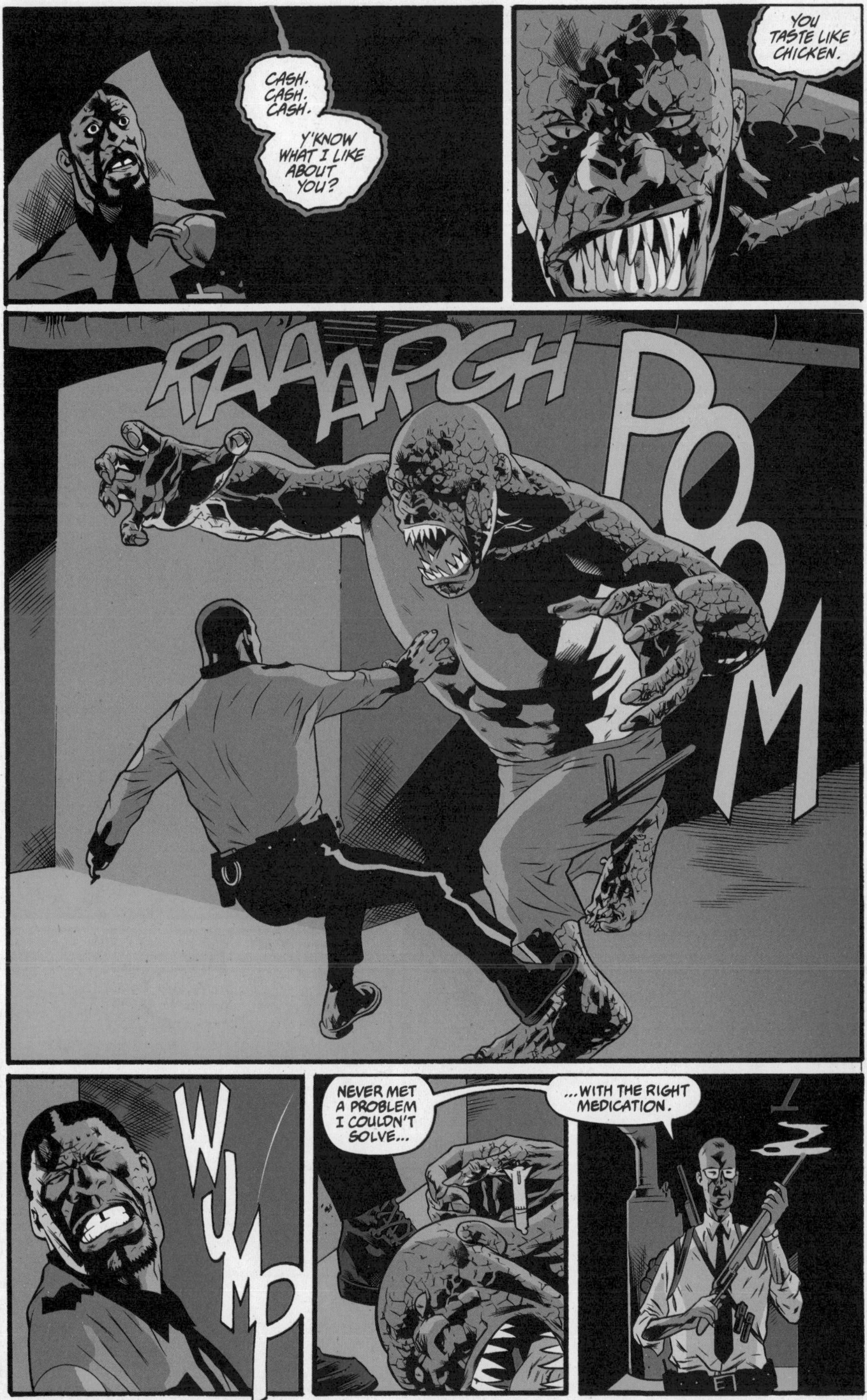
CASH. CASH. CASH.
Y'KNOW WHAT I LIKE ABOUT YOU?
YOU TASTE LIKE CHICKEN.
RAAAARGH
BOOM
WUMP
NEVER MET A PROBLEM I COULDN'T SOLVE...
...WITH THE RIGHT MEDICATION.

THERE WAS NO NEED FOR THIS, SIR. I HAD EVERYTHING--

UNDER CONTROL. I KNOW. HERE, PUT THIS ON.

SECURITY, THIS IS DR. ARKHAM. I'M CALLING IN AN "UNSCHEDULED NAP TIME."

SECURITY HERE. ARE YOU SURE, DOC? WE'RE SHOWING "ALL CLEAR" IN THE BOOTH.

I REPEAT, AN "UNSCHEDULED NAP TIME." OVER!

SSSsss

YOU'RE THE BOSS.

KLIK

"ALL CLEAR!" CAN YOU BELIEVE THAT?!

MR. FRE

I AM BESET ON ALL SIDES BY IDIOTS! IDIOTS AND MADMEN!

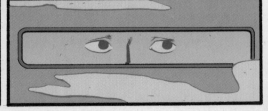

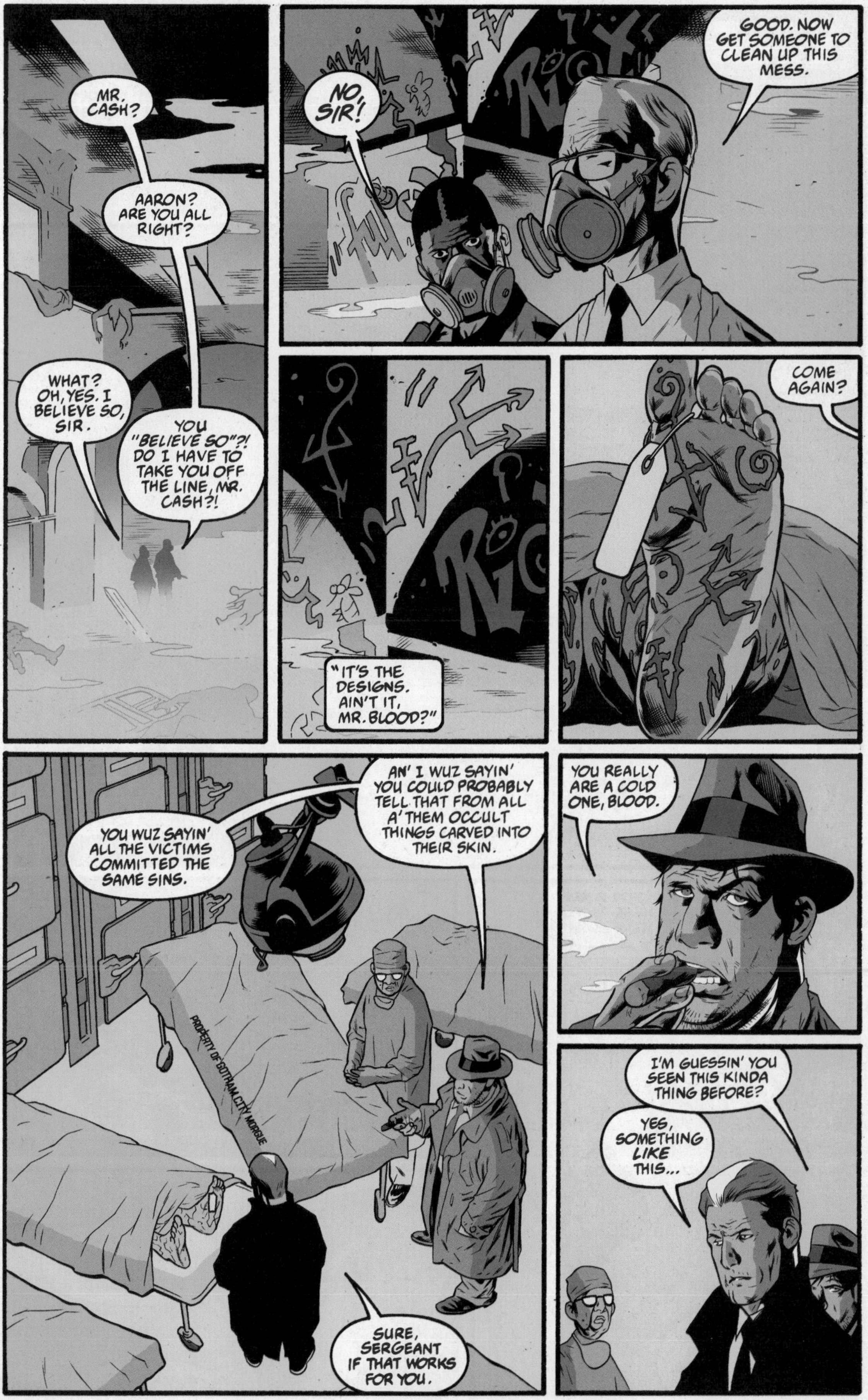
MR. CASH?
AARON? ARE YOU ALL RIGHT?
WHAT? OH, YES. I BELIEVE SO, SIR.
YOU "BELIEVE SO"?! DO I HAVE TO TAKE YOU OFF THE LINE, MR. CASH?!
NO, SIR!
GOOD. NOW GET SOMEONE TO CLEAN UP THIS MESS.
"IT'S THE DESIGNS. AIN'T IT, MR. BLOOD?"
COME AGAIN?
YOU WUZ SAYIN' ALL THE VICTIMS COMMITTED THE SAME SINS.
AN' I WUZ SAYIN' YOU COULD PROBABLY TELL THAT FROM ALL A' THEM OCCULT THINGS CARVED INTO THEIR SKIN.
PROPERTY OF GOTHAM CITY MORGUE
SURE, SERGEANT IF THAT WORKS FOR YOU.
YOU REALLY ARE A COLD ONE, BLOOD.
I'M GUESSIN' YOU SEEN THIS KINDA THING BEFORE?
YES, SOMETHING LIKE THIS...

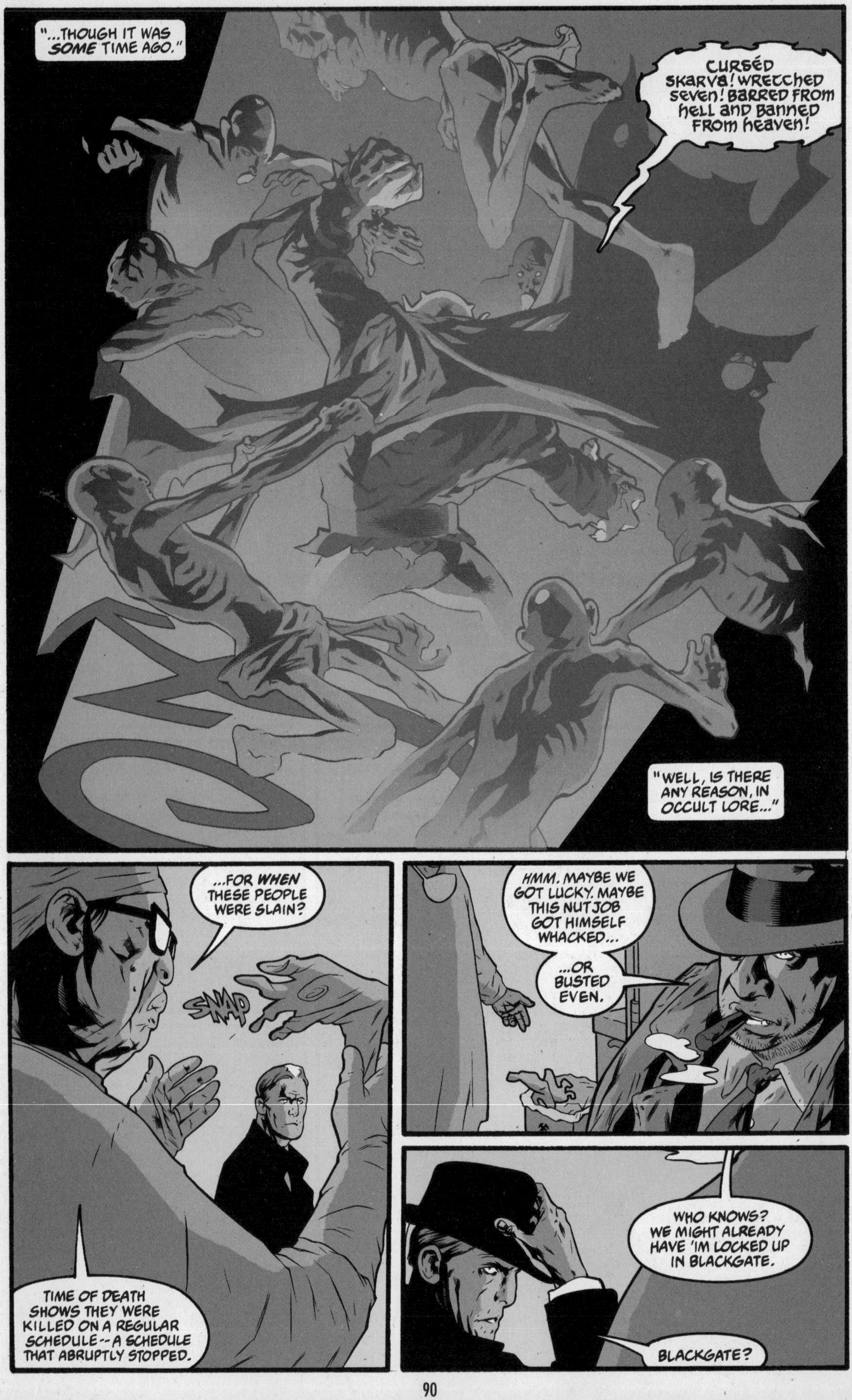
"...THOUGH IT WAS SOME TIME AGO."
CURSÉD SKARVA! WRETCHED SEVEN! BARRED FROM HELL AND BANNED FROM HEAVEN!
"WELL, IS THERE ANY REASON, IN OCCULT LORE..."
...FOR WHEN THESE PEOPLE WERE SLAIN?
SNAP
TIME OF DEATH SHOWS THEY WERE KILLED ON A REGULAR SCHEDULE-- A SCHEDULE THAT ABRUPTLY STOPPED.
HMM. MAYBE WE GOT LUCKY. MAYBE THIS NUT JOB GOT HIMSELF WHACKED...
...OR BUSTED EVEN.
WHO KNOWS? WE MIGHT ALREADY HAVE 'IM LOCKED UP IN BLACKGATE.
BLACKGATE?

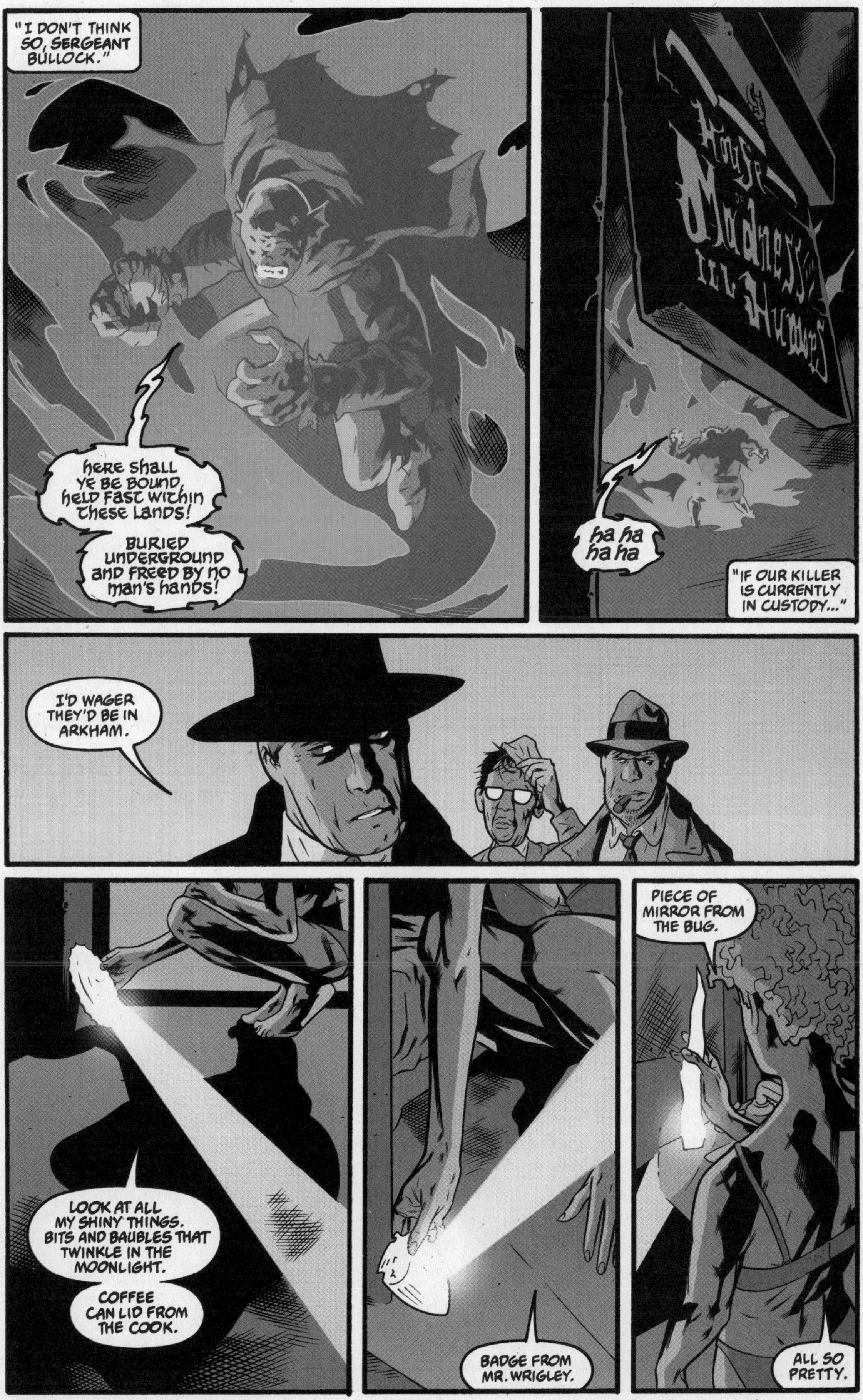

"I DON'T THINK SO, SERGEANT BULLOCK."
HERE SHALL YE BE BOUND, HELD FAST WITHIN THESE LANDS!
BURIED UNDERGROUND AND FREED BY NO MAN'S HANDS!
HA HA HA HA
"IF OUR KILLER IS CURRENTLY IN CUSTODY..."
I'D WAGER THEY'D BE IN ARKHAM.
LOOK AT ALL MY SHINY THINGS. BITS AND BAUBLES THAT TWINKLE IN THE MOONLIGHT.
COFFEE CAN LID FROM THE COOK.
BADGE FROM MR. WRIGLEY.
PIECE OF MIRROR FROM THE BUG.
ALL SO PRETTY.

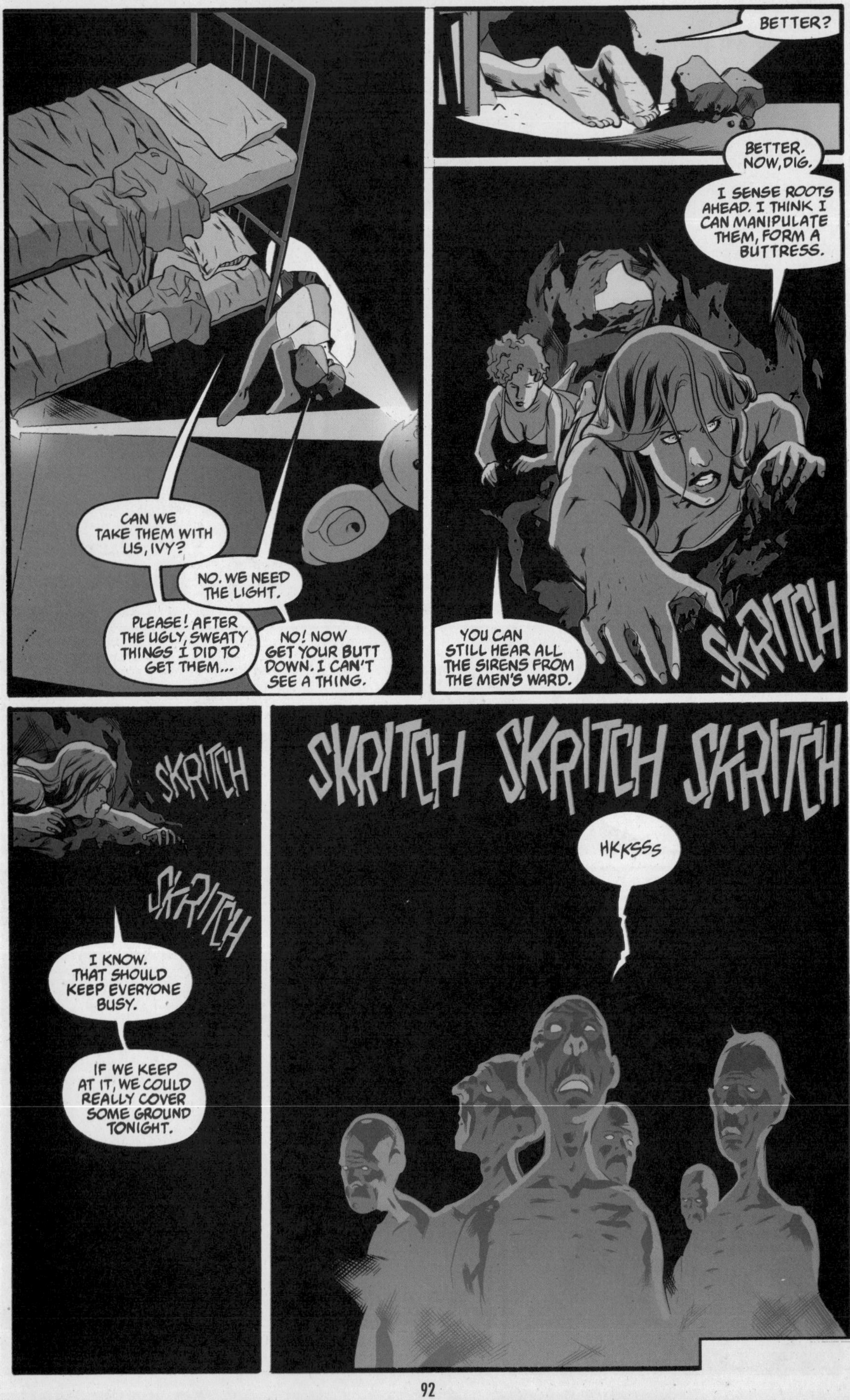
CAN WE TAKE THEM WITH US, IVY?
NO. WE NEED THE LIGHT.
PLEASE! AFTER THE UGLY, SWEATY THINGS I DID TO GET THEM...
NO! NOW GET YOUR BUTT DOWN. I CAN'T SEE A THING.
BETTER?
BETTER. NOW, DIG.
I SENSE ROOTS AHEAD. I THINK I CAN MANIPULATE THEM, FORM A BUTTRESS.
YOU CAN STILL HEAR ALL THE SIRENS FROM THE MEN'S WARD.
SKRITCH
SKRITCH
SKRITCH
I KNOW. THAT SHOULD KEEP EVERYONE BUSY.
IF WE KEEP AT IT, WE COULD REALLY COVER SOME GROUND TONIGHT.
SKRITCH SKRITCH SKRITCH
HKKSSs

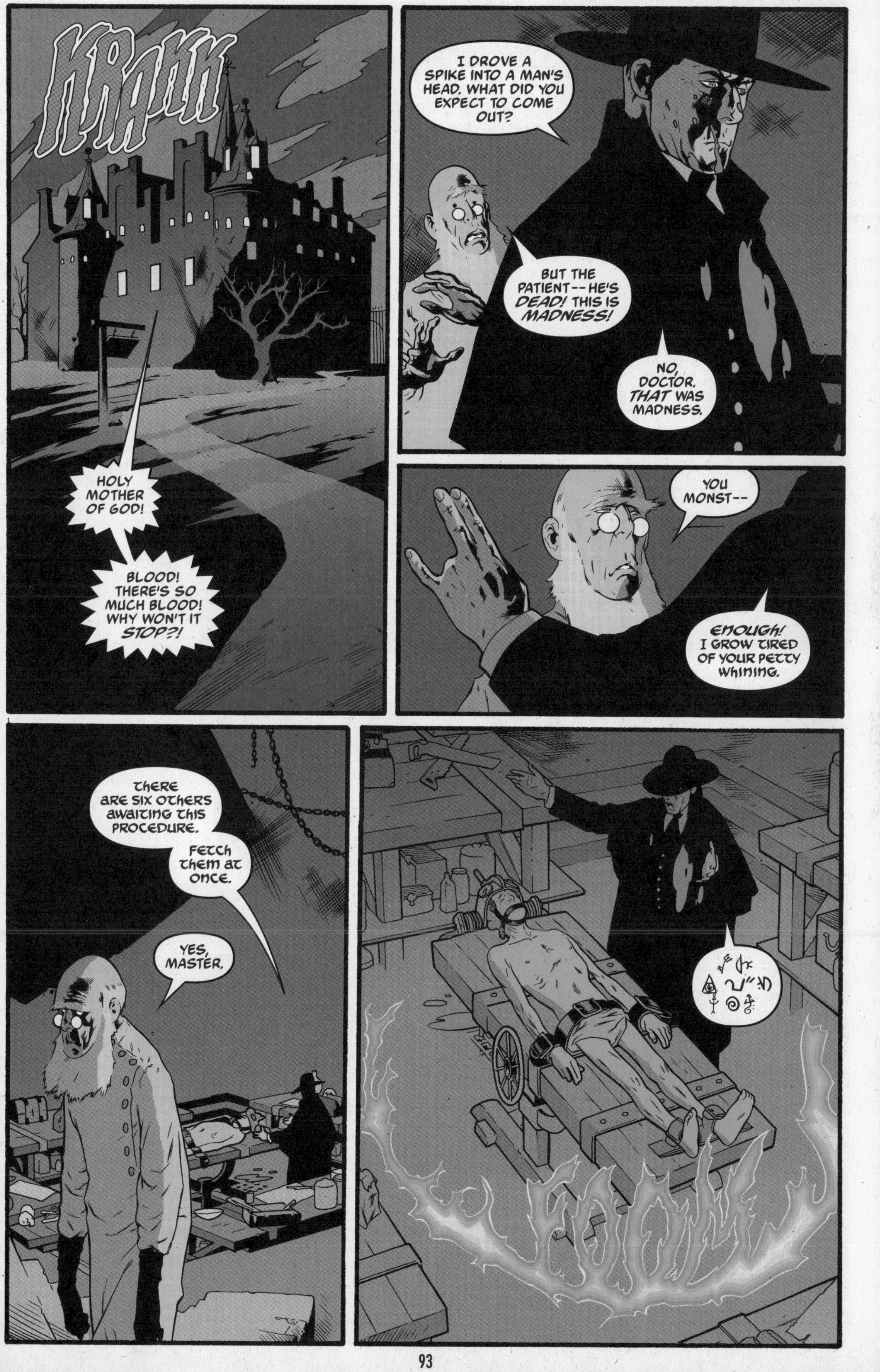
KRAKK
HOLY MOTHER OF GOD!
BLOOD! THERE'S SO MUCH BLOOD! WHY WON'T IT STOP?!
I DROVE A SPIKE INTO A MAN'S HEAD. WHAT DID YOU EXPECT TO COME OUT?
BUT THE PATIENT--HE'S DEAD! THIS IS MADNESS!
NO, DOCTOR. THAT WAS MADNESS.
YOU MONST--
ENOUGH! I GROW TIRED OF YOUR PETTY WHINING.
THERE ARE SIX OTHERS AWAITING THIS PROCEDURE.
FETCH THEM AT ONCE.
YES, MASTER.

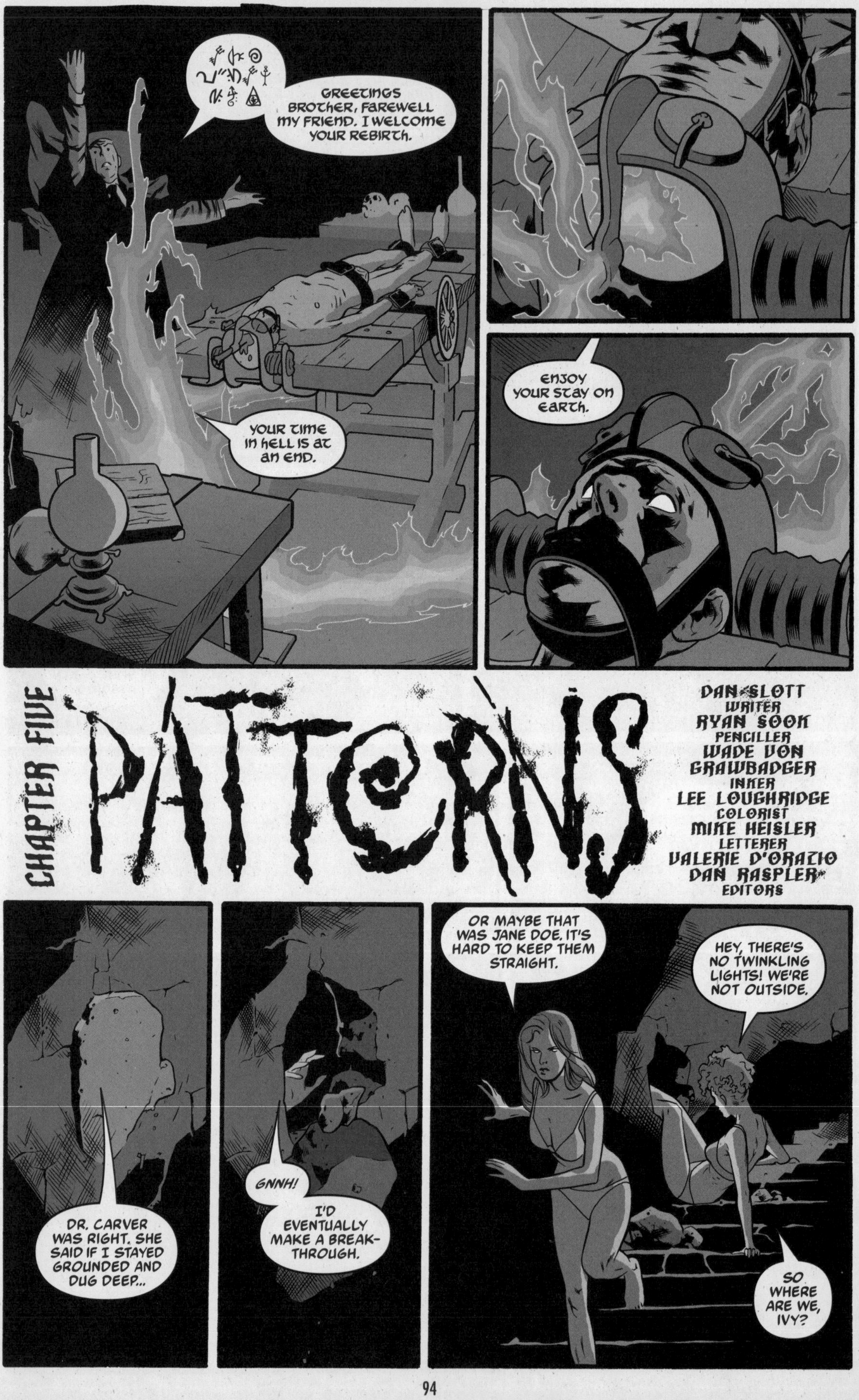
GREETINGS BROTHER, FAREWELL MY FRIEND. I WELCOME YOUR REBIRTH.
YOUR TIME IN HELL IS AT AN END.
ENJOY YOUR STAY ON EARTH.
CHAPTER FIVE
PATTERNS
DAN SLOTT WRITER
RYAN SOOK PENCILLER
WADE VON GRAWBADGER INKER
LEE LOUGHRIDGE COLORIST
MIKE HEISLER LETTERER
VALERIE D'ORAZIO
DAN RASPLER EDITORS
DR. CARVER WAS RIGHT. SHE SAID IF I STAYED GROUNDED AND DUG DEEP...
GNNH!
I'D EVENTUALLY MAKE A BREAK-THROUGH.
OR MAYBE THAT WAS JANE DOE. IT'S HARD TO KEEP THEM STRAIGHT.
HEY, THERE'S NO TWINKLING LIGHTS! WE'RE NOT OUTSIDE.
SO WHERE ARE WE, IVY?

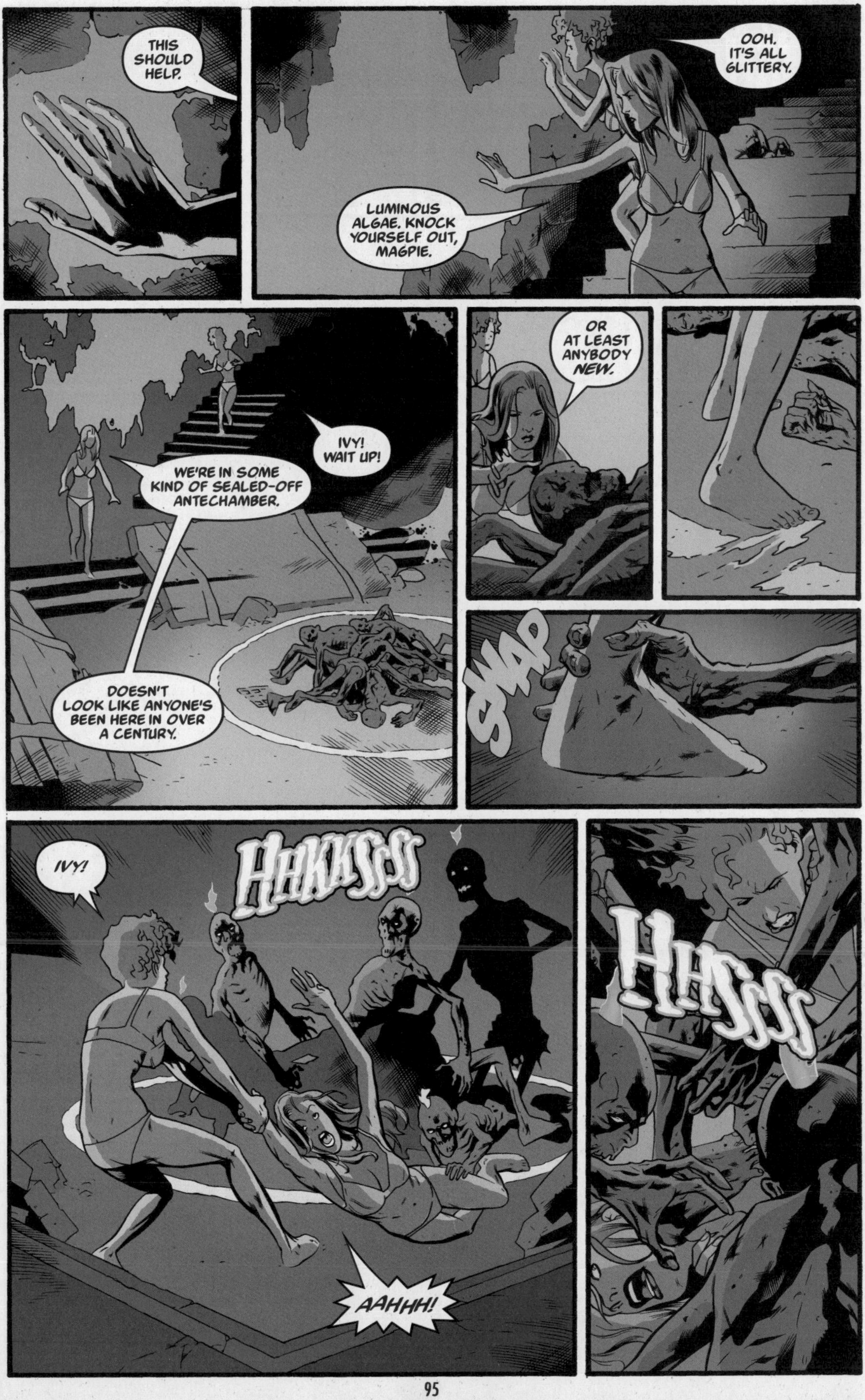
THIS SHOULD HELP.
OOH. IT'S ALL GLITTERY.
LUMINOUS ALGAE. KNOCK YOURSELF OUT, MAGPIE.
IVY! WAIT UP!
WE'RE IN SOME KIND OF SEALED-OFF ANTECHAMBER.
DOESN'T LOOK LIKE ANYONE'S BEEN HERE IN OVER A CENTURY.
OR AT LEAST ANYBODY NEW.
SNAP
IVY!
HHKKSSSS
AAHHH!
HHSSSS

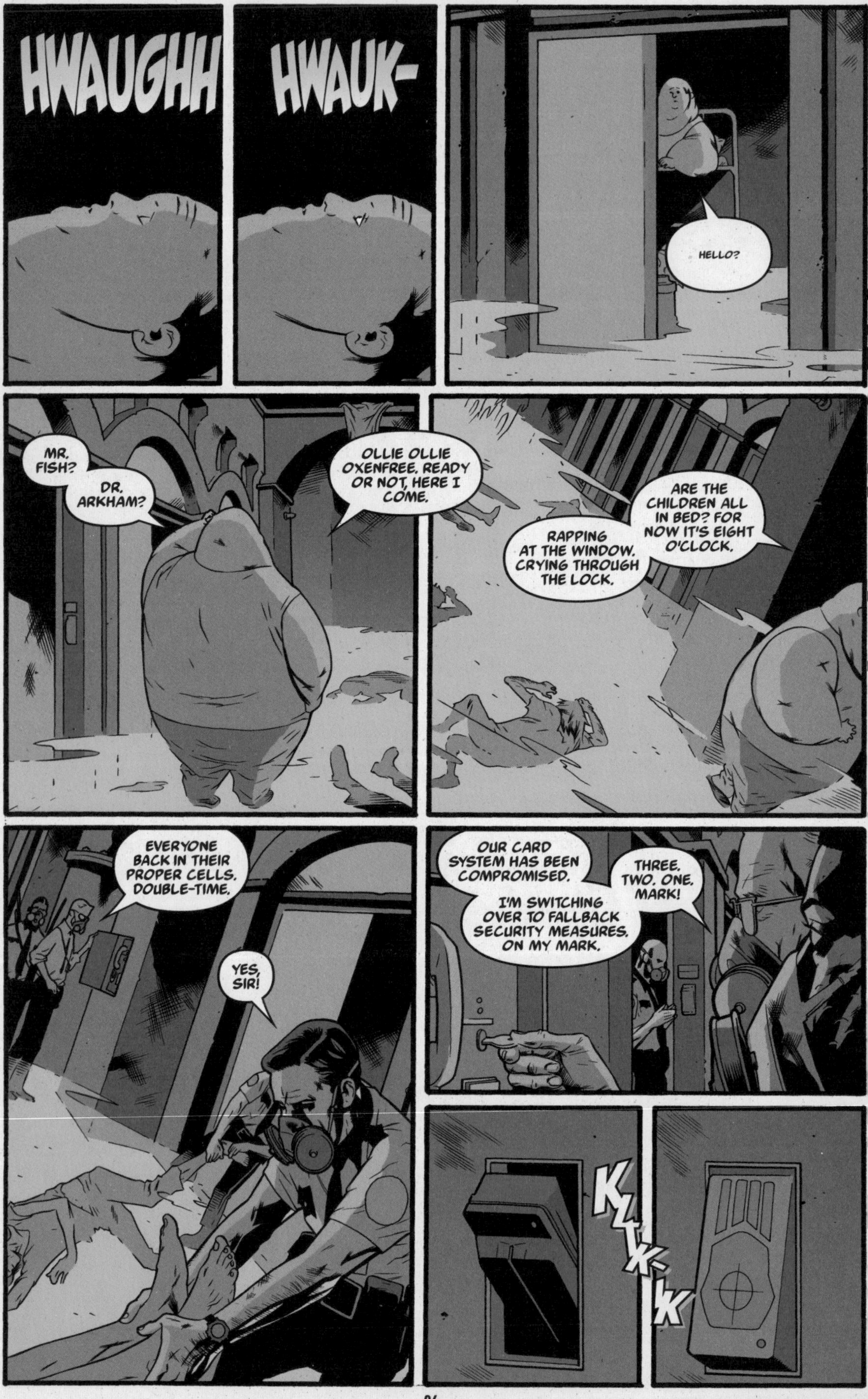
HWAUGHH
HWAUK-
HELLO?
MR. FISH?
DR. ARKHAM?
OLLIE OLLIE OXENFREE. READY OR NOT, HERE I COME.
ARE THE CHILDREN ALL IN BED? FOR NOW IT'S EIGHT O'CLOCK.
RAPPING AT THE WINDOW. CRYING THROUGH THE LOCK.
EVERYONE BACK IN THEIR PROPER CELLS. DOUBLE-TIME.
YES, SIR!
OUR CARD SYSTEM HAS BEEN COMPROMISED.
I'M SWITCHING OVER TO FALLBACK SECURITY MEASURES. ON MY MARK.
THREE. TWO. ONE. MARK!
KLIK-KK

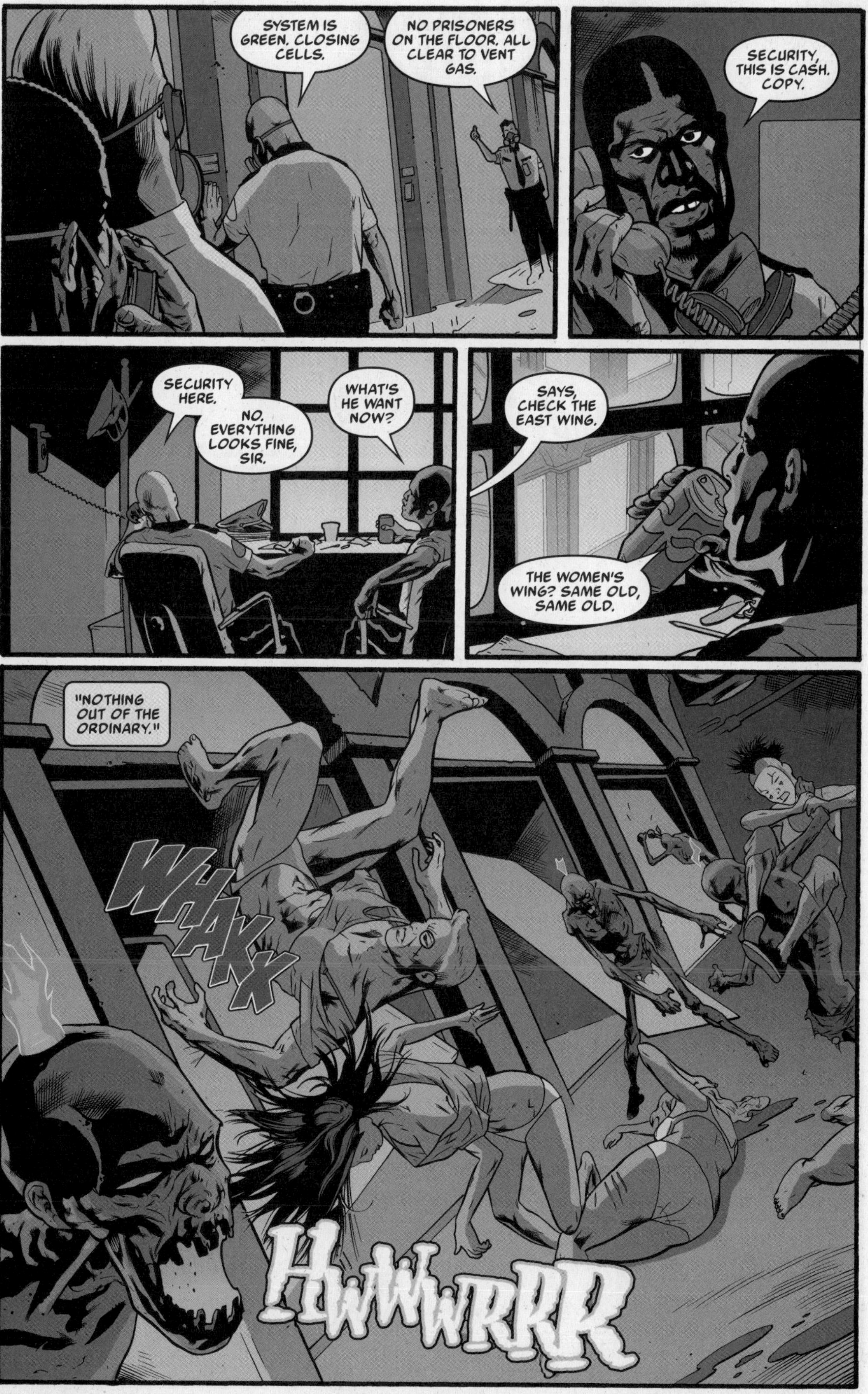
SYSTEM IS GREEN. CLOSING CELLS.
NO PRISONERS ON THE FLOOR. ALL CLEAR TO VENT GAS.
SECURITY, THIS IS CASH. COPY.
SECURITY HERE.
NO. EVERYTHING LOOKS FINE, SIR.
WHAT'S HE WANT NOW?
SAYS, CHECK THE EAST WING.
THE WOMEN'S WING? SAME OLD, SAME OLD.
"NOTHING OUT OF THE ORDINARY."
WHAKK
HWWWRRR

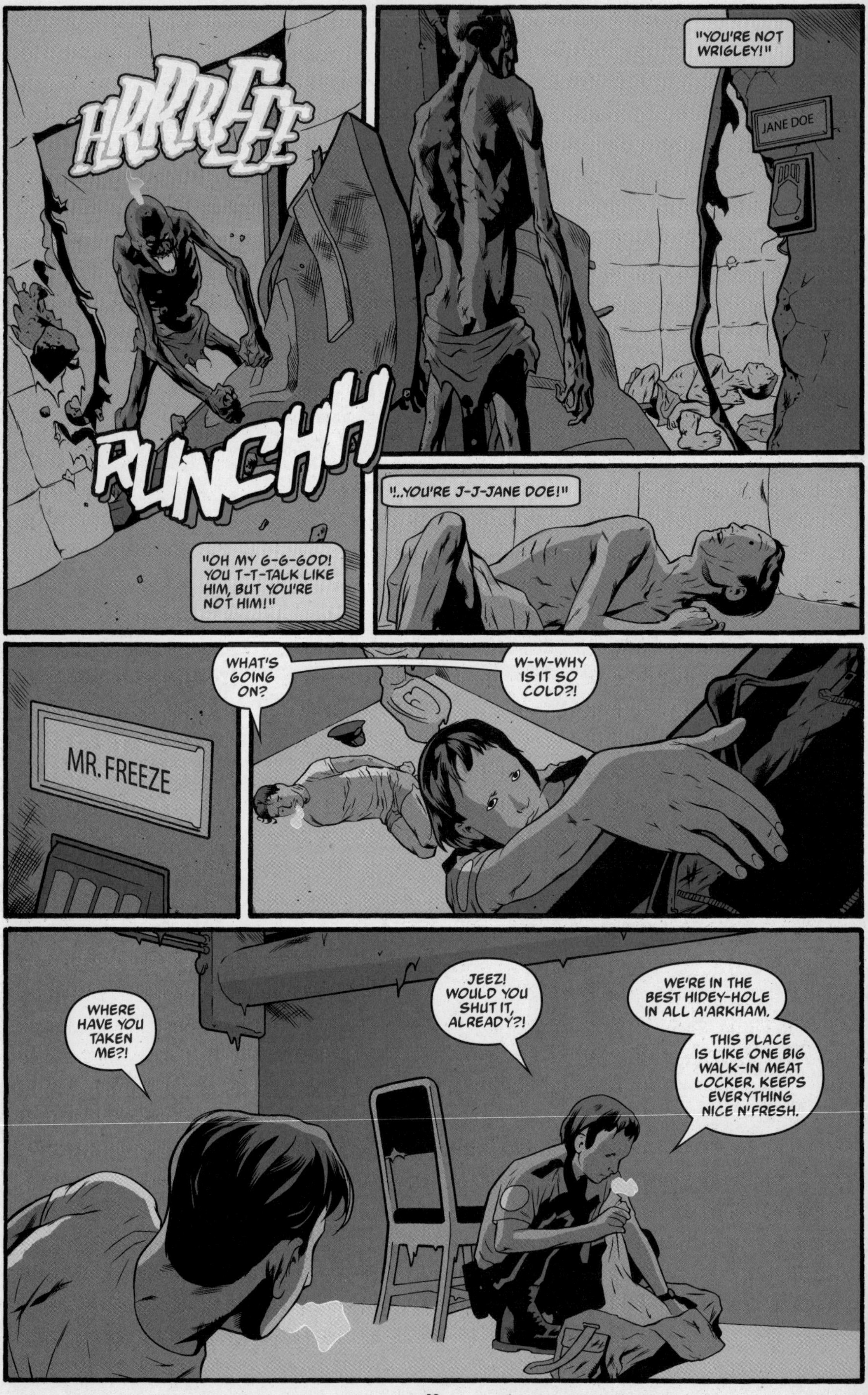
HRKRREEE
RUNCHH
"OH MY G-G-GOD! YOU T-T-TALK LIKE HIM, BUT YOU'RE NOT HIM!"
"YOU'RE NOT WRIGLEY!"
JANE DOE
"...YOU'RE J-J-JANE DOE!"
MR. FREEZE
WHAT'S GOING ON?
W-W-WHY IS IT SO COLD?!
WHERE HAVE YOU TAKEN ME?!
JEEZ! WOULD YOU SHUT IT, ALREADY?!
WE'RE IN THE BEST HIDEY-HOLE IN ALL A'ARKHAM.
THIS PLACE IS LIKE ONE BIG WALK-IN MEAT LOCKER. KEEPS EVERYTHING NICE N'FRESH.

NOW WHERE'D I STASH THAT...

NO, THAT AIN'T IT.

J-J-JESUS!

WUMP

THAT'S RIGHT. YOU HAVEN'T BEEN INTRODUCED. MR. WHITE, MEET DOC CARVER.

AH! HERE WE GO!

THIS IS THE "FISH SKIN" JANE WAS WORKING ON.

THE ONE SHE WAS GONNA USE TO TAKE YOUR PLACE.

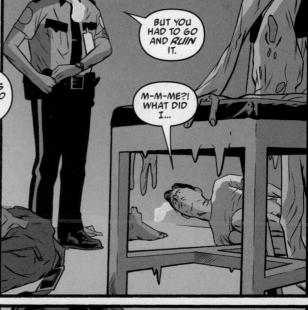

BUT YOU HAD TO GO AND RUIN IT.

M-M-ME?! WHAT DID I...

CLICK

...DO?

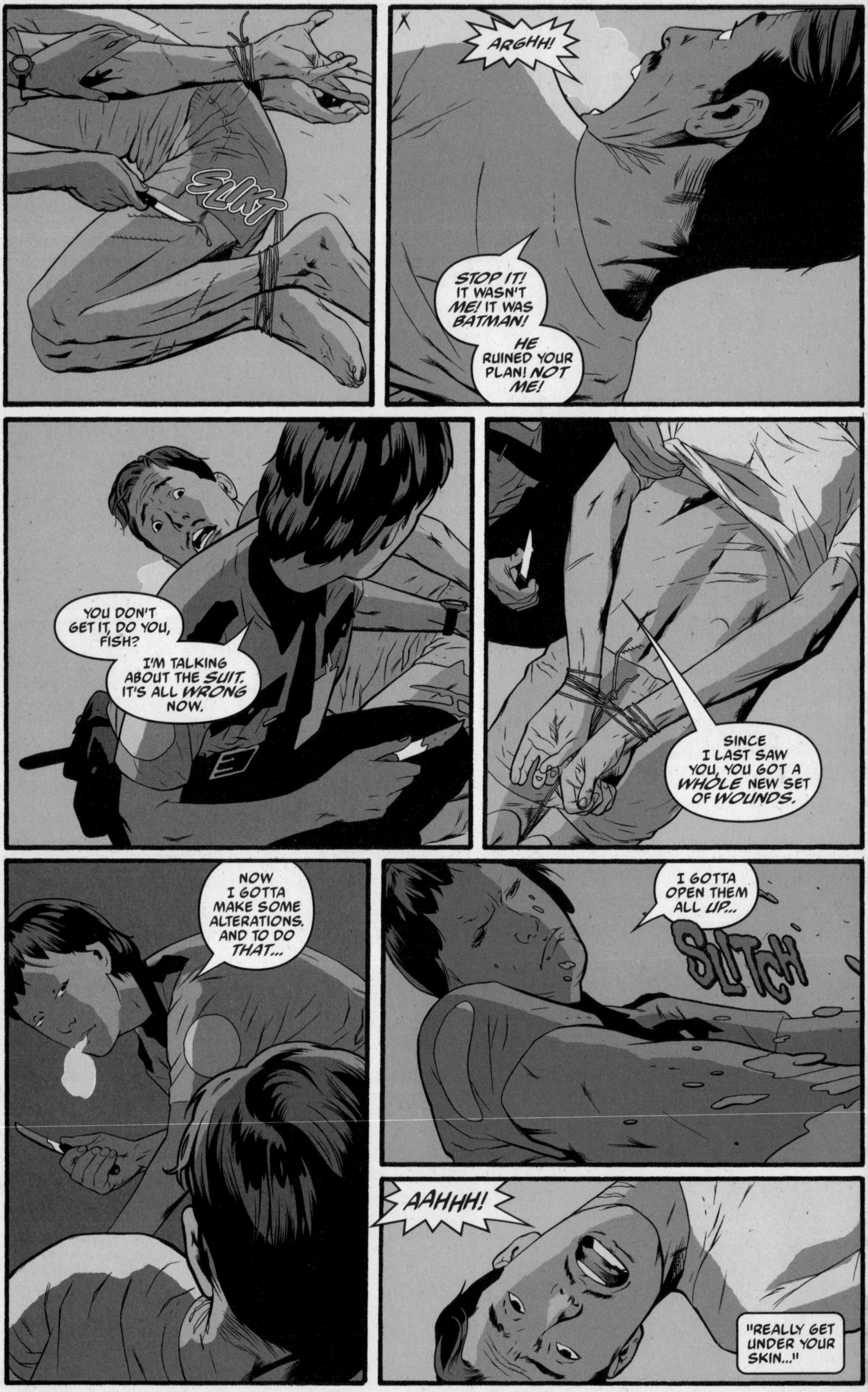
SLIKT
ARGHH!
STOP IT! IT WASN'T ME! IT WAS BATMAN!
HE RUINED YOUR PLAN! NOT ME!
YOU DON'T GET IT, DO YOU, FISH?
I'M TALKING ABOUT THE SUIT. IT'S ALL WRONG NOW.
SINCE I LAST SAW YOU, YOU GOT A WHOLE NEW SET OF WOUNDS.
NOW I GOTTA MAKE SOME ALTERATIONS. AND TO DO THAT...
I GOTTA OPEN THEM ALL UP...
SLITCH
AAHHH!
"REALLY GET UNDER YOUR SKIN..."

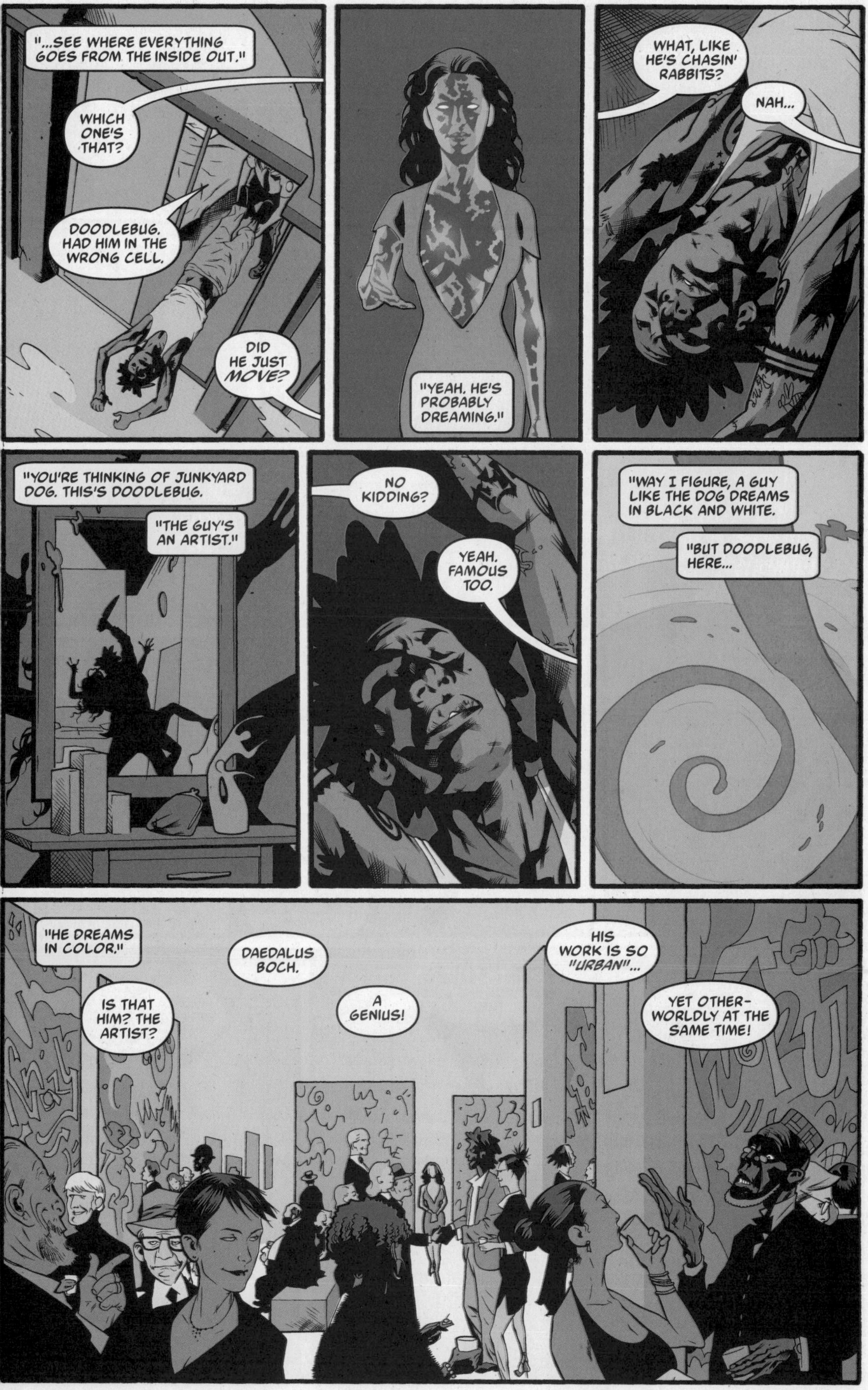
"...SEE WHERE EVERYTHING GOES FROM THE INSIDE OUT."
WHICH ONE'S THAT?
DOODLEBUG. HAD HIM IN THE WRONG CELL.
DID HE JUST MOVE?
"YEAH. HE'S PROBABLY DREAMING."
WHAT, LIKE HE'S CHASIN' RABBITS?
NAH...
"YOU'RE THINKING OF JUNKYARD DOG. THIS'S DOODLEBUG.
"THE GUY'S AN ARTIST."
NO KIDDING?
YEAH. FAMOUS TOO.
"WAY I FIGURE, A GUY LIKE THE DOG DREAMS IN BLACK AND WHITE.
"BUT DOODLEBUG, HERE...
"HE DREAMS IN COLOR."
IS THAT HIM? THE ARTIST?
DAEDALUS BOCH.
A GENIUS!
HIS WORK IS SO "URBAN"...
YET OTHER-WORLDLY AT THE SAME TIME!

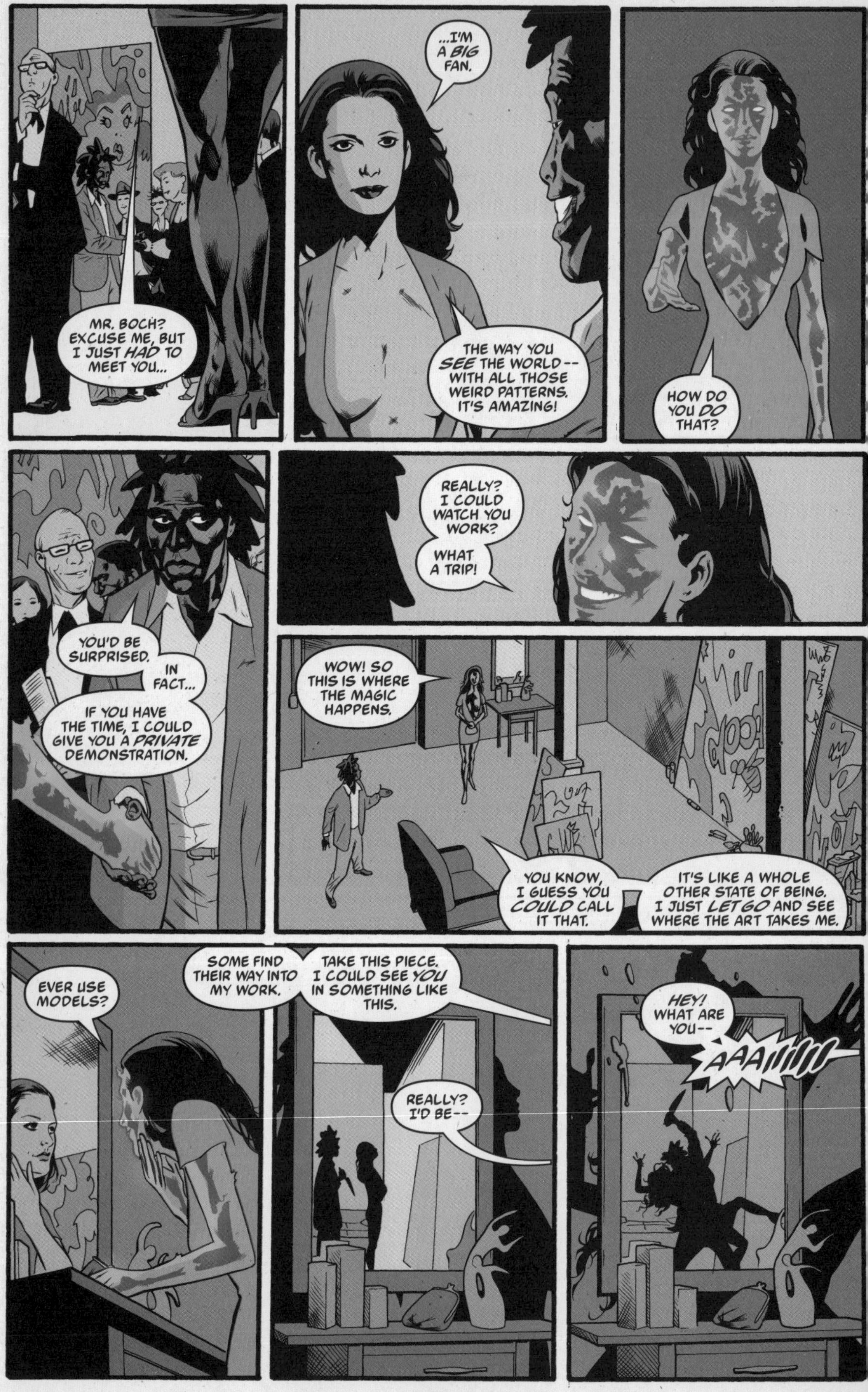
MR. BOCH? EXCUSE ME, BUT I JUST HAD TO MEET YOU...
...I'M A BIG FAN.
THE WAY YOU SEE THE WORLD-- WITH ALL THOSE WEIRD PATTERNS. IT'S AMAZING!
HOW DO YOU DO THAT?
YOU'D BE SURPRISED.
IN FACT...
IF YOU HAVE THE TIME, I COULD GIVE YOU A PRIVATE DEMONSTRATION.
REALLY? I COULD WATCH YOU WORK?
WHAT A TRIP!
WOW! SO THIS IS WHERE THE MAGIC HAPPENS.
YOU KNOW, I GUESS YOU COULD CALL IT THAT.
IT'S LIKE A WHOLE OTHER STATE OF BEING. I JUST LET GO AND SEE WHERE THE ART TAKES ME.
EVER USE MODELS?
SOME FIND THEIR WAY INTO MY WORK.
TAKE THIS PIECE. I COULD SEE YOU IN SOMETHING LIKE THIS.
REALLY? I'D BE--
HEY! WHAT ARE YOU--
AAAIIIIII

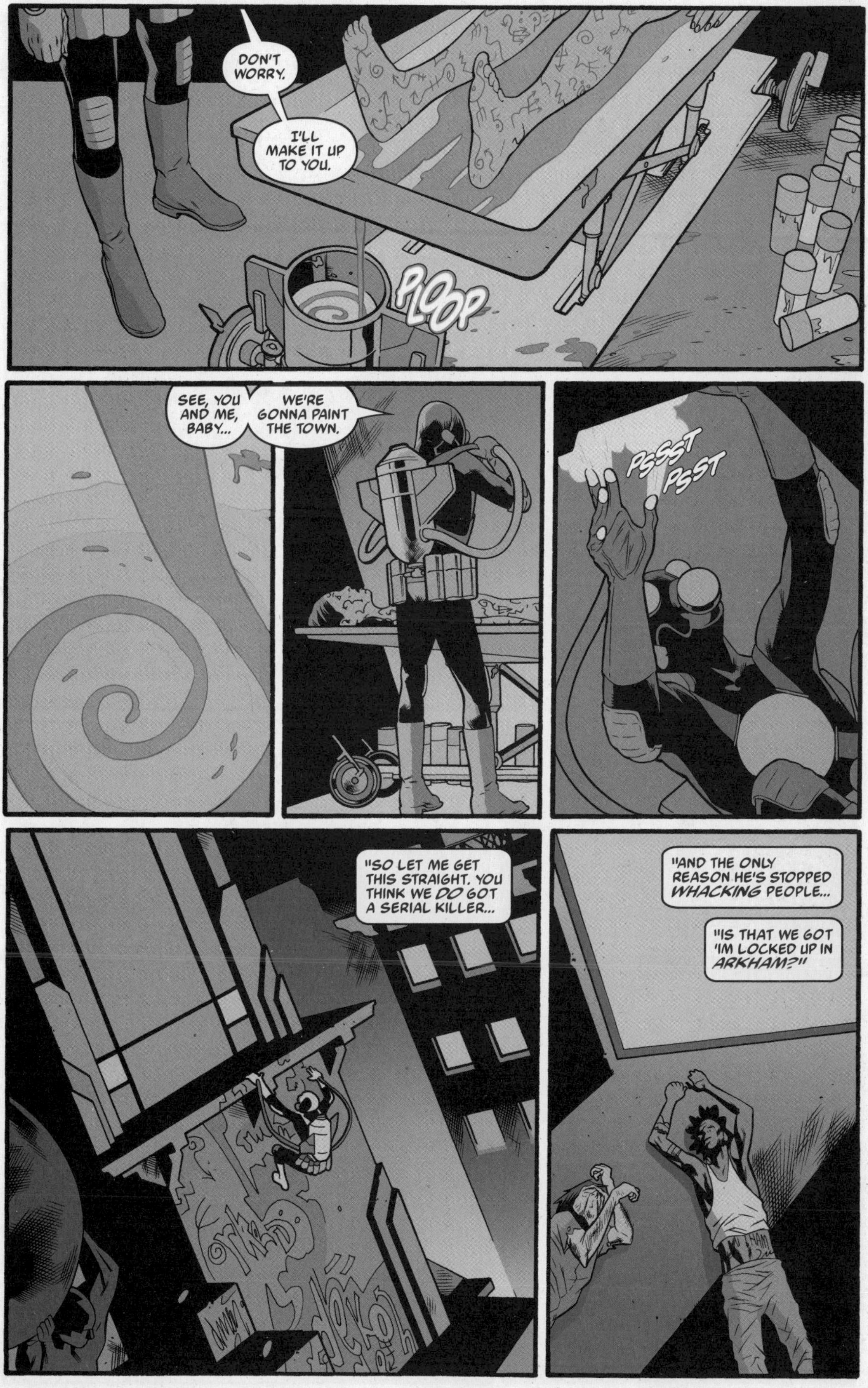
DON'T WORRY.
I'LL MAKE IT UP TO YOU.
PLOOP
SEE, YOU AND ME, BABY...
WE'RE GONNA PAINT THE TOWN.
PSSST PSST
"SO LET ME GET THIS STRAIGHT. YOU THINK WE DO GOT A SERIAL KILLER...
"AND THE ONLY REASON HE'S STOPPED WHACKING PEOPLE...
"IS THAT WE GOT 'IM LOCKED UP IN ARKHAM?"

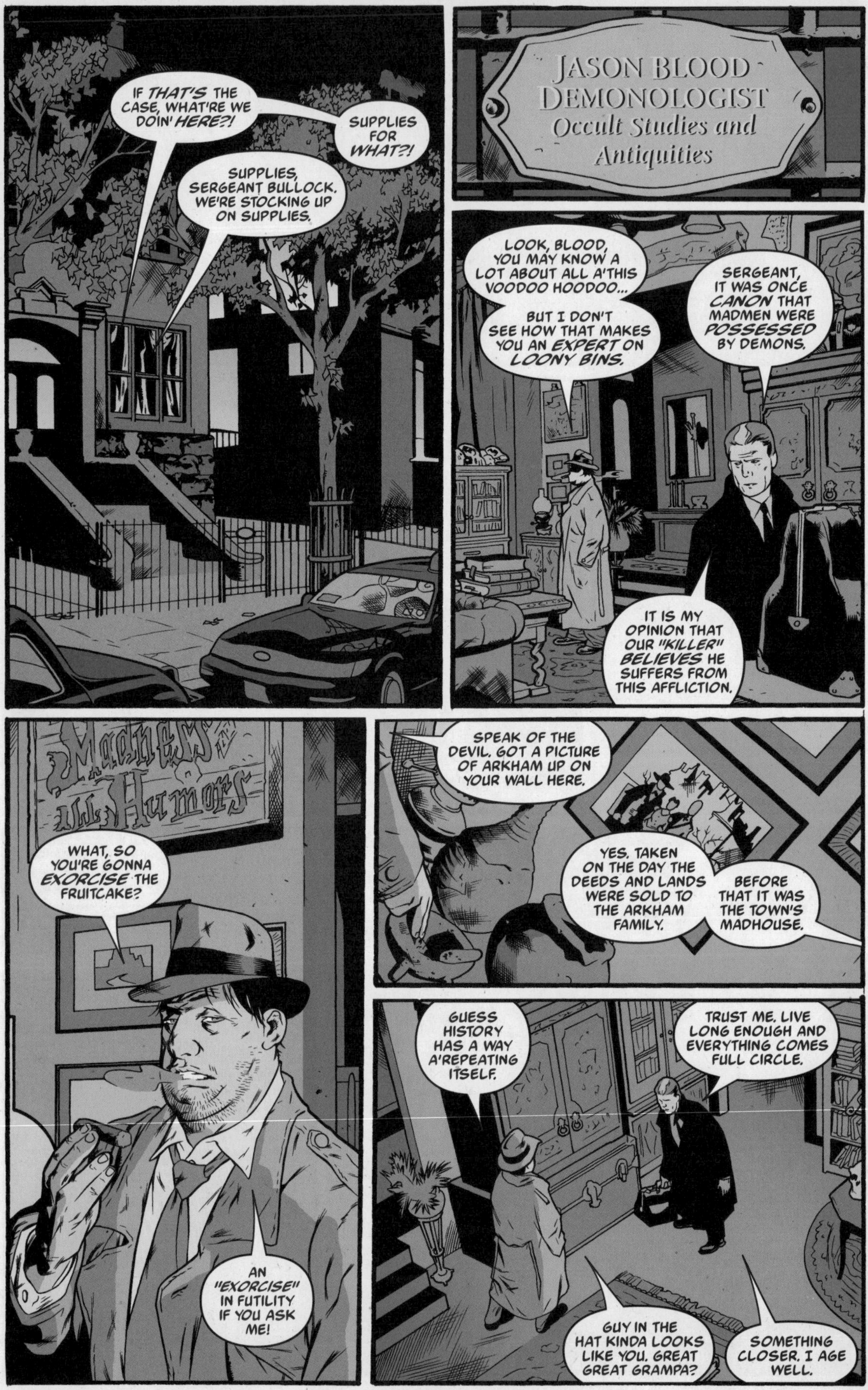
IF THAT'S THE CASE, WHAT'RE WE DOIN' HERE?!
SUPPLIES, SERGEANT BULLOCK. WE'RE STOCKING UP ON SUPPLIES.
SUPPLIES FOR WHAT?!
JASON BLOOD DEMONOLOGIST Occult Studies and Antiquities
LOOK, BLOOD, YOU MAY KNOW A LOT ABOUT ALL A'THIS VOODOO HOODOO...
BUT I DON'T SEE HOW THAT MAKES YOU AN EXPERT ON LOONY BINS.
SERGEANT, IT WAS ONCE CANON THAT MADMEN WERE POSSESSED BY DEMONS.
IT IS MY OPINION THAT OUR "KILLER" BELIEVES HE SUFFERS FROM THIS AFFLICTION.
WHAT, SO YOU'RE GONNA EXORCISE THE FRUITCAKE?
AN "EXORCISE" IN FUTILITY IF YOU ASK ME!
SPEAK OF THE DEVIL. GOT A PICTURE OF ARKHAM UP ON YOUR WALL HERE.
YES. TAKEN ON THE DAY THE DEEDS AND LANDS WERE SOLD TO THE ARKHAM FAMILY.
BEFORE THAT IT WAS THE TOWN'S MADHOUSE.
GUESS HISTORY HAS A WAY A'REPEATING ITSELF.
TRUST ME. LIVE LONG ENOUGH AND EVERYTHING COMES FULL CIRCLE.
GUY IN THE HAT KINDA LOOKS LIKE YOU. GREAT GREAT GRAMPA?
SOMETHING CLOSER. I AGE WELL.

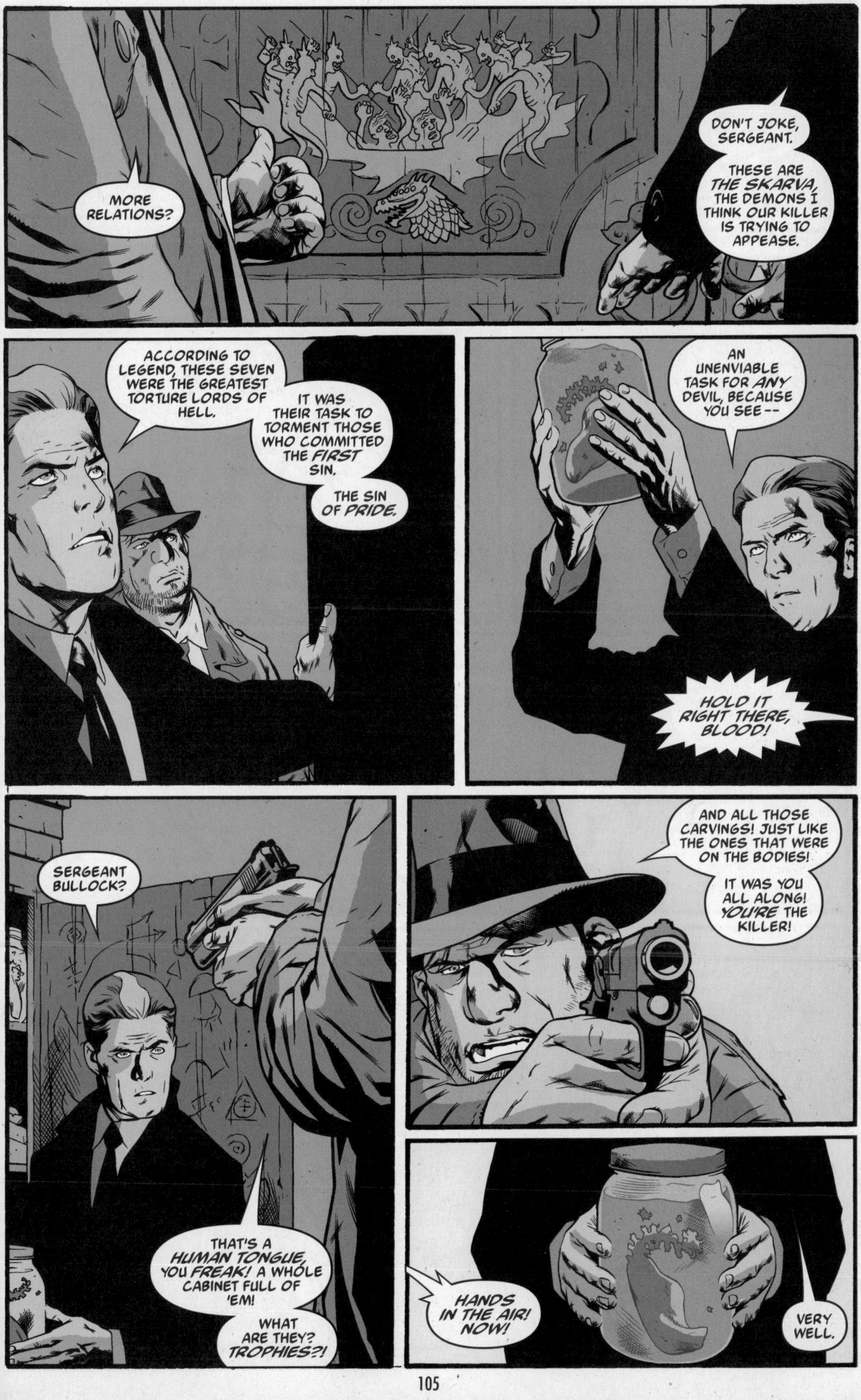
MORE RELATIONS?
DON'T JOKE, SERGEANT.
THESE ARE THE SKARVA, THE DEMONS I THINK OUR KILLER IS TRYING TO APPEASE.
ACCORDING TO LEGEND, THESE SEVEN WERE THE GREATEST TORTURE LORDS OF HELL.
IT WAS THEIR TASK TO TORMENT THOSE WHO COMMITTED THE FIRST SIN.
THE SIN OF PRIDE.
AN UNENVIABLE TASK FOR ANY DEVIL, BECAUSE YOU SEE --
HOLD IT RIGHT THERE, BLOOD!
SERGEANT BULLOCK?
THAT'S A HUMAN TONGUE, YOU FREAK! A WHOLE CABINET FULL OF 'EM!
WHAT ARE THEY? TROPHIES?!
AND ALL THOSE CARVINGS! JUST LIKE THE ONES THAT WERE ON THE BODIES!
IT WAS YOU ALL ALONG! YOU'RE THE KILLER!
HANDS IN THE AIR! NOW!
VERY WELL.

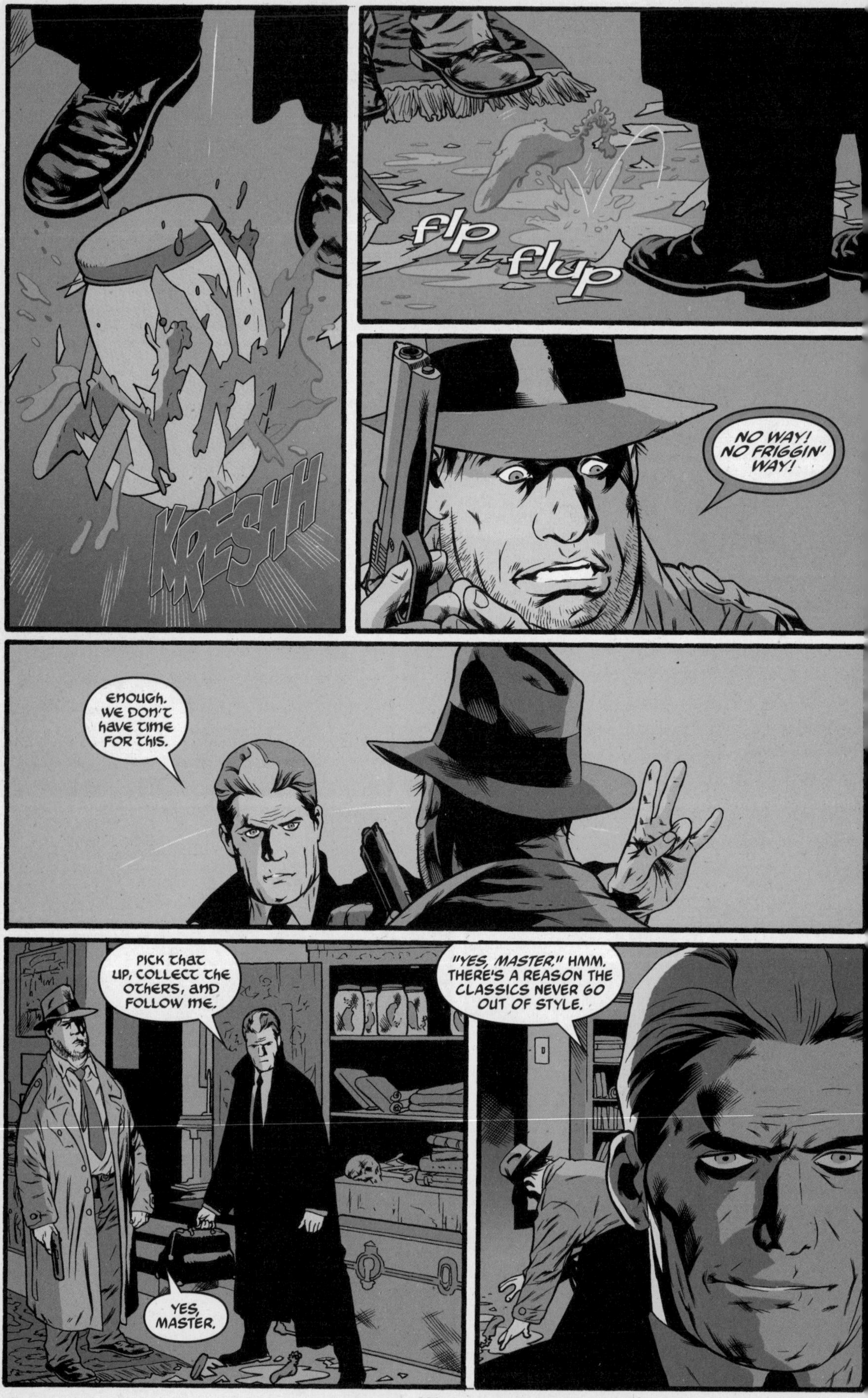
KRESHH
flp
flup
NO WAY! NO FRIGGIN' WAY!
ENOUGH. WE DON'T HAVE TIME FOR THIS.
PICK THAT UP, COLLECT THE OTHERS, AND FOLLOW ME.
YES, MASTER.
"YES, MASTER." HMM. THERE'S A REASON THE CLASSICS NEVER GO OUT OF STYLE.

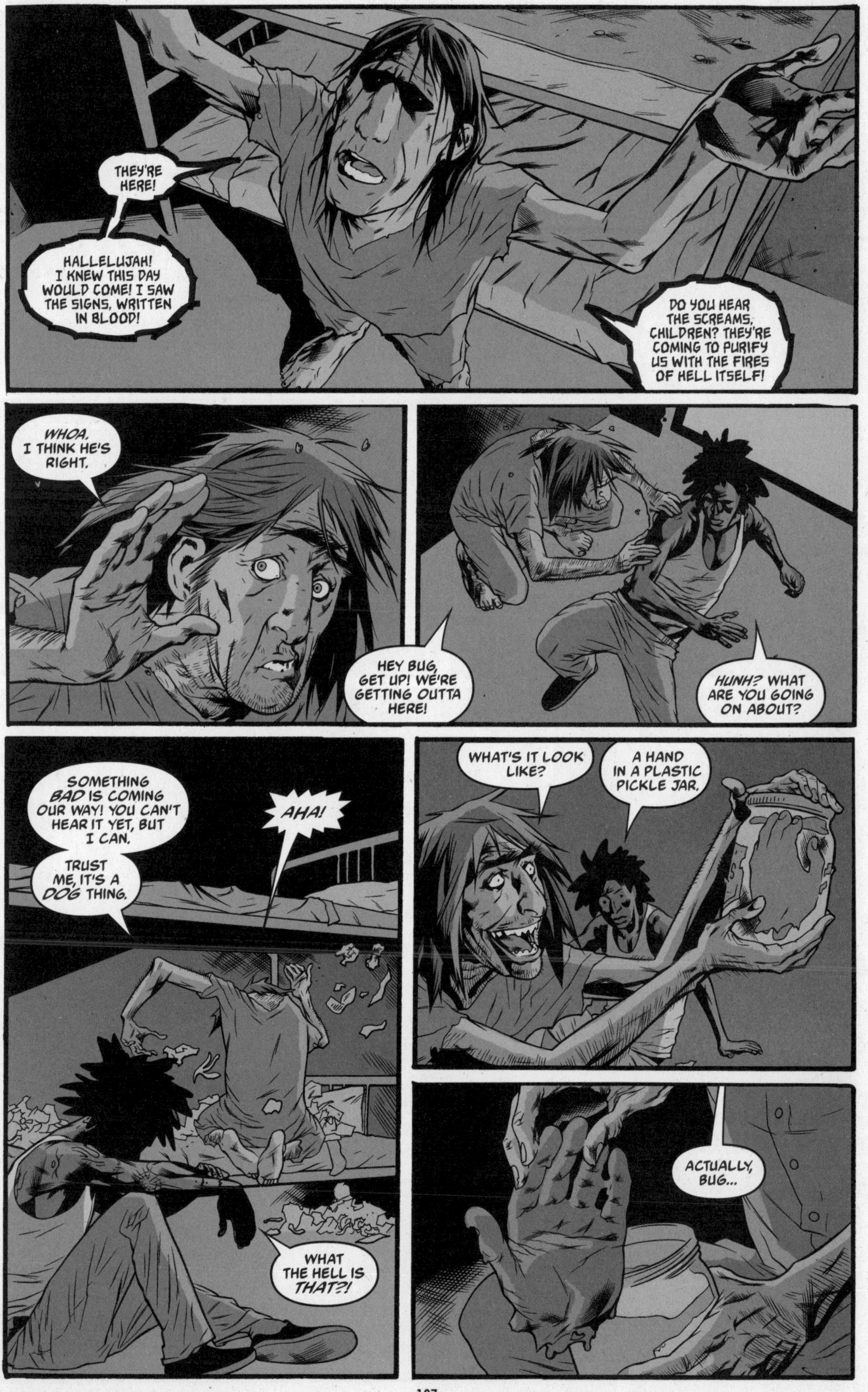
THEY'RE HERE!
HALLELUJAH! I KNEW THIS DAY WOULD COME! I SAW THE SIGNS, WRITTEN IN BLOOD!
DO YOU HEAR THE SCREAMS, CHILDREN? THEY'RE COMING TO PURIFY US WITH THE FIRES OF HELL ITSELF!
WHOA. I THINK HE'S RIGHT.
HEY BUG, GET UP! WE'RE GETTING OUTTA HERE!
HUNH? WHAT ARE YOU GOING ON ABOUT?
SOMETHING BAD IS COMING OUR WAY! YOU CAN'T HEAR IT YET, BUT I CAN.
TRUST ME, IT'S A DOG THING.
AHA!
WHAT THE HELL IS THAT?!
WHAT'S IT LOOK LIKE?
A HAND IN A PLASTIC PICKLE JAR.
ACTUALLY, BUG...

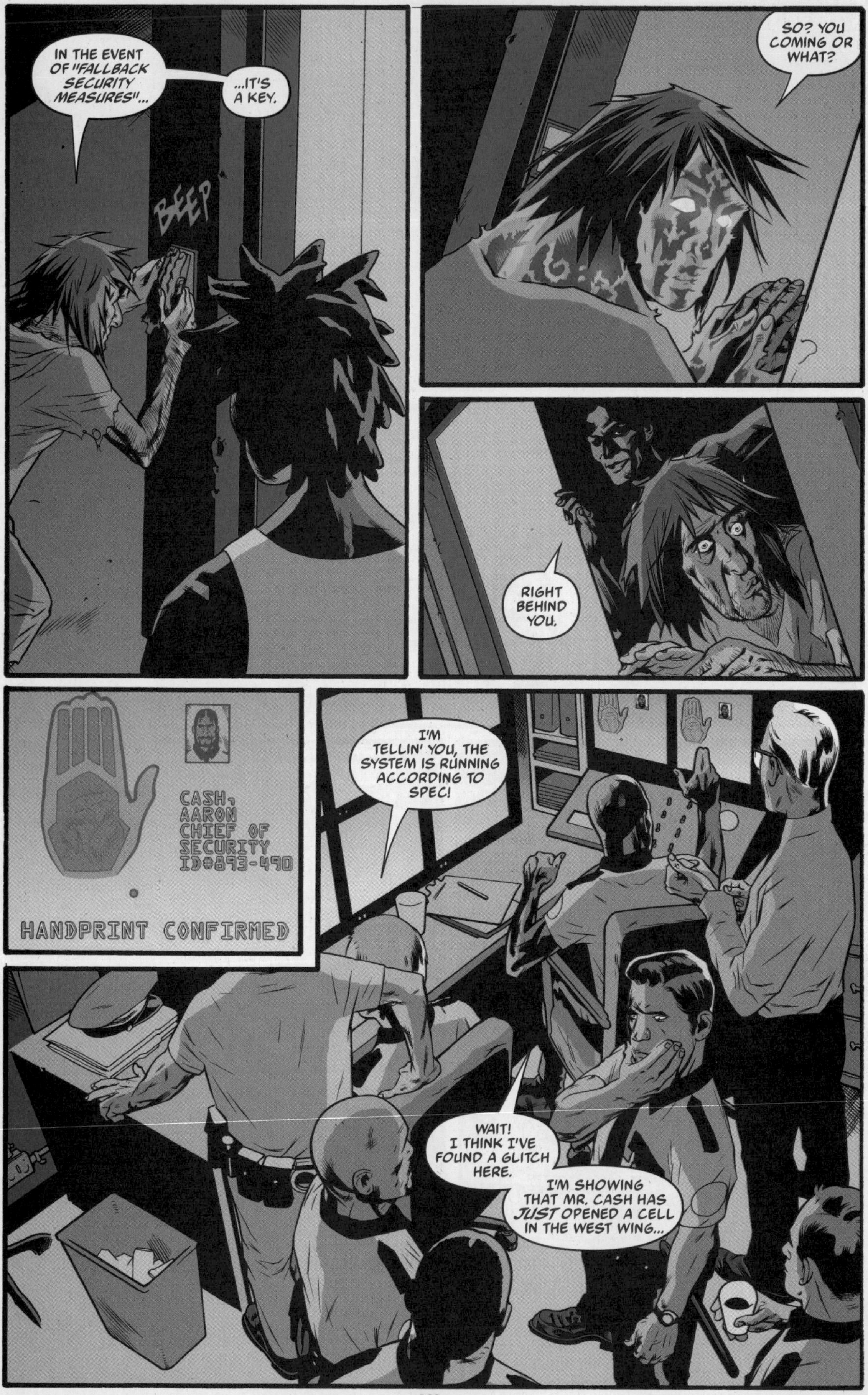
IN THE EVENT OF "FALLBACK SECURITY MEASURES"...
...IT'S A KEY.
BEEP
SO? YOU COMING OR WHAT?
RIGHT BEHIND YOU.
CASH, AARON CHIEF OF SECURITY ID#893-490
HANDPRINT CONFIRMED
I'M TELLIN' YOU, THE SYSTEM IS RUNNING ACCORDING TO SPEC!
WAIT! I THINK I'VE FOUND A GLITCH HERE.
I'M SHOWING THAT MR. CASH HAS *JUST* OPENED A CELL IN THE WEST WING...

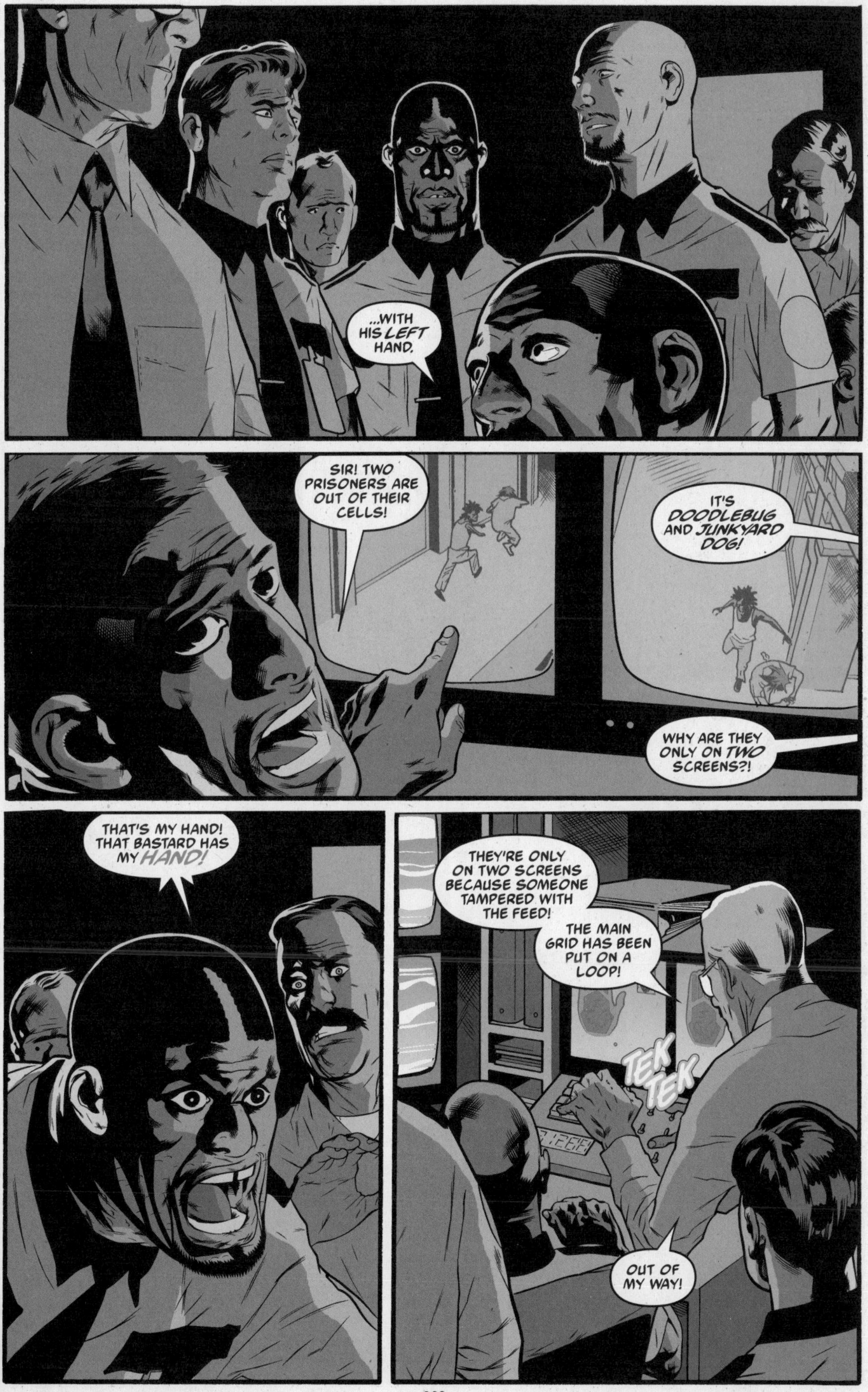
...WITH HIS LEFT HAND.
SIR! TWO PRISONERS ARE OUT OF THEIR CELLS!
IT'S DOODLEBUG AND JUNKYARD DOG!
WHY ARE THEY ONLY ON TWO SCREENS?!
THAT'S MY HAND! THAT BASTARD HAS MY HAND!
THEY'RE ONLY ON TWO SCREENS BECAUSE SOMEONE TAMPERED WITH THE FEED!
THE MAIN GRID HAS BEEN PUT ON A LOOP!
TEK TEK
OUT OF MY WAY!

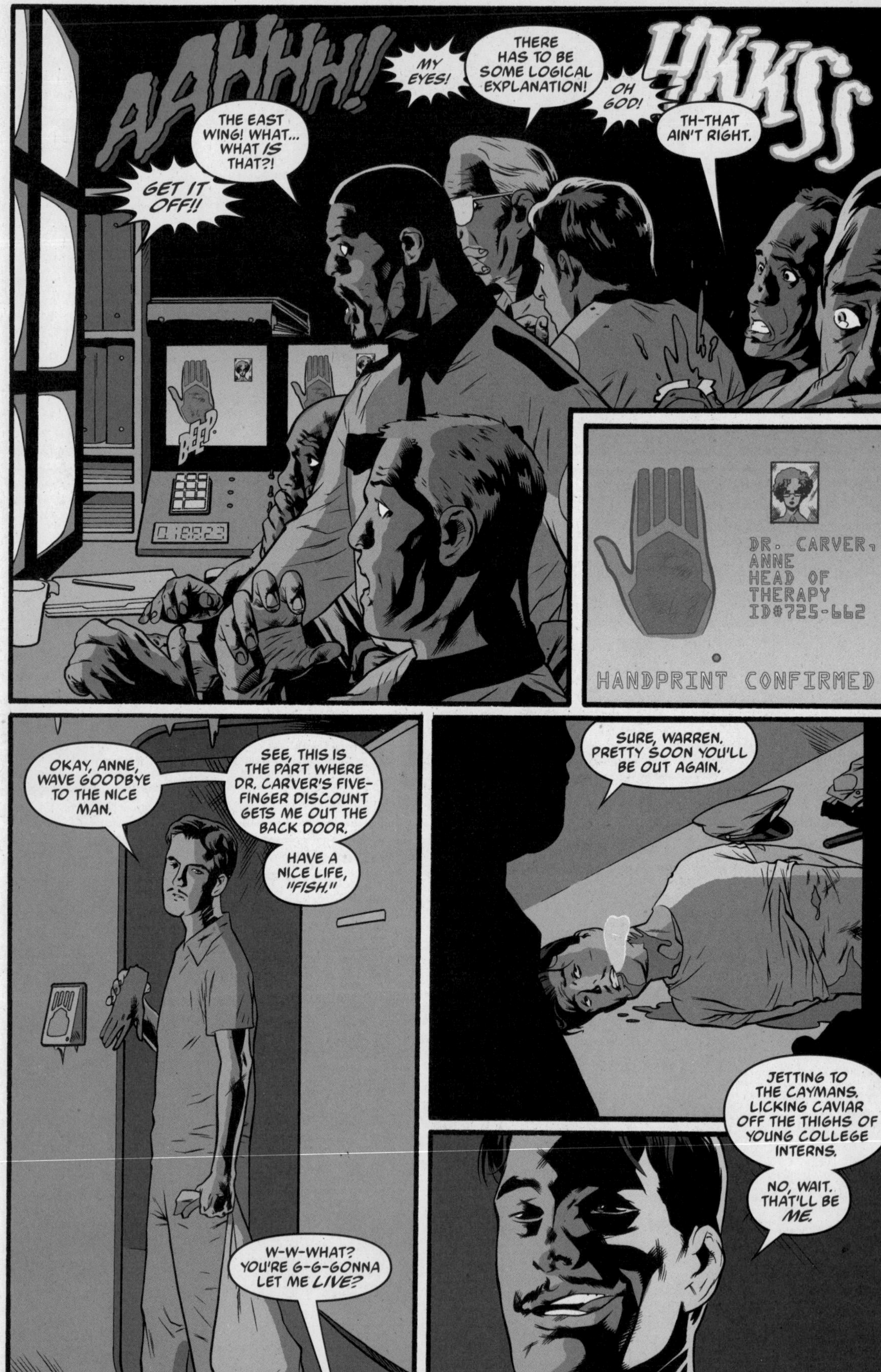
AAHHH!!
THE EAST WING! WHAT... WHAT *IS* THAT?!
GET IT OFF!!
MY EYES!
THERE HAS TO BE SOME LOGICAL EXPLANATION!
OH GOD!
HKKSS
TH-THAT AIN'T RIGHT.
BEEP
DR. CARVER, ANNE
HEAD OF THERAPY
ID#725-662
HANDPRINT CONFIRMED
OKAY, ANNE, WAVE GOODBYE TO THE NICE MAN.
SEE, THIS IS THE PART WHERE DR. CARVER'S FIVE-FINGER DISCOUNT GETS ME OUT THE BACK DOOR.
HAVE A NICE LIFE, "FISH."
W-W-WHAT? YOU'RE G-G-GONNA LET ME *LIVE?*
SURE, WARREN. PRETTY SOON YOU'LL BE OUT AGAIN.
JETTING TO THE CAYMANS. LICKING CAVIAR OFF THE THIGHS OF YOUNG COLLEGE INTERNS.
NO, WAIT. THAT'LL BE *ME.*

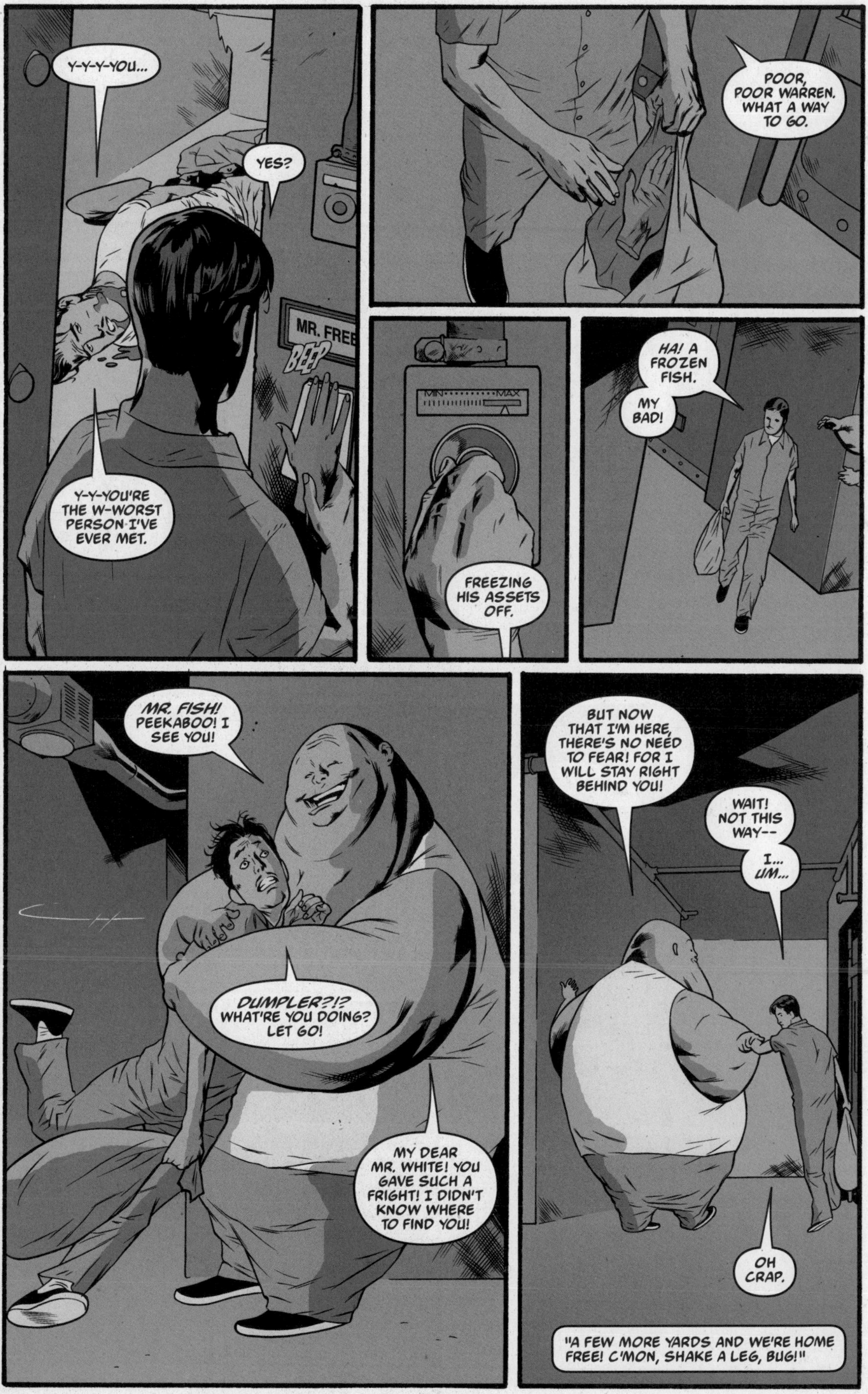
Y-Y-Y-YOU...
YES?
MR. FREE
BEEP
Y-Y-YOU'RE THE W-WORST PERSON I'VE EVER MET.
POOR, POOR WARREN. WHAT A WAY TO GO.
MIN MAX
FREEZING HIS ASSETS OFF.
HA! A FROZEN FISH.
MY BAD!
MR. FISH! PEEKABOO! I SEE YOU!
DUMPLER?!? WHAT'RE YOU DOING? LET GO!
MY DEAR MR. WHITE! YOU GAVE SUCH A FRIGHT! I DIDN'T KNOW WHERE TO FIND YOU!
BUT NOW THAT I'M HERE, THERE'S NO NEED TO FEAR! FOR I WILL STAY RIGHT BEHIND YOU!
WAIT! NOT THIS WAY--
I... UM...
OH CRAP.
"A FEW MORE YARDS AND WE'RE HOME FREE! C'MON, SHAKE A LEG, BUG!"

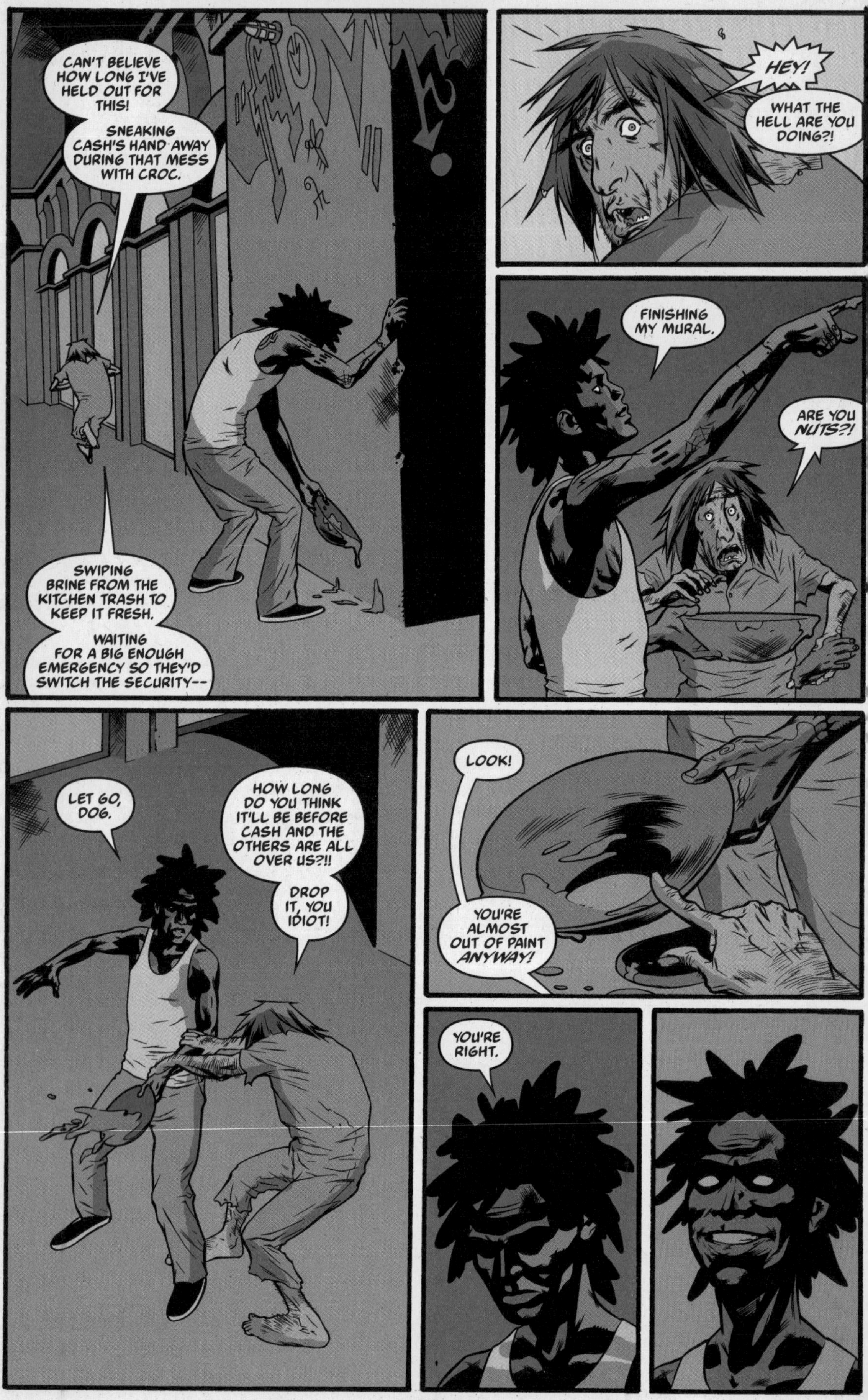
CAN'T BELIEVE HOW LONG I'VE HELD OUT FOR THIS!
SNEAKING CASH'S HAND AWAY DURING THAT MESS WITH CROC.
SWIPING BRINE FROM THE KITCHEN TRASH TO KEEP IT FRESH.
WAITING FOR A BIG ENOUGH EMERGENCY SO THEY'D SWITCH THE SECURITY--
HEY!
WHAT THE HELL ARE YOU DOING?!
FINISHING MY MURAL.
ARE YOU NUTS?!
LET GO, DOG.
HOW LONG DO YOU THINK IT'LL BE BEFORE CASH AND THE OTHERS ARE ALL OVER US?!!
DROP IT, YOU IDIOT!
LOOK!
YOU'RE ALMOST OUT OF PAINT ANYWAY!
YOU'RE RIGHT.

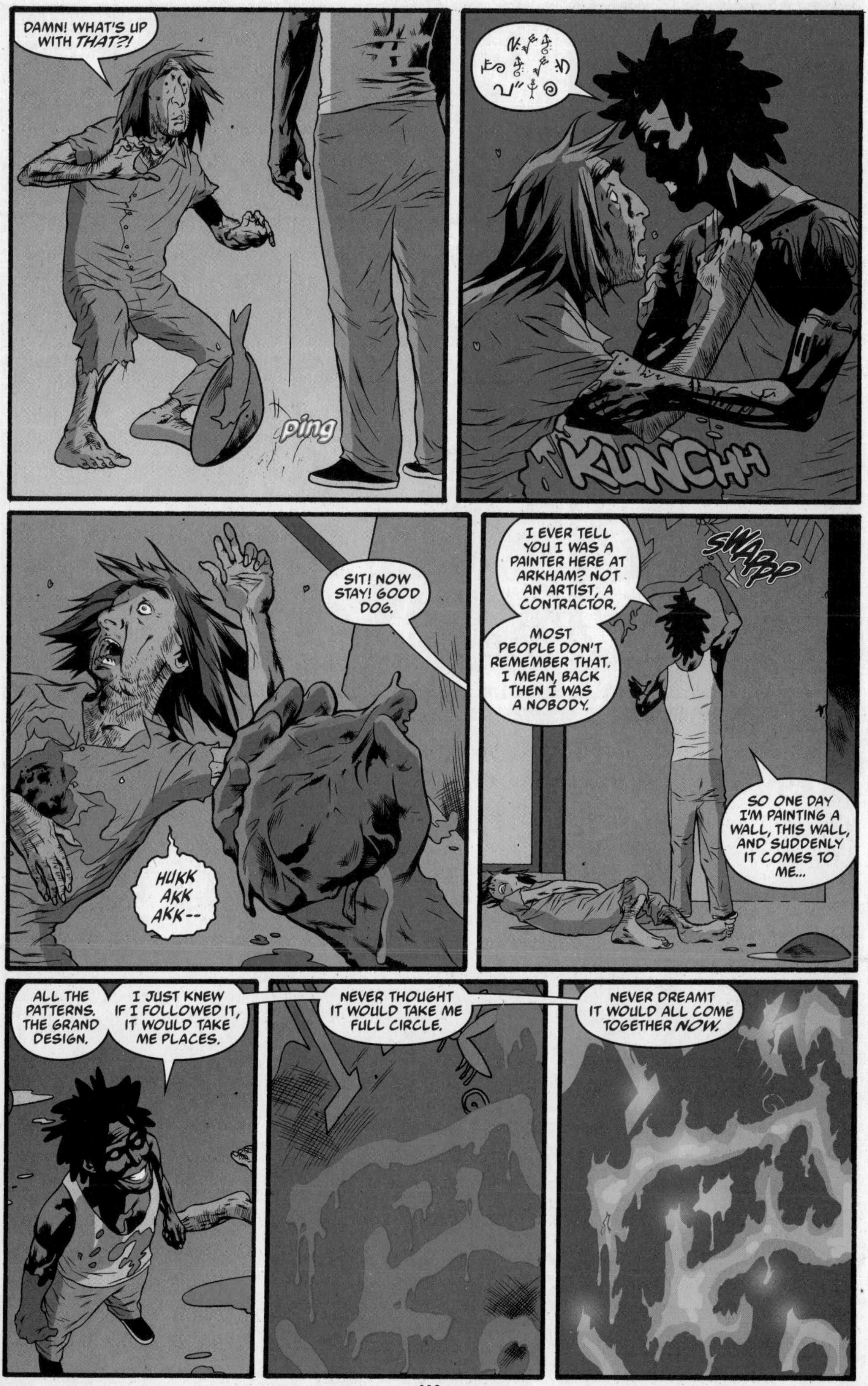
DAMN! WHAT'S UP WITH THAT?!
ping
KUNCHH
SIT! NOW STAY! GOOD DOG.
HUKK AKK AKK--
I EVER TELL YOU I WAS A PAINTER HERE AT ARKHAM? NOT AN ARTIST, A CONTRACTOR.
MOST PEOPLE DON'T REMEMBER THAT. I MEAN, BACK THEN I WAS A NOBODY.
SWABPP
SO ONE DAY I'M PAINTING A WALL, THIS WALL, AND SUDDENLY IT COMES TO ME...
ALL THE PATTERNS. THE GRAND DESIGN.
I JUST KNEW IF I FOLLOWED IT, IT WOULD TAKE ME PLACES.
NEVER THOUGHT IT WOULD TAKE ME FULL CIRCLE.
NEVER DREAMT IT WOULD ALL COME TOGETHER NOW.

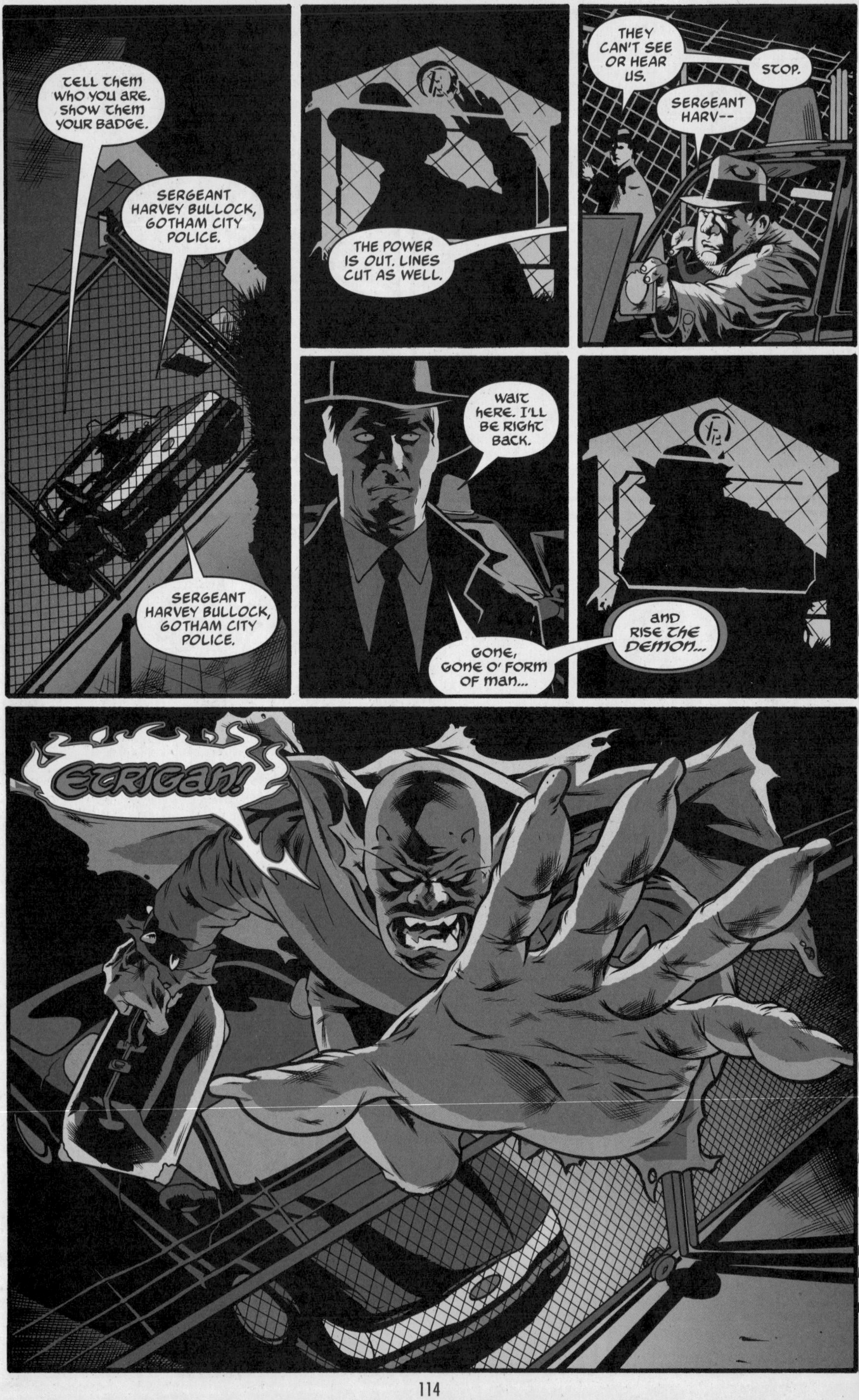
TELL THEM WHO YOU ARE. SHOW THEM YOUR BADGE.
SERGEANT HARVEY BULLOCK, GOTHAM CITY POLICE.
SERGEANT HARVEY BULLOCK, GOTHAM CITY POLICE.
THE POWER IS OUT. LINES CUT AS WELL.
THEY CAN'T SEE OR HEAR US.
STOP.
SERGEANT HARV--
WAIT HERE. I'LL BE RIGHT BACK.
GONE, GONE O' FORM OF MAN...
AND RISE THE DEMON...
ETRIGAN!

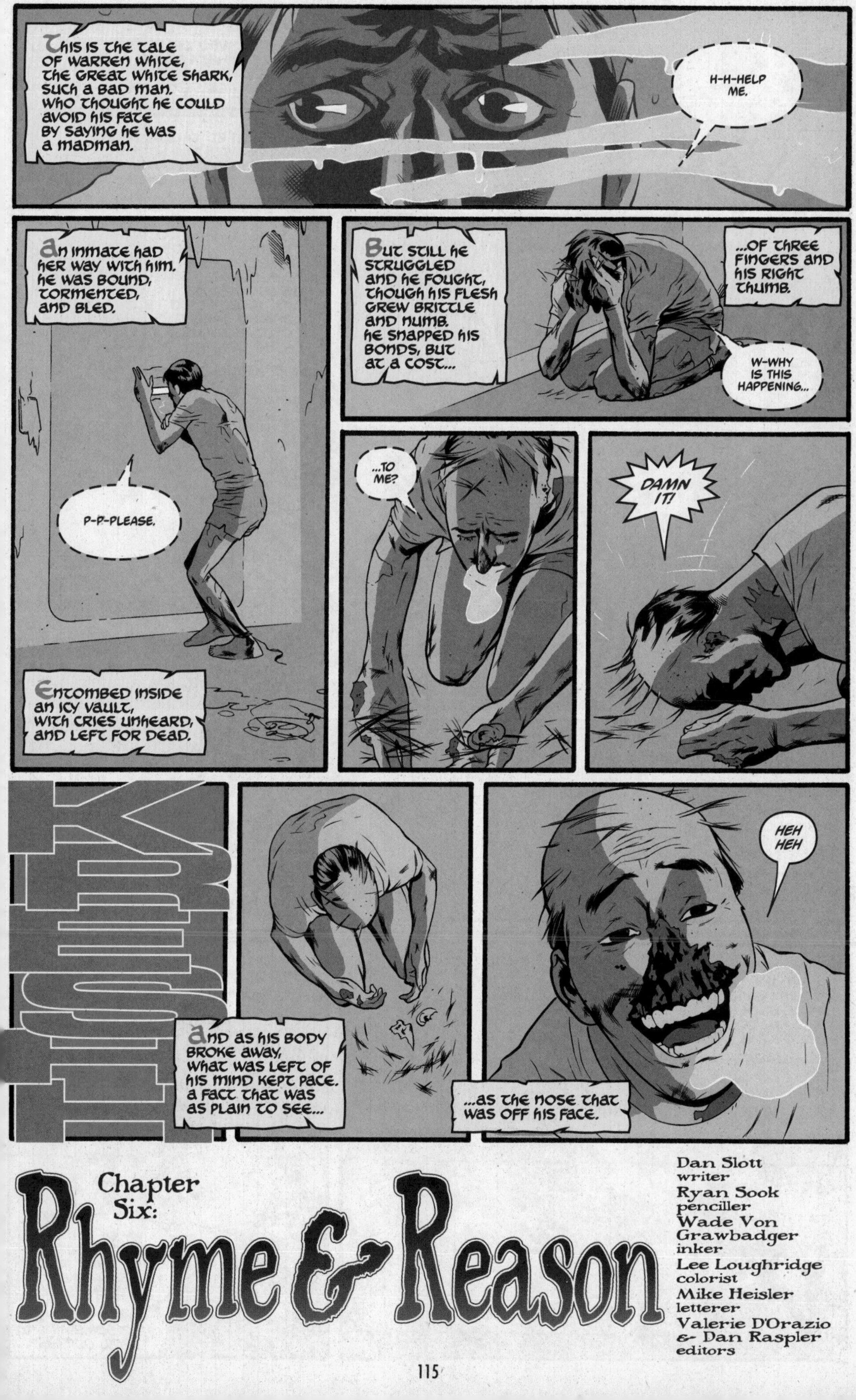
This is the tale of Warren White, the Great White Shark, such a bad man. Who thought he could avoid his fate by saying he was a madman.
H-H-HELP ME.
An inmate had her way with him. He was bound, tormented, and bled.
P-P-PLEASE.
Entombed inside an icy vault, with cries unheard, and left for dead.
But still he struggled and he fought, though his flesh grew brittle and numb. He snapped his bonds, but at a cost...
...of three fingers and his right thumb.
W-WHY IS THIS HAPPENING...
...TO ME?
DAMN IT!
And as his body broke away, what was left of his mind kept pace. A fact that was as plain to see...
...as the nose that was off his face.
HEH HEH

Chapter Six: Rhyme & Reason

Dan Slott
writer
Ryan Sook
penciller
Wade Von Grawbadger
inker
Lee Loughridge
colorist
Mike Heisler
letterer
Valerie D'Orazio & Dan Raspler
editors

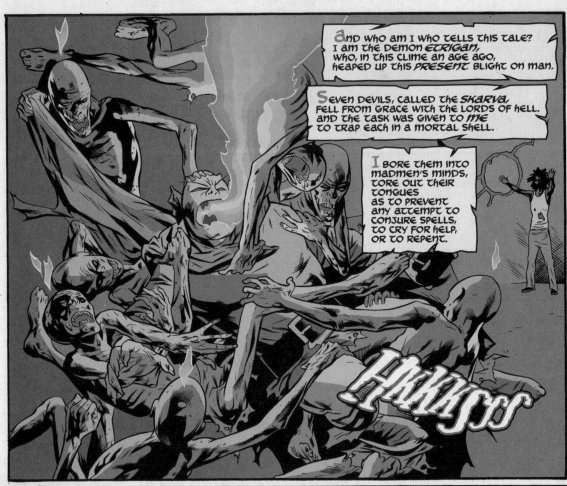

AND WHO AM I WHO TELLS THIS TALE? I AM THE DEMON *ETRIGAN*, WHO, IN THIS CLIME AN AGE AGO, HEAPED UP THIS *PRESENT* BLIGHT ON MAN.

SEVEN DEVILS, CALLED THE *SKARVA*, FELL FROM GRACE WITH THE LORDS OF HELL. AND THE TASK WAS GIVEN TO *ME* TO TRAP EACH IN A MORTAL SHELL.

I BORE THEM INTO MADMEN'S MINDS, TORE OUT THEIR TONGUES AS TO PREVENT ANY ATTEMPT TO CONJURE SPELLS, TO CRY FOR HELP, OR TO REPENT.

HRKKSSS

A MODERN MADMAN AIDS THEM NOW, AN ARTIST WHO FOLLOWS HIS "MUSE" AND TAPS INTO AN ARCANE MIGHT THAT HE IS MOST UNWISE TO USE!

I HAD A PLAN TO MAKE THINGS RIGHT, TO PUT EV'RY PIECE BACK IN PLACE, BUT FAR TOO SOON I LOST THE FIGHT...

TIED UP IN DEFEAT AND DISGRACE.

GRRR! SHOGGOTH SLIME?! A STICKY TRAP! I AM HELD AT BAY!

BUT DO NOT THINK THIS MEANS THAT YOU HAVE WON THE DAY!

ANY OF YOU KNOW THIS GUY? DIDN'T THINK SO. YET HE CRASHES MY OPENING.

WHAT'S IN THE BAG? SOMETHING TO SPOIL OUR FUN?

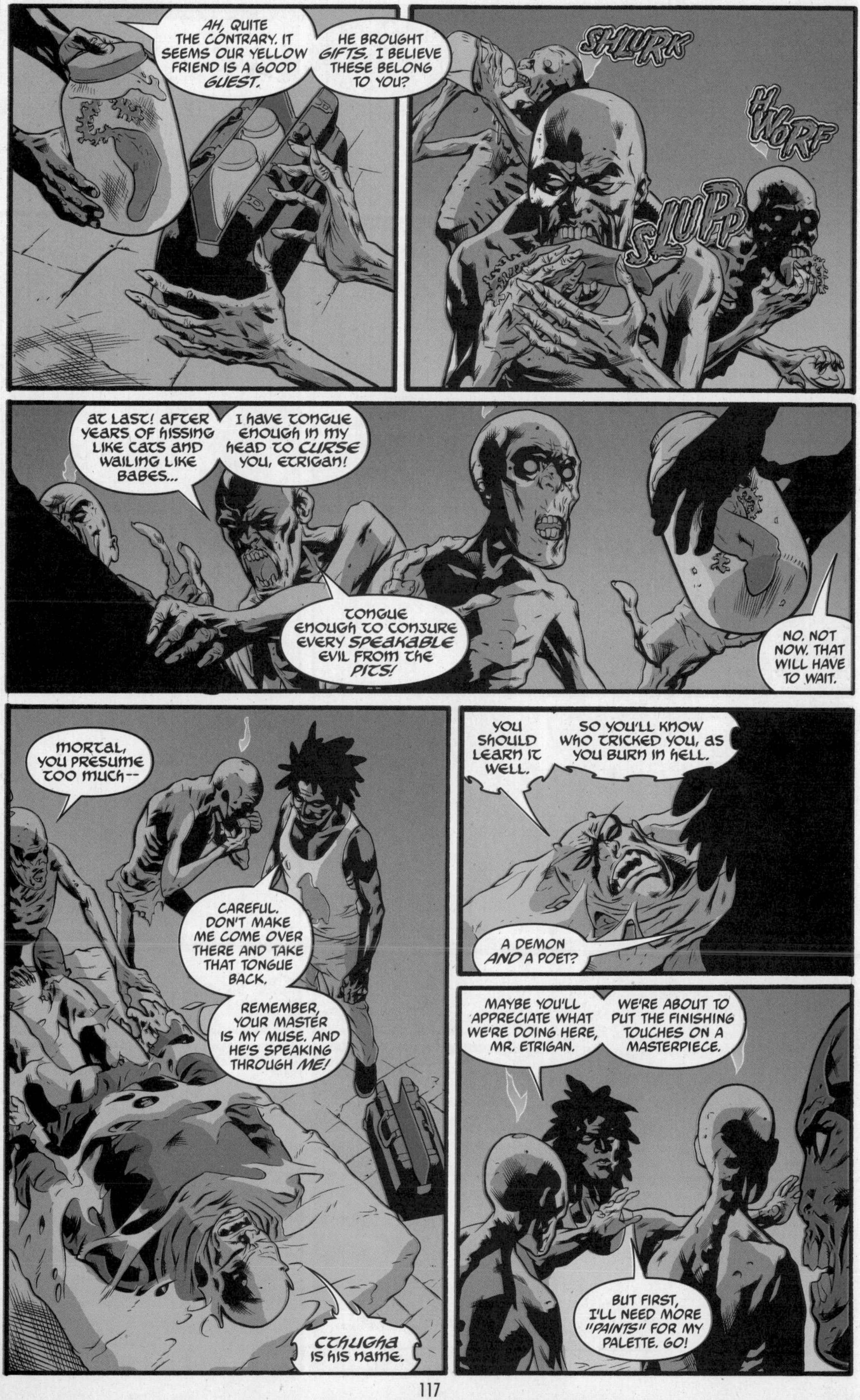
AH, QUITE THE CONTRARY. IT SEEMS OUR YELLOW FRIEND IS A GOOD GUEST.
HE BROUGHT GIFTS. I BELIEVE THESE BELONG TO YOU?
SHLURK
HWORF
SLUPP
AT LAST! AFTER YEARS OF HISSING LIKE CATS AND WAILING LIKE BABES...
I HAVE TONGUE ENOUGH IN MY HEAD TO CURSE YOU, ETRIGAN!
TONGUE ENOUGH TO CONJURE EVERY SPEAKABLE EVIL FROM THE PITS!
NO. NOT NOW. THAT WILL HAVE TO WAIT.
MORTAL, YOU PRESUME TOO MUCH--
CAREFUL. DON'T MAKE ME COME OVER THERE AND TAKE THAT TONGUE BACK.
REMEMBER, YOUR MASTER IS MY MUSE. AND HE'S SPEAKING THROUGH ME!
CTHUGHA IS HIS NAME.
YOU SHOULD LEARN IT WELL.
SO YOU'LL KNOW WHO TRICKED YOU, AS YOU BURN IN HELL.
A DEMON AND A POET?
MAYBE YOU'LL APPRECIATE WHAT WE'RE DOING HERE, MR. ETRIGAN.
WE'RE ABOUT TO PUT THE FINISHING TOUCHES ON A MASTERPIECE.
BUT FIRST, I'LL NEED MORE "PAINTS" FOR MY PALETTE. GO!

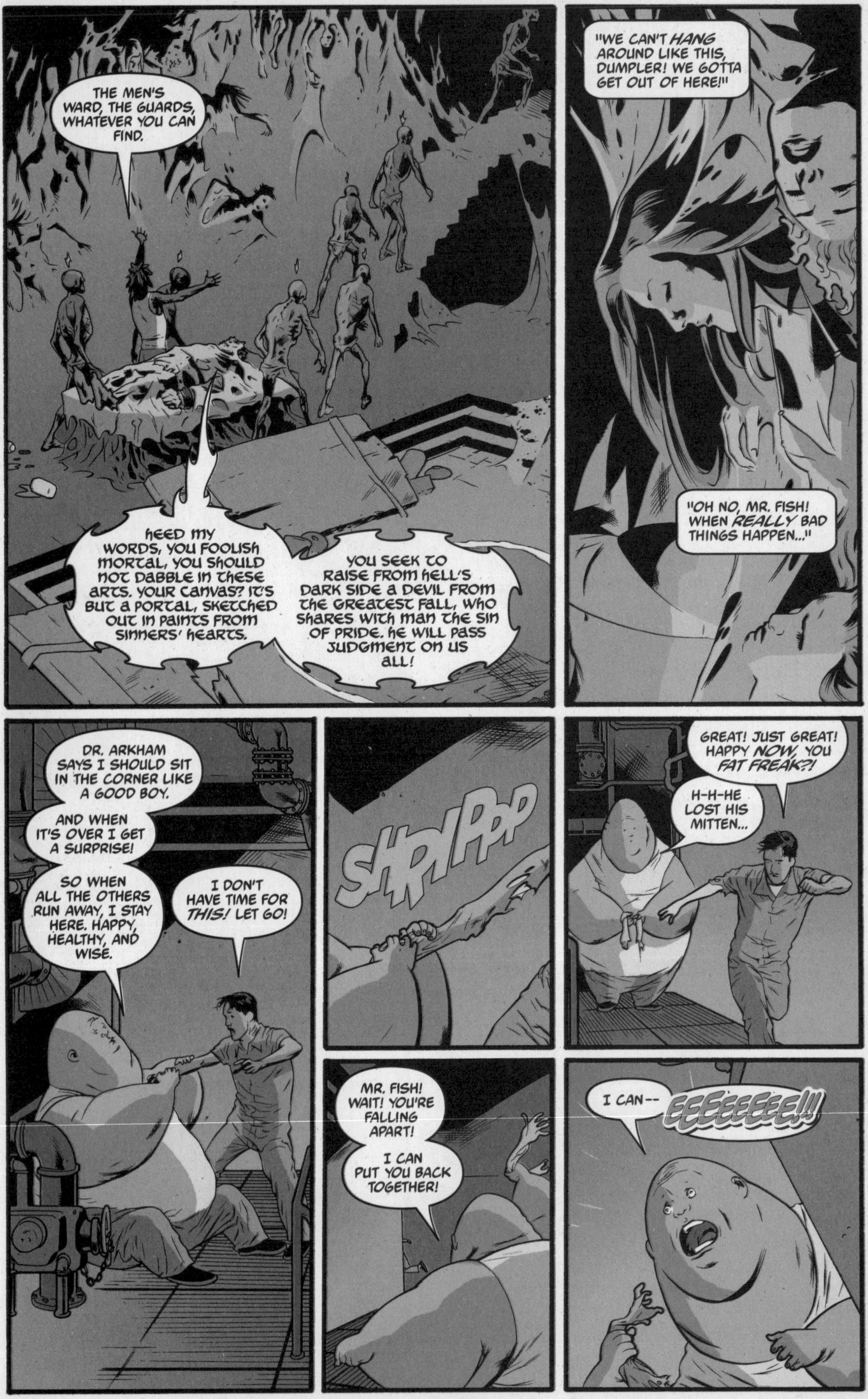
THE MEN'S WARD, THE GUARDS, WHATEVER YOU CAN FIND.
HEED MY WORDS, YOU FOOLISH MORTAL, YOU SHOULD NOT DABBLE IN THESE ARTS. YOUR CANVAS? IT'S BUT A PORTAL, SKETCHED OUT IN PAINTS FROM SINNERS' HEARTS.
YOU SEEK TO RAISE FROM HELL'S DARK SIDE A DEVIL FROM THE GREATEST FALL, WHO SHARES WITH MAN THE SIN OF PRIDE. HE WILL PASS JUDGMENT ON US ALL!
"WE CAN'T HANG AROUND LIKE THIS, DUMPLER! WE GOTTA GET OUT OF HERE!"
"OH NO, MR. FISH! WHEN REALLY BAD THINGS HAPPEN..."
DR. ARKHAM SAYS I SHOULD SIT IN THE CORNER LIKE A GOOD BOY.
AND WHEN IT'S OVER I GET A SURPRISE!
SO WHEN ALL THE OTHERS RUN AWAY, I STAY HERE. HAPPY, HEALTHY, AND WISE.
I DON'T HAVE TIME FOR THIS! LET GO!
SHRIPPP
GREAT! JUST GREAT! HAPPY NOW, YOU FAT FREAK?!
H-H-HE LOST HIS MITTEN...
MR. FISH! WAIT! YOU'RE FALLING APART!
I CAN PUT YOU BACK TOGETHER!
I CAN--
EEEEEEEE!!!

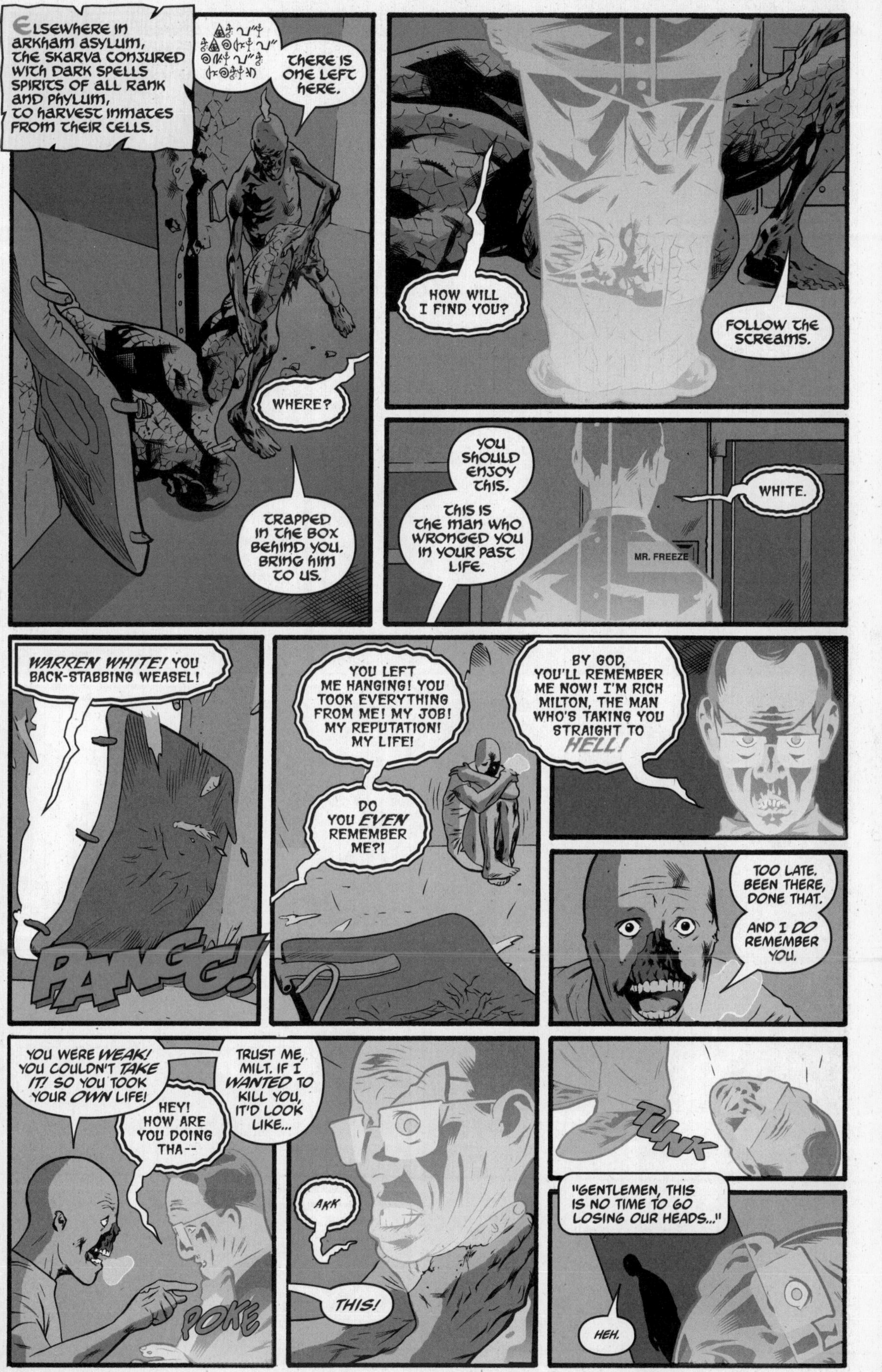
Elsewhere in Arkham Asylum, the Skarva conjured with dark spells spirits of all rank and phylum, to harvest inmates from their cells.
There is one left here.
Where?
Trapped in the box behind you. Bring him to us.
How will I find you?
Follow the screams.
You should enjoy this.
This is the man who wronged you in your past life.
White.
MR. FREEZE
WARREN WHITE! YOU BACK-STABBING WEASEL!
PANGG!
YOU LEFT ME HANGING! YOU TOOK EVERYTHING FROM ME! MY JOB! MY REPUTATION! MY LIFE!
DO YOU EVEN REMEMBER ME?!
BY GOD, YOU'LL REMEMBER ME NOW! I'M RICH MILTON, THE MAN WHO'S TAKING YOU STRAIGHT TO HELL!
TOO LATE. BEEN THERE, DONE THAT.
AND I DO REMEMBER YOU.
YOU WERE WEAK! YOU COULDN'T TAKE IT! SO YOU TOOK YOUR OWN LIFE!
HEY! HOW ARE YOU DOING THA--
TRUST ME, MILT. IF I WANTED TO KILL YOU, IT'D LOOK LIKE...
POKE
AKK
THIS!
TUNK
"GENTLEMEN, THIS IS NO TIME TO GO LOSING OUR HEADS..."
HEH.

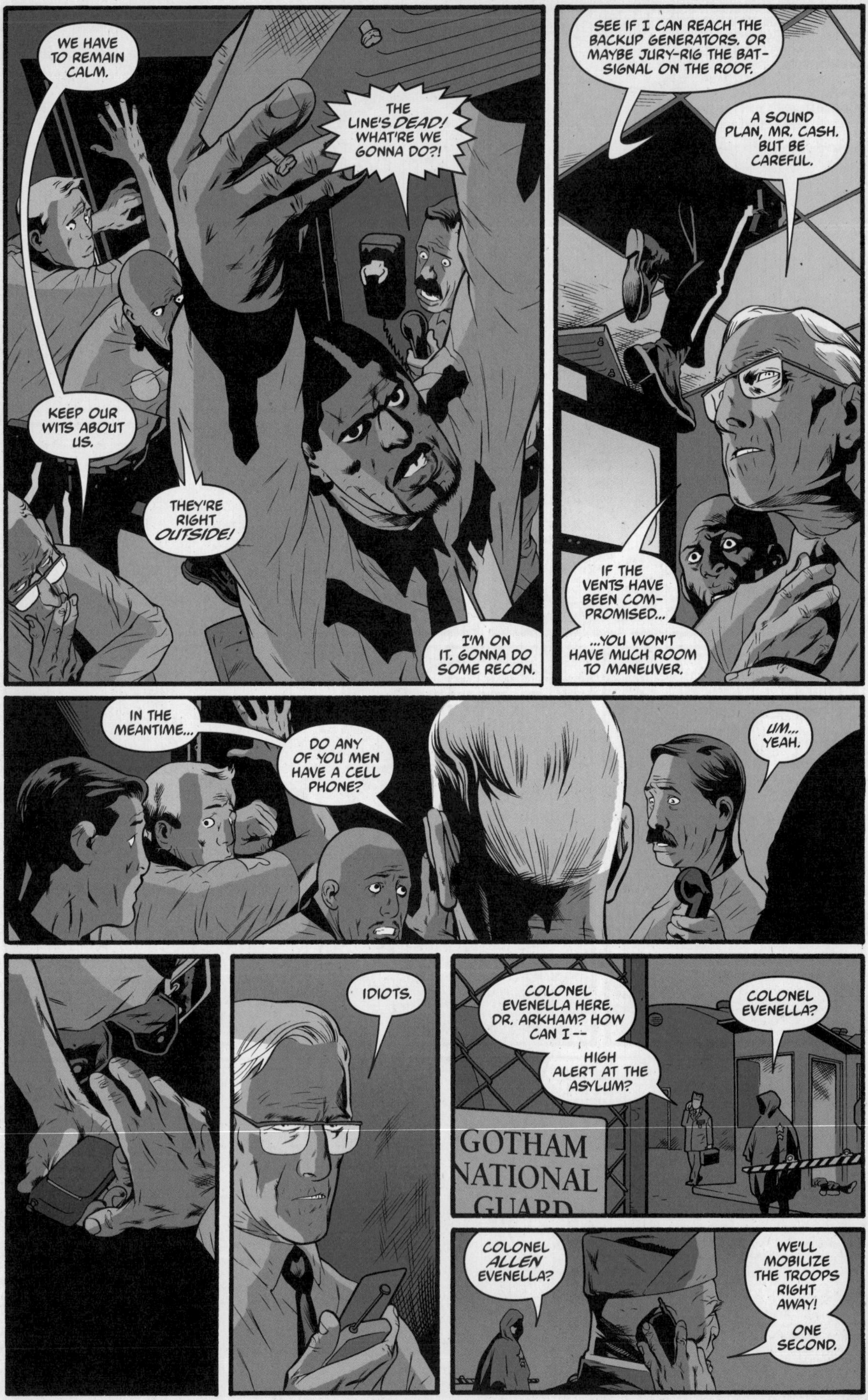
WE HAVE TO REMAIN CALM.
THE LINE'S DEAD! WHAT'RE WE GONNA DO?!
KEEP OUR WITS ABOUT US.
THEY'RE RIGHT OUTSIDE!
I'M ON IT. GONNA DO SOME RECON.
SEE IF I CAN REACH THE BACKUP GENERATORS. OR MAYBE JURY-RIG THE BAT-SIGNAL ON THE ROOF.
A SOUND PLAN, MR. CASH. BUT BE CAREFUL.
IF THE VENTS HAVE BEEN COM-PROMISED...
...YOU WON'T HAVE MUCH ROOM TO MANEUVER.
IN THE MEANTIME...
DO ANY OF YOU MEN HAVE A CELL PHONE?
UM... YEAH.
IDIOTS.
COLONEL EVENELLA HERE. DR. ARKHAM? HOW CAN I --
HIGH ALERT AT THE ASYLUM?
COLONEL EVENELLA?
GOTHAM NATIONAL GUARD
COLONEL ALLEN EVENELLA?
WE'LL MOBILIZE THE TROOPS RIGHT AWAY!
ONE SECOND.

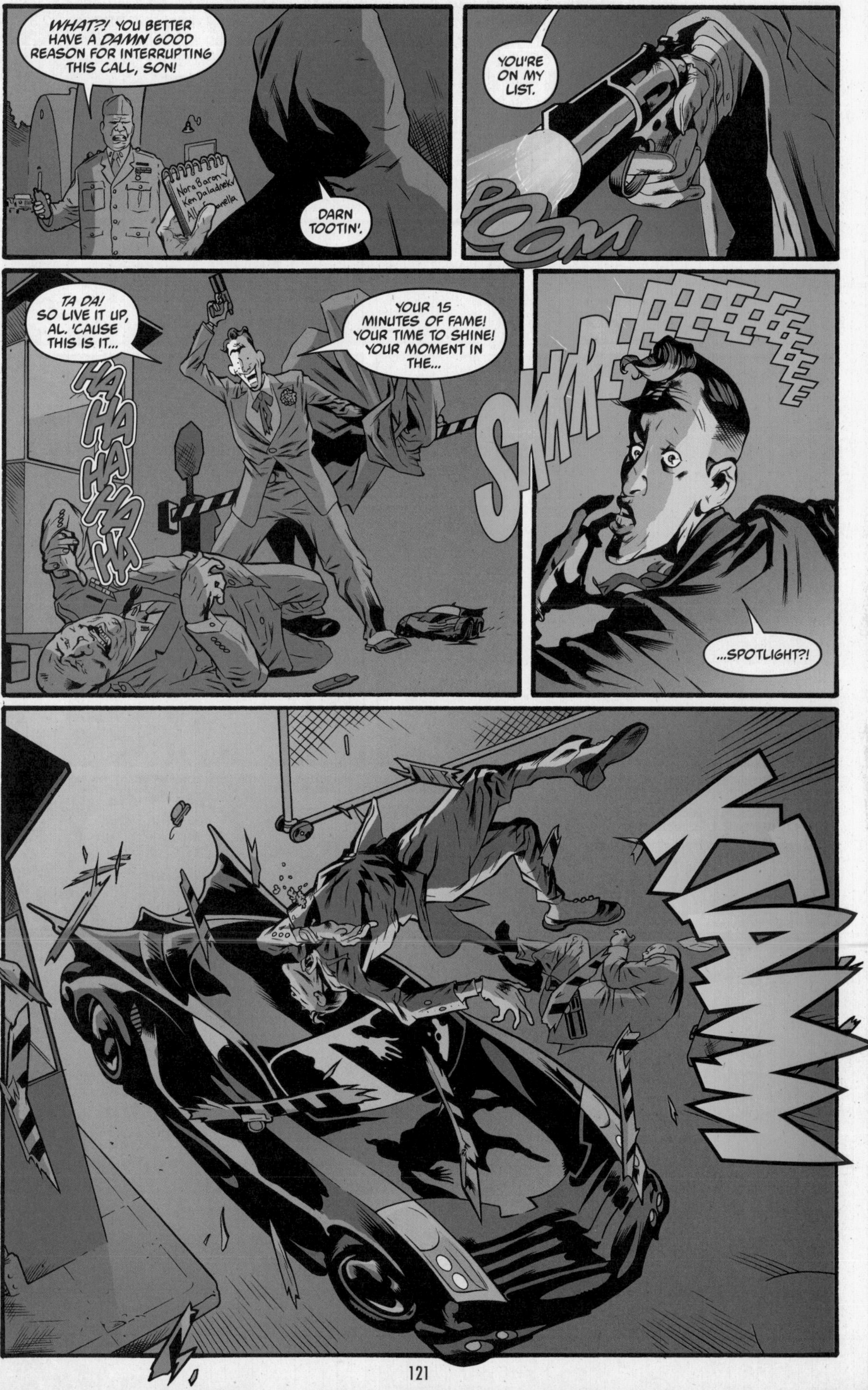

WHAT?! YOU BETTER HAVE A DAMN GOOD REASON FOR INTERRUPTING THIS CALL, SON!
Nora Baron
Ken Daladnek
DARN TOOTIN'.
YOU'RE ON MY LIST.
POOM!
TA DA! SO LIVE IT UP, AL. 'CAUSE THIS IS IT...
HA HA HA HA HA HA
YOUR 15 MINUTES OF FAME! YOUR TIME TO SHINE! YOUR MOMENT IN THE...
SKKREEEEEEEEEEEE
...SPOTLIGHT?!
KLAMM

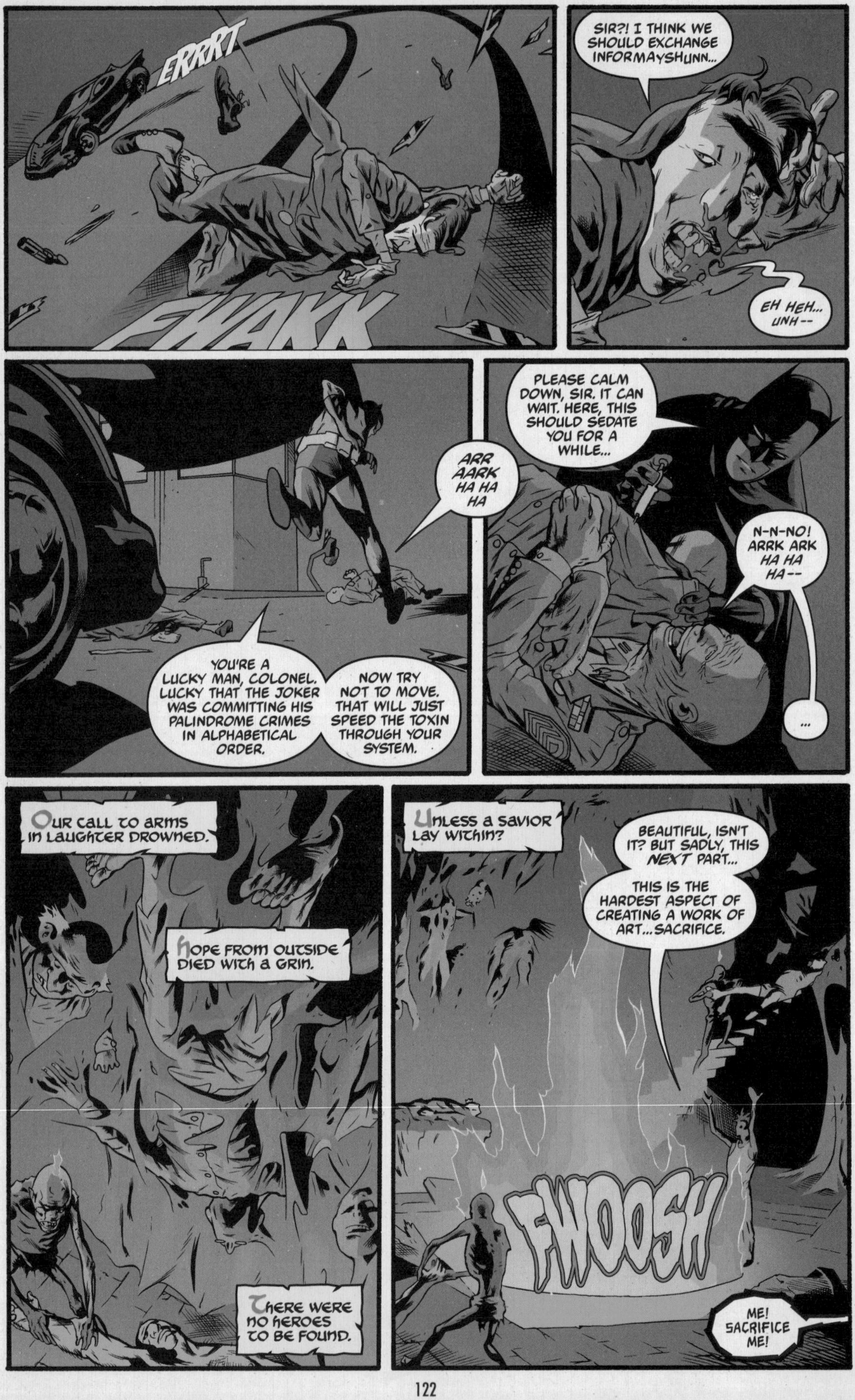
ERRRT
FWAKK
SIR?! I THINK WE SHOULD EXCHANGE INFORMAYSHUNN...
EH HEH... UNH --
ARR AARK HA HA HA
YOU'RE A LUCKY MAN, COLONEL. LUCKY THAT THE JOKER WAS COMMITTING HIS PALINDROME CRIMES IN ALPHABETICAL ORDER.
NOW TRY NOT TO MOVE. THAT WILL JUST SPEED THE TOXIN THROUGH YOUR SYSTEM.
PLEASE CALM DOWN, SIR. IT CAN WAIT. HERE, THIS SHOULD SEDATE YOU FOR A WHILE...
N-N-NO! ARRK ARK HA HA HA--
...
Our call to arms in laughter drowned.
Hope from outside died with a grin.
There were no heroes to be found.
Unless a savior lay within?
BEAUTIFUL, ISN'T IT? BUT SADLY, THIS NEXT PART...
THIS IS THE HARDEST ASPECT OF CREATING A WORK OF ART...SACRIFICE.
FWOOSH
ME! SACRIFICE ME!

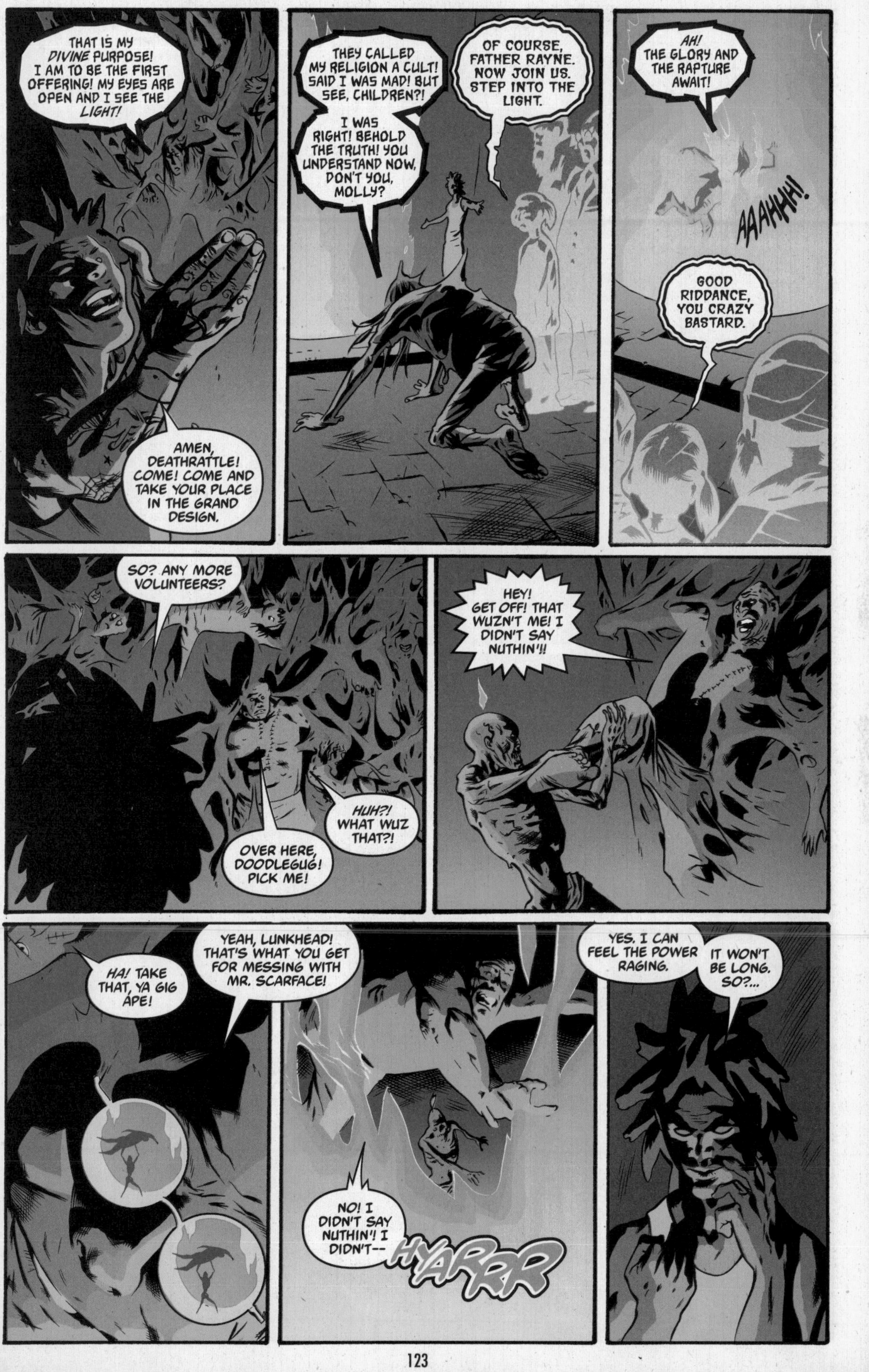
THAT IS MY *DIVINE* PURPOSE! I AM TO BE THE FIRST OFFERING! MY EYES ARE OPEN AND I SEE THE *LIGHT!*
AMEN, DEATHRATTLE! COME! COME AND TAKE YOUR PLACE IN THE GRAND DESIGN.
THEY CALLED MY RELIGION A CULT! SAID I WAS MAD! BUT SEE, CHILDREN?!
I WAS RIGHT! BEHOLD THE TRUTH! YOU UNDERSTAND NOW, DON'T YOU, MOLLY?
OF COURSE, FATHER RAYNE. NOW JOIN US. STEP INTO THE LIGHT.
AH! THE GLORY AND THE RAPTURE AWAIT!
AAAHHH!
GOOD RIDDANCE, YOU CRAZY BASTARD.
SO? ANY MORE VOLUNTEERS?
OVER HERE, DOODLEGUG! PICK ME!
HUH?! WHAT WUZ THAT?!
HEY! GET OFF! THAT WUZN'T ME! I DIDN'T SAY NUTHIN'!!
HA! TAKE THAT, YA GIG APE!
YEAH, LUNKHEAD! THAT'S WHAT YOU GET FOR MESSING WITH MR. SCARFACE!
NO! I DIDN'T SAY NUTHIN'! I DIDN'T--
HYARRR
YES. I CAN FEEL THE POWER RAGING.
IT WON'T BE LONG. SO?...

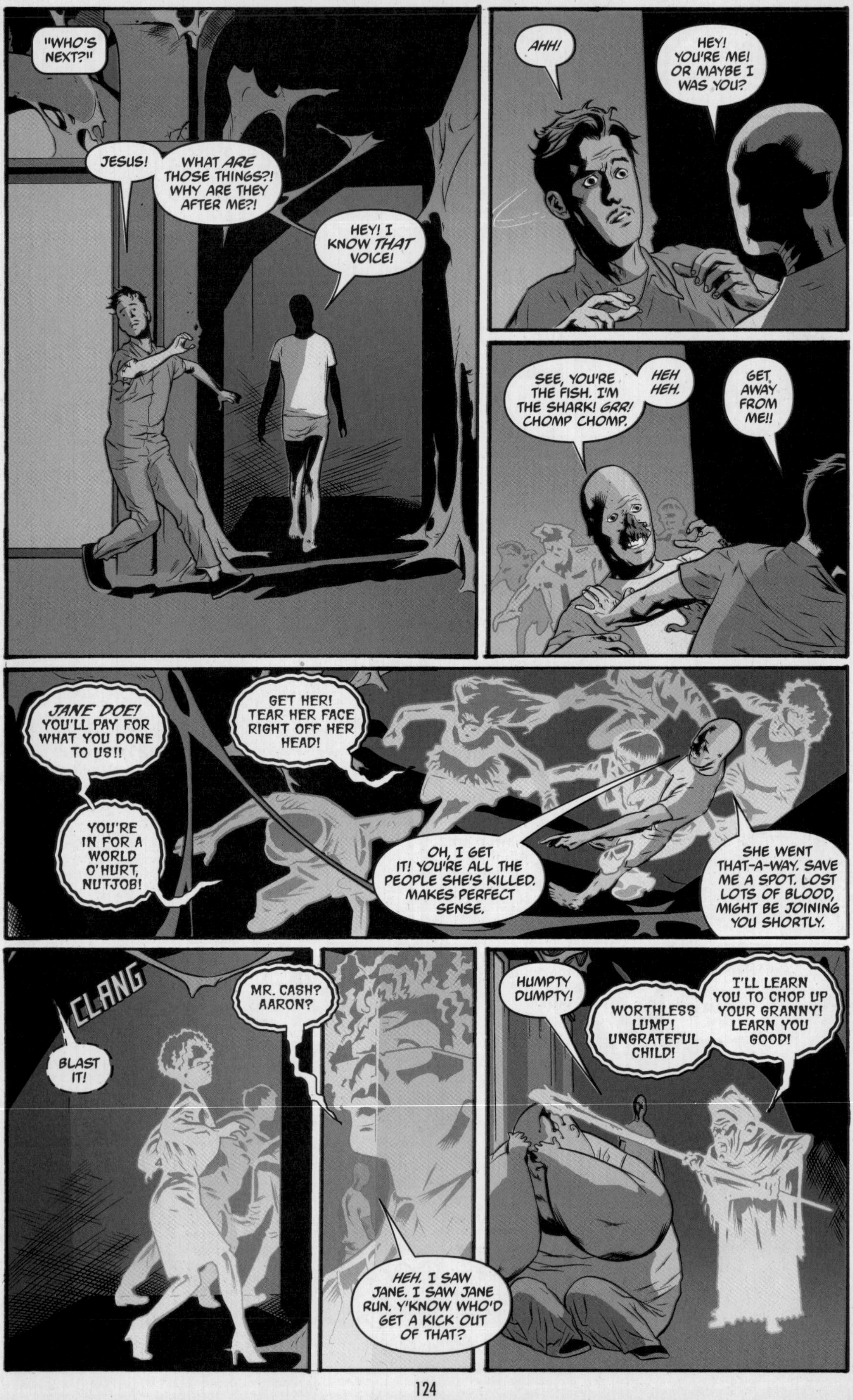
"WHO'S NEXT?"
JESUS!
WHAT ARE THOSE THINGS?! WHY ARE THEY AFTER ME?!
HEY! I KNOW THAT VOICE!
AHH!
HEY! YOU'RE ME! OR MAYBE I WAS YOU?
SEE, YOU'RE THE FISH. I'M THE SHARK! GRR! CHOMP CHOMP.
HEH HEH.
GET AWAY FROM ME!!
JANE DOE! YOU'LL PAY FOR WHAT YOU DONE TO US!!
YOU'RE IN FOR A WORLD O' HURT, NUTJOB!
GET HER! TEAR HER FACE RIGHT OFF HER HEAD!
OH, I GET IT! YOU'RE ALL THE PEOPLE SHE'S KILLED. MAKES PERFECT SENSE.
SHE WENT THAT-A-WAY. SAVE ME A SPOT. LOST LOTS OF BLOOD, MIGHT BE JOINING YOU SHORTLY.
CLANG
BLAST IT!
MR. CASH? AARON?
HEH. I SAW JANE. I SAW JANE RUN. Y'KNOW WHO'D GET A KICK OUT OF THAT?
HUMPTY DUMPTY!
WORTHLESS LUMP! UNGRATEFUL CHILD!
I'LL LEARN YOU TO CHOP UP YOUR GRANNY! LEARN YOU GOOD!

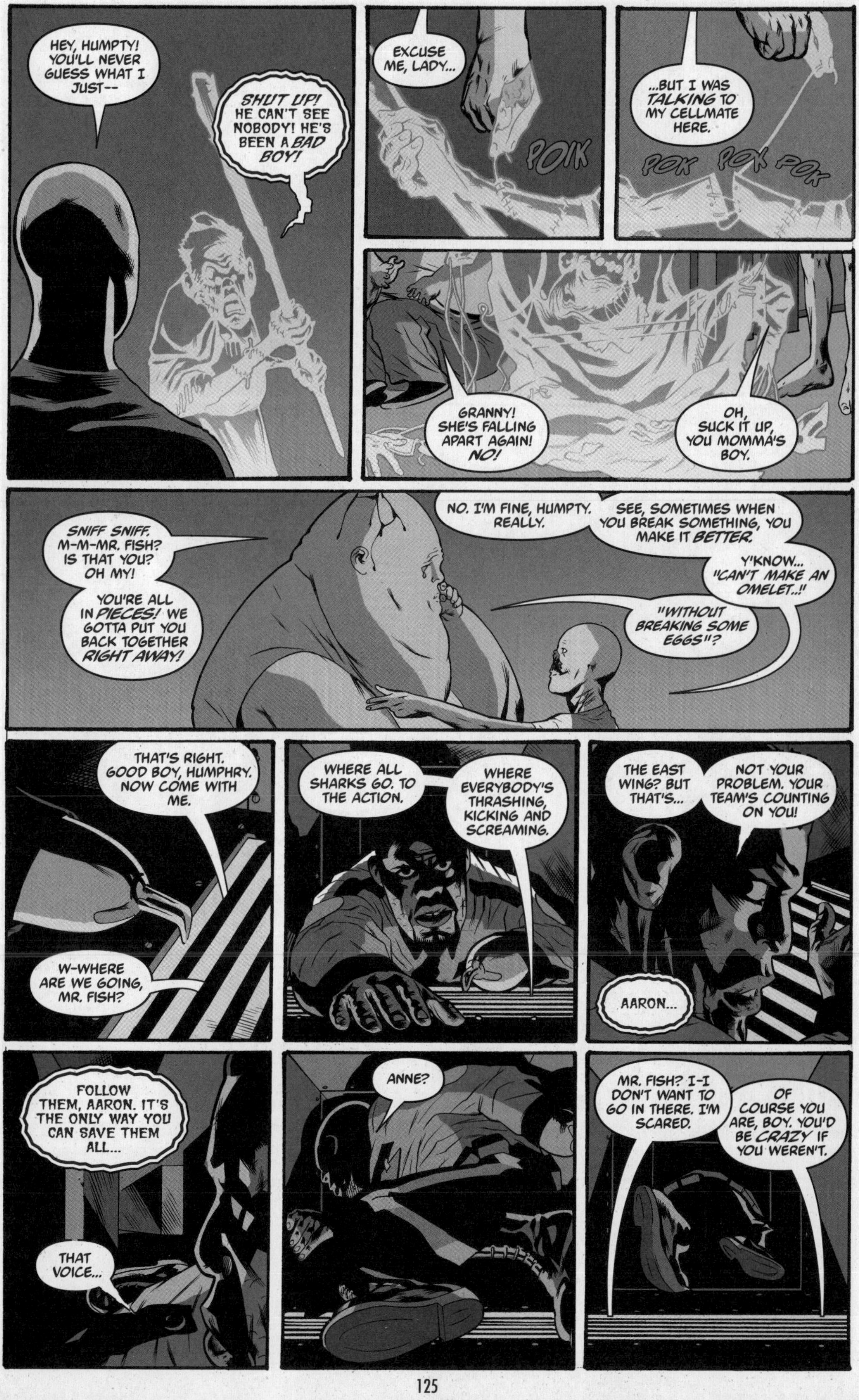
HEY, HUMPTY! YOU'LL NEVER GUESS WHAT I JUST--
SHUT UP! HE CAN'T SEE NOBODY! HE'S BEEN A BAD BOY!
EXCUSE ME, LADY...
POIK
...BUT I WAS TALKING TO MY CELLMATE HERE.
POK POK POK
GRANNY! SHE'S FALLING APART AGAIN! NO!
OH, SUCK IT UP, YOU MOMMA'S BOY.
SNIFF SNIFF. M-M-MR. FISH? IS THAT YOU? OH MY!
YOU'RE ALL IN PIECES! WE GOTTA PUT YOU BACK TOGETHER RIGHT AWAY!
NO. I'M FINE, HUMPTY. REALLY.
SEE, SOMETIMES WHEN YOU BREAK SOMETHING, YOU MAKE IT BETTER.
Y'KNOW... "CAN'T MAKE AN OMELET..!"
"WITHOUT BREAKING SOME EGGS"?
THAT'S RIGHT. GOOD BOY, HUMPHRY. NOW COME WITH ME.
W-WHERE ARE WE GOING, MR. FISH?
WHERE ALL SHARKS GO. TO THE ACTION.
WHERE EVERYBODY'S THRASHING, KICKING AND SCREAMING.
THE EAST WING? BUT THAT'S...
NOT YOUR PROBLEM. YOUR TEAM'S COUNTING ON YOU!
AARON...
FOLLOW THEM, AARON. IT'S THE ONLY WAY YOU CAN SAVE THEM ALL...
THAT VOICE...
ANNE?
MR. FISH? I-I DON'T WANT TO GO IN THERE. I'M SCARED.
OF COURSE YOU ARE, BOY. YOU'D BE CRAZY IF YOU WEREN'T.

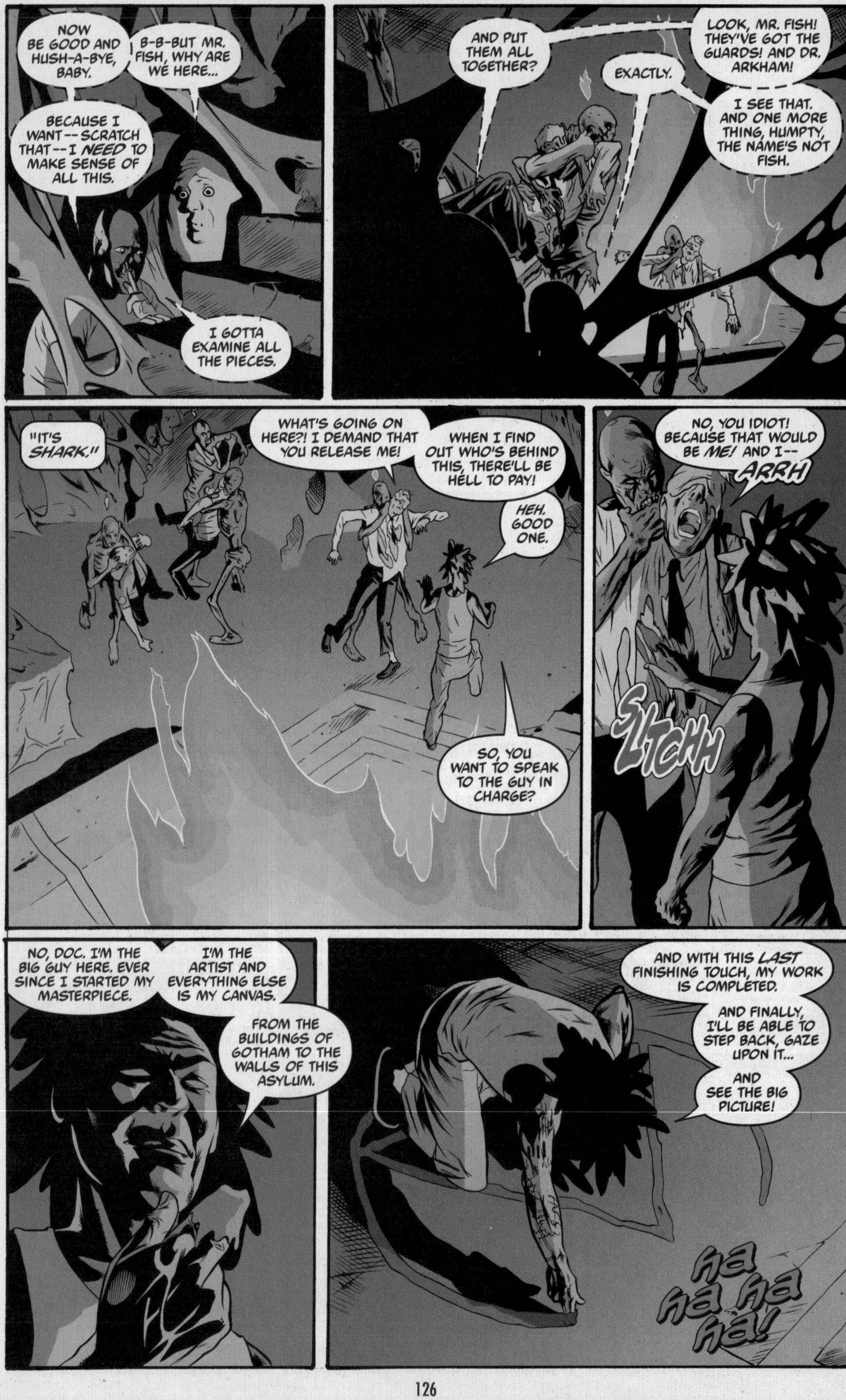

NOW BE GOOD AND HUSH-A-BYE, BABY.
B-B-BUT MR. FISH, WHY ARE WE HERE...
BECAUSE I WANT--SCRATCH THAT--I NEED TO MAKE SENSE OF ALL THIS.
I GOTTA EXAMINE ALL THE PIECES.
AND PUT THEM ALL TOGETHER?
EXACTLY.
LOOK, MR. FISH! THEY'VE GOT THE GUARDS! AND DR. ARKHAM!
I SEE THAT. AND ONE MORE THING, HUMPTY, THE NAME'S NOT FISH.
"IT'S SHARK."
WHAT'S GOING ON HERE?! I DEMAND THAT YOU RELEASE ME!
WHEN I FIND OUT WHO'S BEHIND THIS, THERE'LL BE HELL TO PAY!
HEH. GOOD ONE.
SO, YOU WANT TO SPEAK TO THE GUY IN CHARGE?
NO, YOU IDIOT! BECAUSE THAT WOULD BE ME! AND I--
ARRH
SLITCHH
NO, DOC. I'M THE BIG GUY HERE. EVER SINCE I STARTED MY MASTERPIECE.
I'M THE ARTIST AND EVERYTHING ELSE IS MY CANVAS.
FROM THE BUILDINGS OF GOTHAM TO THE WALLS OF THIS ASYLUM.
AND WITH THIS LAST FINISHING TOUCH, MY WORK IS COMPLETED.
AND FINALLY, I'LL BE ABLE TO STEP BACK, GAZE UPON IT...
AND SEE THE BIG PICTURE!
ha ha ha ha ha!

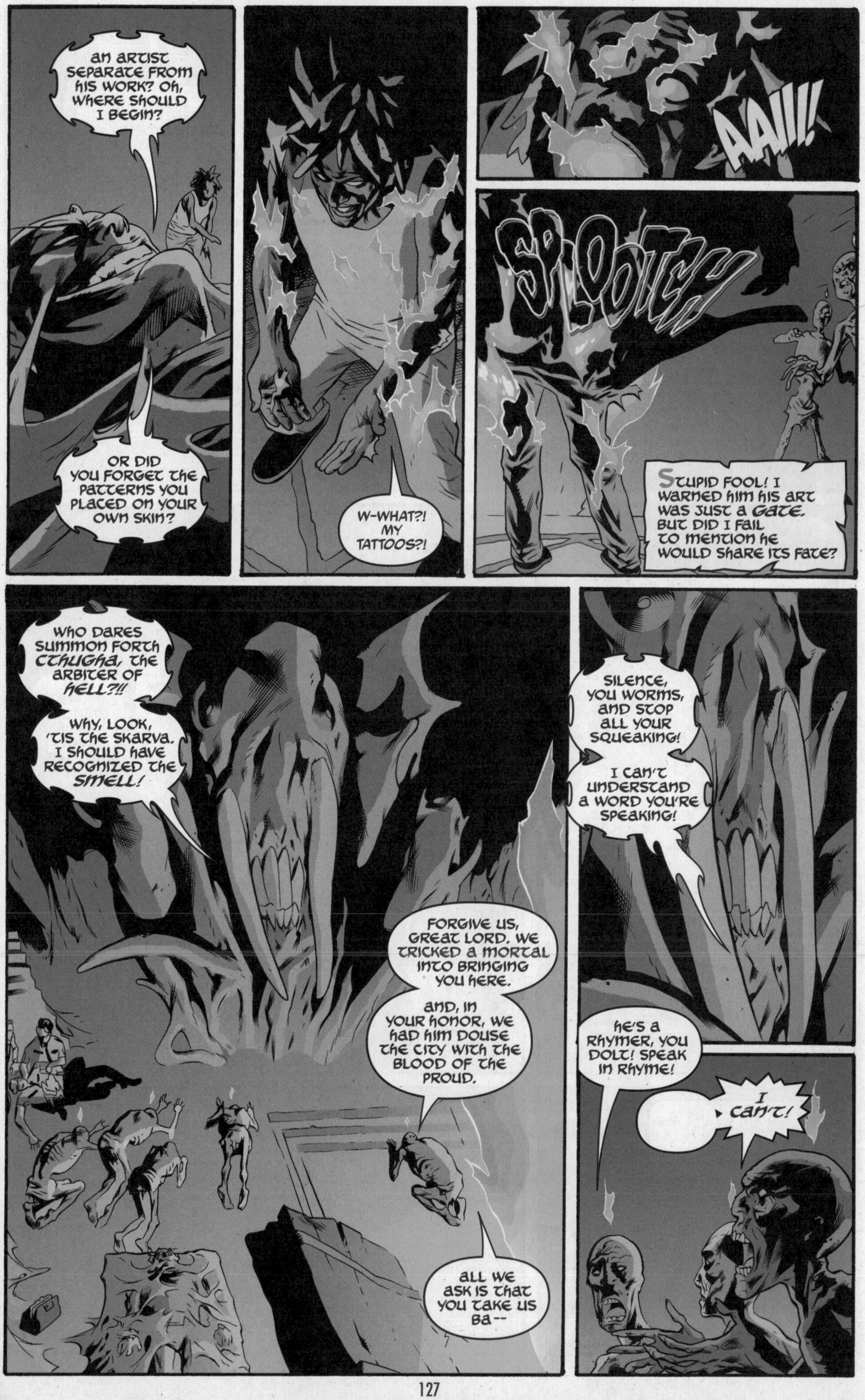

AN ARTIST SEPARATE FROM HIS WORK? OH, WHERE SHOULD I BEGIN?
OR DID YOU FORGET THE PATTERNS YOU PLACED ON YOUR OWN SKIN?
W-WHAT?! MY TATTOOS?!
AAIII!
SPLOOTCH
STUPID FOOL! I WARNED HIM HIS ART WAS JUST A GATE. BUT DID I FAIL TO MENTION HE WOULD SHARE ITS FATE?
WHO DARES SUMMON FORTH CTHUGHA, THE ARBITER OF HELL?!!
WHY, LOOK, 'TIS THE SKARVA. I SHOULD HAVE RECOGNIZED THE SMELL!
FORGIVE US, GREAT LORD. WE TRICKED A MORTAL INTO BRINGING YOU HERE.
AND, IN YOUR HONOR, WE HAD HIM DOUSE THE CITY WITH THE BLOOD OF THE PROUD.
ALL WE ASK IS THAT YOU TAKE US BA--
SILENCE, YOU WORMS, AND STOP ALL YOUR SQUEAKING!
I CAN'T UNDERSTAND A WORD YOU'RE SPEAKING!
HE'S A RHYMER, YOU DOLT! SPEAK IN RHYME!
I CAN'T!

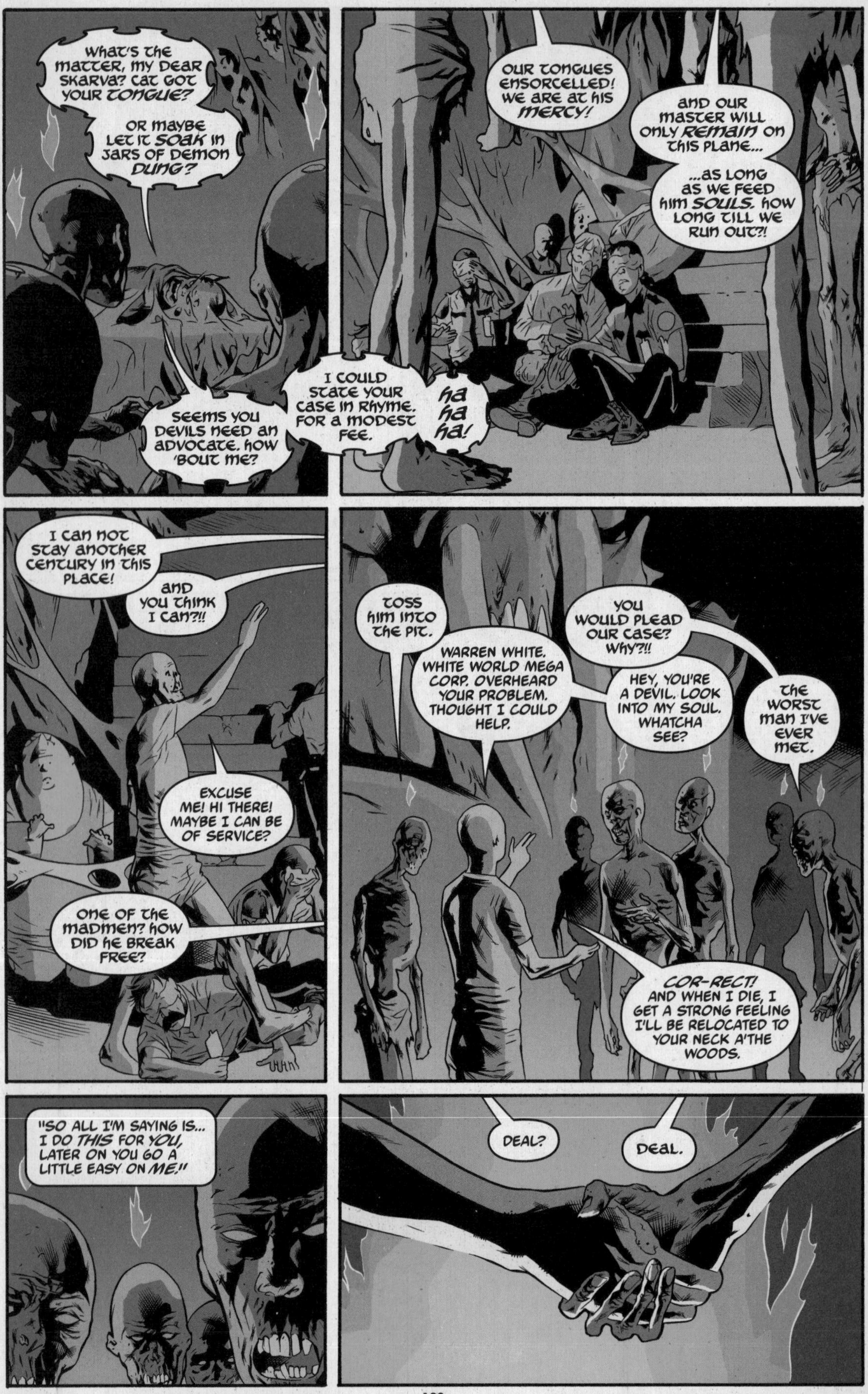
WHAT'S THE MATTER, MY DEAR SKARVA? CAT GOT YOUR TONGUE?
OR MAYBE LET IT SOAK IN JARS OF DEMON DUNG?
OUR TONGUES ENSORCELLED! WE ARE AT HIS MERCY!
AND OUR MASTER WILL ONLY REMAIN ON THIS PLANE...
...AS LONG AS WE FEED HIM SOULS. HOW LONG TILL WE RUN OUT?!
SEEMS YOU DEVILS NEED AN ADVOCATE. HOW 'BOUT ME?
I COULD STATE YOUR CASE IN RHYME. FOR A MODEST FEE.
HA HA HA!
I CAN NOT STAY ANOTHER CENTURY IN THIS PLACE!
AND YOU THINK I CAN?!!
EXCUSE ME! HI THERE! MAYBE I CAN BE OF SERVICE?
ONE OF THE MADMEN? HOW DID HE BREAK FREE?
TOSS HIM INTO THE PIT.
WARREN WHITE. WHITE WORLD MEGA CORP. OVERHEARD YOUR PROBLEM. THOUGHT I COULD HELP.
YOU WOULD PLEAD OUR CASE? WHY?!!
HEY, YOU'RE A DEVIL. LOOK INTO MY SOUL. WHATCHA SEE?
THE WORST MAN I'VE EVER MET.
COR-RECT! AND WHEN I DIE, I GET A STRONG FEELING I'LL BE RELOCATED TO YOUR NECK A'THE WOODS.
"SO ALL I'M SAYING IS... I DO THIS FOR YOU, LATER ON YOU GO A LITTLE EASY ON ME."
DEAL?
DEAL.

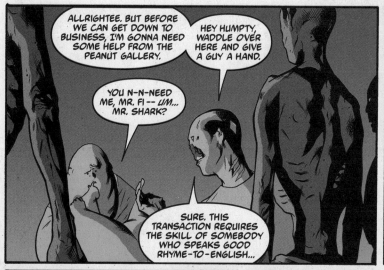

ALLRIGHTEE. BUT BEFORE WE CAN GET DOWN TO BUSINESS, I'M GONNA NEED SOME HELP FROM THE PEANUT GALLERY.

HEY HUMPTY, WADDLE OVER HERE AND GIVE A GUY A HAND.

YOU N-N-NEED ME, MR. FI-- UM... MR. SHARK?

SURE. THIS TRANSACTION REQUIRES THE SKILL OF SOMEBODY WHO SPEAKS GOOD RHYME-TO-ENGLISH...

SKLUTCH

"...AND THAT MAKES YOU THE MAN FOR THE JOB."

UN-FREAKIN'-BELIEVABLE. THIS IS SO OVER MY HEAD.

TO HELL WITH BATMAN. THIS'S A JOB FOR SUPERMAN...

...OR A PRIEST.

NO, AARON.

YOU'LL DO JUST FINE. YOU ALWAYS HAVE.

ANNE!?! BUT I CAN--

YOU'RE HERE! AND I CAN FEEL YOU! HOW IS THIS...?

THERE'S NO TIME TO EXPLAIN. MY TIME IS SHORT.

I WAS BROUGHT BACK HERE IN THE NAME OF VENGEANCE.

BUT THANKS TO YOU, I WAS REMINDED OF SOMETHING FAR MORE IMPORTANT...

"A SENSE OF DUTY. TO THIS PLACE, AND TO THOSE MEN."

SAVE THEM, AARON. THEIR FATE IS IN YOUR HANDS.

ANNE! DON'T GO! THERE'S SO MUCH I WANT TO--

YOU WERE THERE FOR ME, AARON. BE THERE FOR THEM...

SPEAK! THE HANDS OF TIME GIVE CHASE! QUICKLY, MORTALS, STATE YOUR CASE!

UM... HOME AGAIN, HOME AGAIN, JIGGITY JIG. SO THEY CAN GO BUTCHER PIG AFTER PIG...

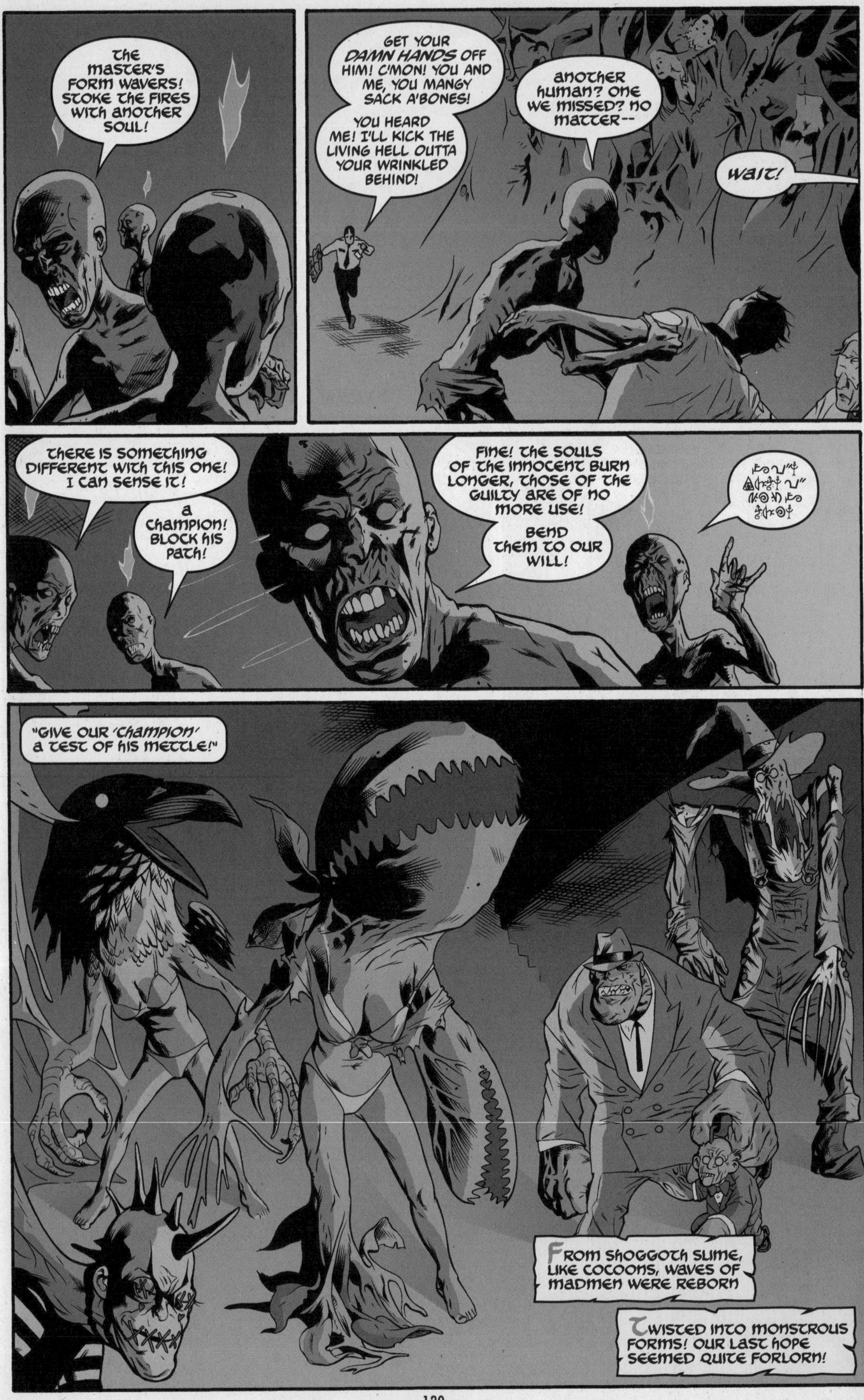
THE MASTER'S FORM WAVERS! STOKE THE FIRES WITH ANOTHER SOUL!
GET YOUR DAMN HANDS OFF HIM! C'MON! YOU AND ME, YOU MANGY SACK A'BONES!
YOU HEARD ME! I'LL KICK THE LIVING HELL OUTTA YOUR WRINKLED BEHIND!
ANOTHER HUMAN? ONE WE MISSED? NO MATTER--
WAIT!
THERE IS SOMETHING DIFFERENT WITH THIS ONE! I CAN SENSE IT!
A CHAMPION! BLOCK HIS PATH!
FINE! THE SOULS OF THE INNOCENT BURN LONGER, THOSE OF THE GUILTY ARE OF NO MORE USE!
BEND THEM TO OUR WILL!
"GIVE OUR 'CHAMPION' A TEST OF HIS METTLE!"
FROM SHOGGOTH SLIME, LIKE COCOONS, WAVES OF MADMEN WERE REBORN
TWISTED INTO MONSTROUS FORMS! OUR LAST HOPE SEEMED QUITE FORLORN!

BUT NOT TO THIS BRAVE JAILER WHO WITH FURY FACED THE TIDE!

YOU'VE *GOT* TO BE KIDDIN' ME!

THWOK

PANG!

AS CTHUGHA WEIGHED THE CASE THAT THE SHARK AND HUMPTY TRIED.

ᚳᚩᚢᛟᛞ ᚢ ᚪᛏᛋᚦᛏ ᚳᚩᚢᛞ ᚦᚻᚷᚩᛟᛖᚱ

I THANK YOU, FOR SPEAKING *SPELLS* ALOUD...

THAT FREE *MONSTERS* FROM THIS SLIMY SHROUD!

SNAP

WHITE AND THE EGG MAN WORKED FAST...

HA HA HA!

THE MORTAL FAST APPROACHES! WHAT SHALL WE DO?

NOT TO WORRY. LOOK INTO HIS SOUL. I KNOW WHAT HE'S AFRAID OF.

WITH WIT AND FAIRY TALE RHYME.

BUT THE ARBITER OF HELL? HE WAS RUNNING OUT OF TIME.

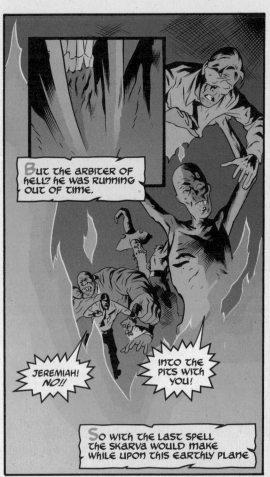

JEREMIAH! NO!!

INTO THE PITS WITH YOU!

SO WITH THE LAST SPELL THE SKARVA WOULD MAKE WHILE UPON THIS EARTHLY PLANE

THEY TRANSFORMED THE FIEND WHO COULD FREEZE THE BLOOD IN THE JAILER'S EVERY VEIN.

BUT THE STAKES WERE HIGH AND HIS DUTY CLEAR. SO HE REACHED DOWN DEEP INSIDE.

WHERE HE FOUND THE STRENGTH TO CLEAR THE BEAST'S MAW

AND TEAR A PIECE OFF ITS HIDE

UM... AND THEY ALL LIVED HAPPILY EVER AFTER.

THE END.

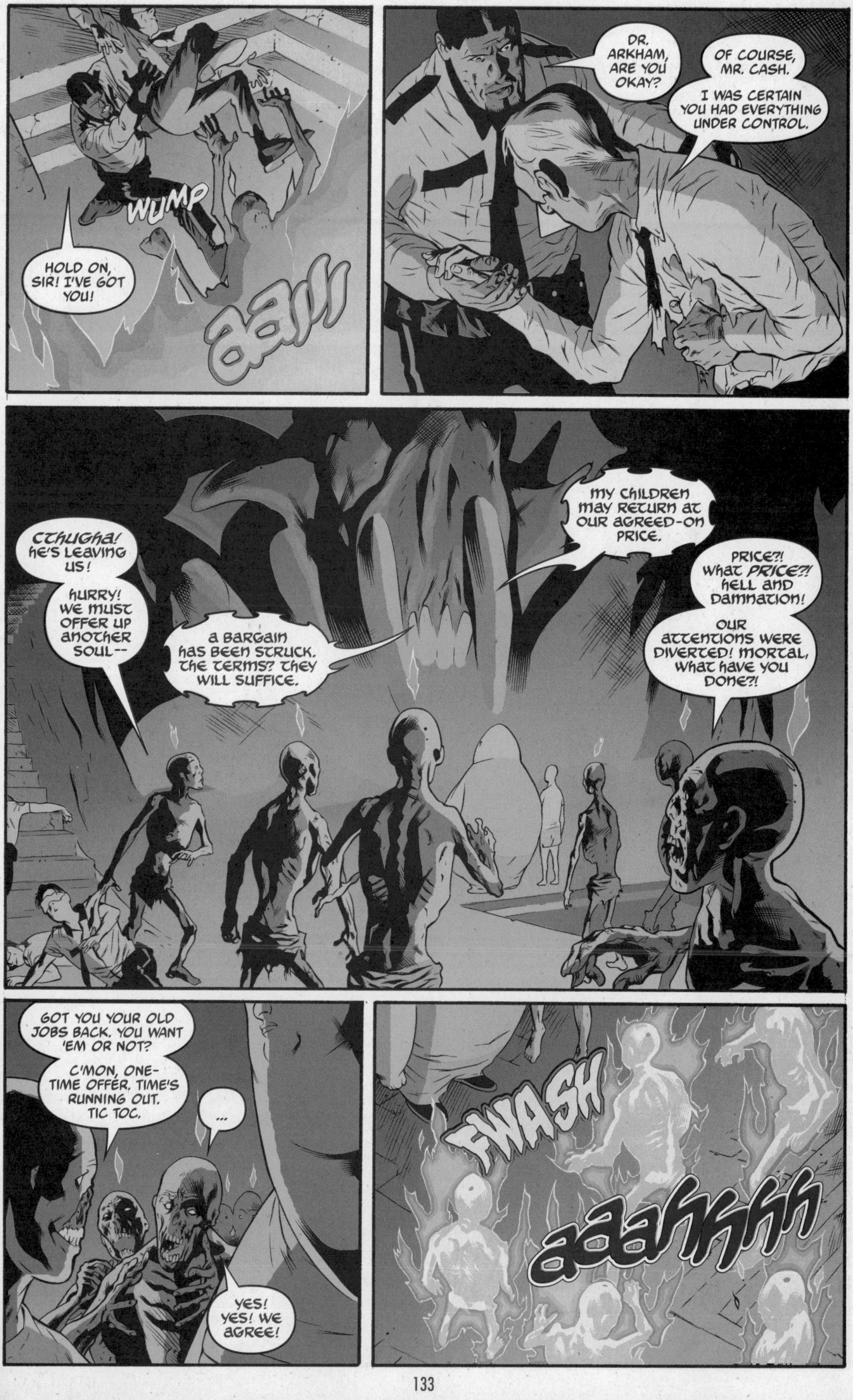
WUMP
HOLD ON, SIR! I'VE GOT YOU!
AAII
DR. ARKHAM, ARE YOU OKAY?
OF COURSE, MR. CASH.
I WAS CERTAIN YOU HAD EVERYTHING UNDER CONTROL.
CTHUGHA! HE'S LEAVING US!
HURRY! WE MUST OFFER UP ANOTHER SOUL--
MY CHILDREN MAY RETURN AT OUR AGREED-ON PRICE.
A BARGAIN HAS BEEN STRUCK. THE TERMS? THEY WILL SUFFICE.
PRICE?! WHAT PRICE?! HELL AND DAMNATION!
OUR ATTENTIONS WERE DIVERTED! MORTAL, WHAT HAVE YOU DONE?!
GOT YOU YOUR OLD JOBS BACK. YOU WANT 'EM OR NOT?
C'MON, ONE-TIME OFFER. TIME'S RUNNING OUT. TIC TOC.
...
YES! YES! WE AGREE!
FWASH
AAAHHHH

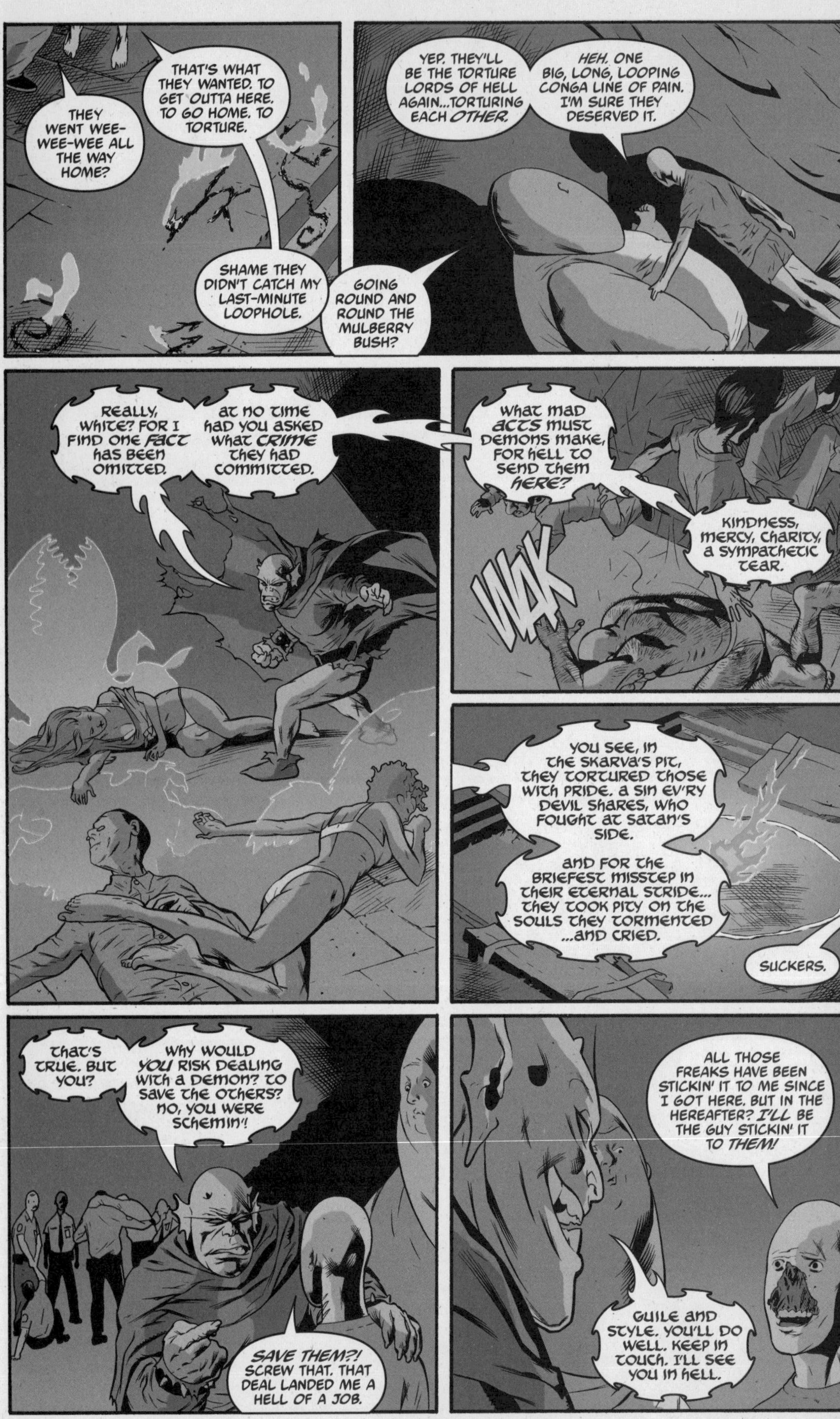
THEY WENT WEE-WEE-WEE ALL THE WAY HOME?
THAT'S WHAT THEY WANTED. TO GET OUTTA HERE. TO GO HOME. TO TORTURE.
SHAME THEY DIDN'T CATCH MY LAST-MINUTE LOOPHOLE.
GOING ROUND AND ROUND THE MULBERRY BUSH?
YEP. THEY'LL BE THE TORTURE LORDS OF HELL AGAIN...TORTURING EACH OTHER.
HEH. ONE BIG, LONG, LOOPING CONGA LINE OF PAIN. I'M SURE THEY DESERVED IT.
REALLY, WHITE? FOR I FIND ONE FACT HAS BEEN OMITTED.
AT NO TIME HAD YOU ASKED WHAT CRIME THEY HAD COMMITTED.
WHAT MAD ACTS MUST DEMONS MAKE, FOR HELL TO SEND THEM HERE?
WAK
KINDNESS, MERCY, CHARITY, A SYMPATHETIC TEAR.
YOU SEE, IN THE SKARVA'S PIT, THEY TORTURED THOSE WITH PRIDE. A SIN EV'RY DEVIL SHARES, WHO FOUGHT AT SATAN'S SIDE.
AND FOR THE BRIEFEST MISSTEP IN THEIR ETERNAL STRIDE... THEY TOOK PITY ON THE SOULS THEY TORMENTED ...AND CRIED.
SUCKERS.
THAT'S TRUE. BUT YOU?
WHY WOULD YOU RISK DEALING WITH A DEMON? TO SAVE THE OTHERS? NO, YOU WERE SCHEMIN'!
SAVE THEM?! SCREW THAT. THAT DEAL LANDED ME A HELL OF A JOB.
ALL THOSE FREAKS HAVE BEEN STICKIN' IT TO ME SINCE I GOT HERE. BUT IN THE HEREAFTER? I'LL BE THE GUY STICKIN' IT TO THEM!
GUILE AND STYLE. YOU'LL DO WELL. KEEP IN TOUCH. I'LL SEE YOU IN HELL.

AND WITH A FIRM PACT MADE, ALL THE SPIRITS DID FADE, AND SO THE LIVING HELL WAS CONCLUDED.

RIP HER APART!

TEAR HER TO SHREDS!

RIP THE SKIN FROM HER BONES!

EMERGENCY EXIT

YET THE SANE AND DERANGED...

I-I-I'M SORRY. I'M...

BOTH REMAINED QUITE UNCHANGED. BECAUSE MORTALS CAN BE SO DELUDED.

WHAT'S GOING ON? WHERE DID THEY..?

DON'T THINK ABOUT IT, JANE. C'MON, GET UP! ON YOUR FEET, GIRL!

JUST GET OUT! THERE'LL BE PLENTY OF TIME TO FIGURE THIS OUT...

...ONCE YOU'RE OUTSIDE! WITH A NEW FACE! A NEW LIFE!

EMERGENCY EXIT

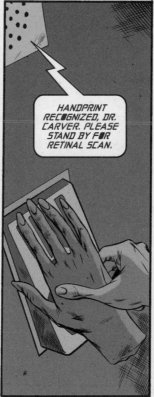

HANDPRINT RECOGNIZED, DR. CARVER. PLEASE STAND BY FOR RETINAL SCAN.

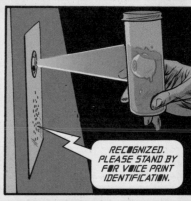

RECOGNIZED. PLEASE STAND BY FOR VOICE PRINT IDENTIFICATION.

CLICK

WHAT ARE YOU DOING?! STOP! PLEASE! DEAR GOD! ARRRRRGHHH!

RECOGNIZED.

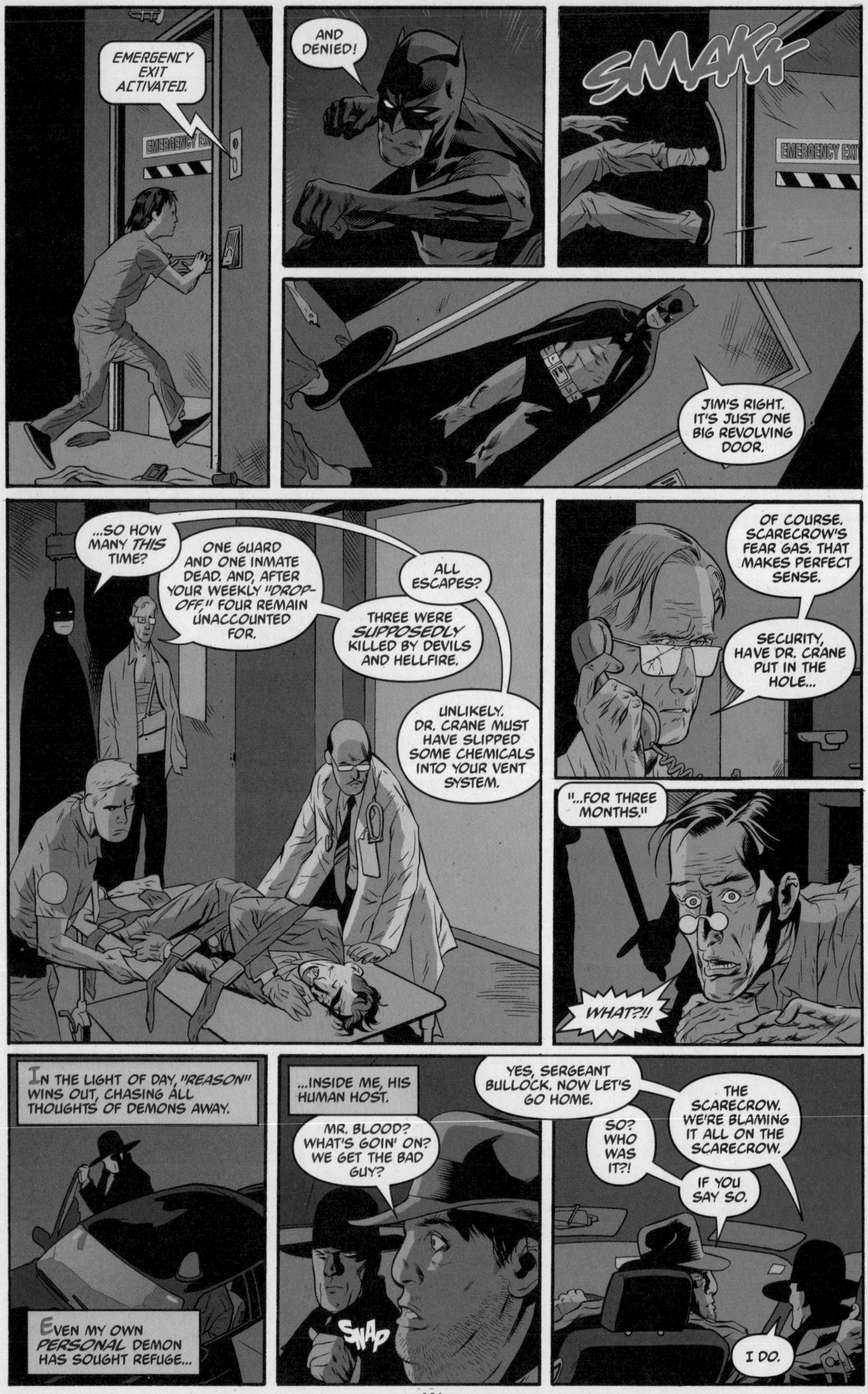
EMERGENCY EXIT ACTIVATED.
EMERGENCY EXIT
AND DENIED!
SMAKK
EMERGENCY EXIT
JIM'S RIGHT. IT'S JUST ONE BIG REVOLVING DOOR.
...SO HOW MANY THIS TIME?
ONE GUARD AND ONE INMATE DEAD. AND, AFTER YOUR WEEKLY "DROP-OFF," FOUR REMAIN UNACCOUNTED FOR.
ALL ESCAPES?
THREE WERE SUPPOSEDLY KILLED BY DEVILS AND HELLFIRE.
UNLIKELY. DR. CRANE MUST HAVE SLIPPED SOME CHEMICALS INTO YOUR VENT SYSTEM.
OF COURSE. SCARECROW'S FEAR GAS. THAT MAKES PERFECT SENSE.
SECURITY, HAVE DR. CRANE PUT IN THE HOLE...
"...FOR THREE MONTHS."
WHAT?!!
IN THE LIGHT OF DAY, "REASON" WINS OUT, CHASING ALL THOUGHTS OF DEMONS AWAY.
EVEN MY OWN PERSONAL DEMON HAS SOUGHT REFUGE...
...INSIDE ME, HIS HUMAN HOST.
MR. BLOOD? WHAT'S GOIN' ON? WE GET THE BAD GUY?
SNAP
YES, SERGEANT BULLOCK. NOW LET'S GO HOME.
SO? WHO WAS IT?!
THE SCARECROW. WE'RE BLAMING IT ALL ON THE SCARECROW.
IF YOU SAY SO.
I DO.

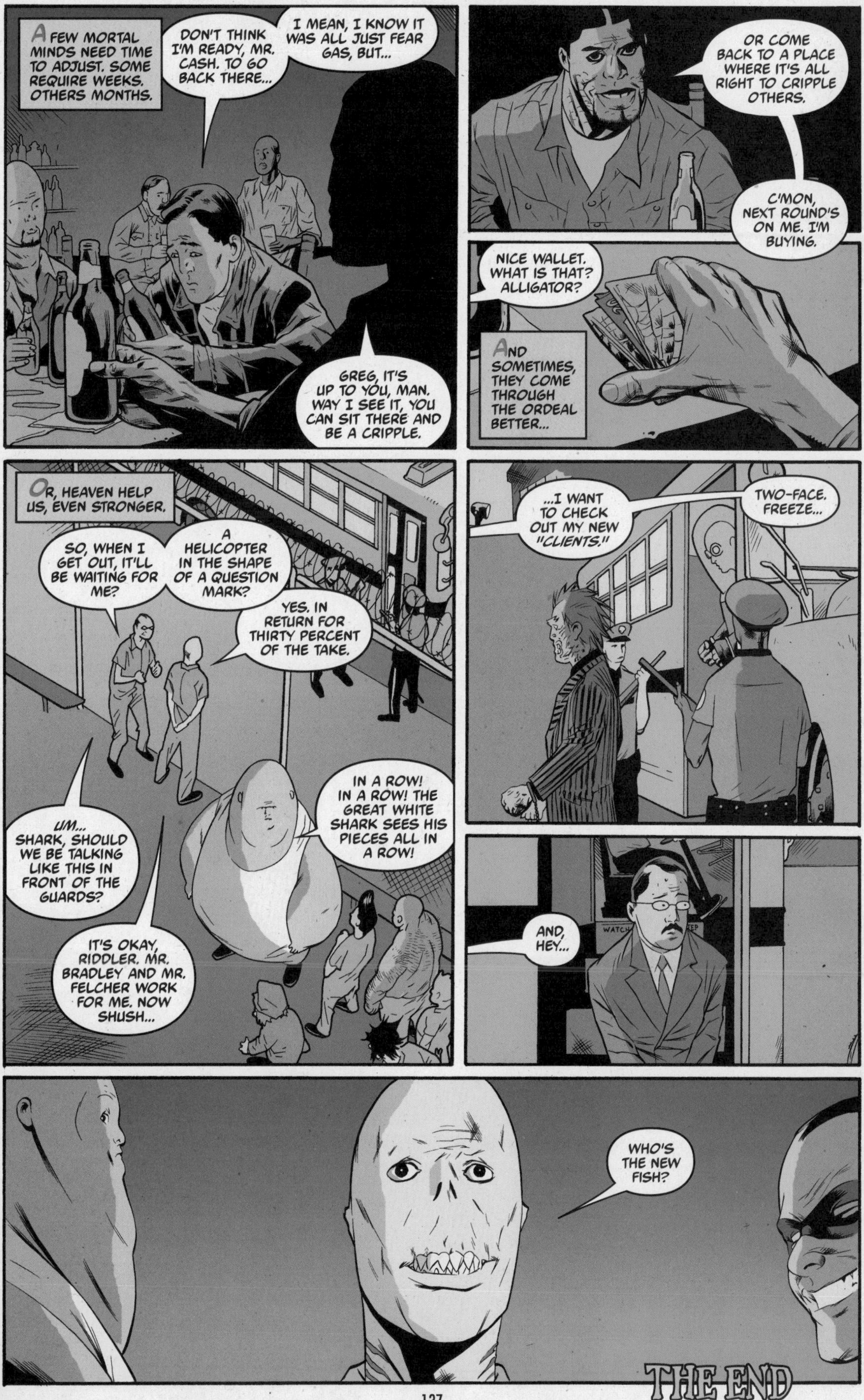
A FEW MORTAL MINDS NEED TIME TO ADJUST. SOME REQUIRE WEEKS. OTHERS MONTHS.
DON'T THINK I'M READY, MR. CASH. TO GO BACK THERE...
I MEAN, I KNOW IT WAS ALL JUST FEAR GAS, BUT...
GREG, IT'S UP TO YOU, MAN. WAY I SEE IT, YOU CAN SIT THERE AND BE A CRIPPLE.
OR COME BACK TO A PLACE WHERE IT'S ALL RIGHT TO CRIPPLE OTHERS.
C'MON, NEXT ROUND'S ON ME. I'M BUYING.
NICE WALLET. WHAT IS THAT? ALLIGATOR?
AND SOMETIMES, THEY COME THROUGH THE ORDEAL BETTER...
OR, HEAVEN HELP US, EVEN STRONGER.
SO, WHEN I GET OUT, IT'LL BE WAITING FOR ME?
A HELICOPTER IN THE SHAPE OF A QUESTION MARK?
YES. IN RETURN FOR THIRTY PERCENT OF THE TAKE.
UM... SHARK, SHOULD WE BE TALKING LIKE THIS IN FRONT OF THE GUARDS?
IN A ROW! IN A ROW! THE GREAT WHITE SHARK SEES HIS PIECES ALL IN A ROW!
IT'S OKAY, RIDDLER. MR. BRADLEY AND MR. FELCHER WORK FOR ME. NOW SHUSH...
...I WANT TO CHECK OUT MY NEW "CLIENTS."
TWO-FACE. FREEZE...
AND, HEY...
WHO'S THE NEW FISH?
THE END

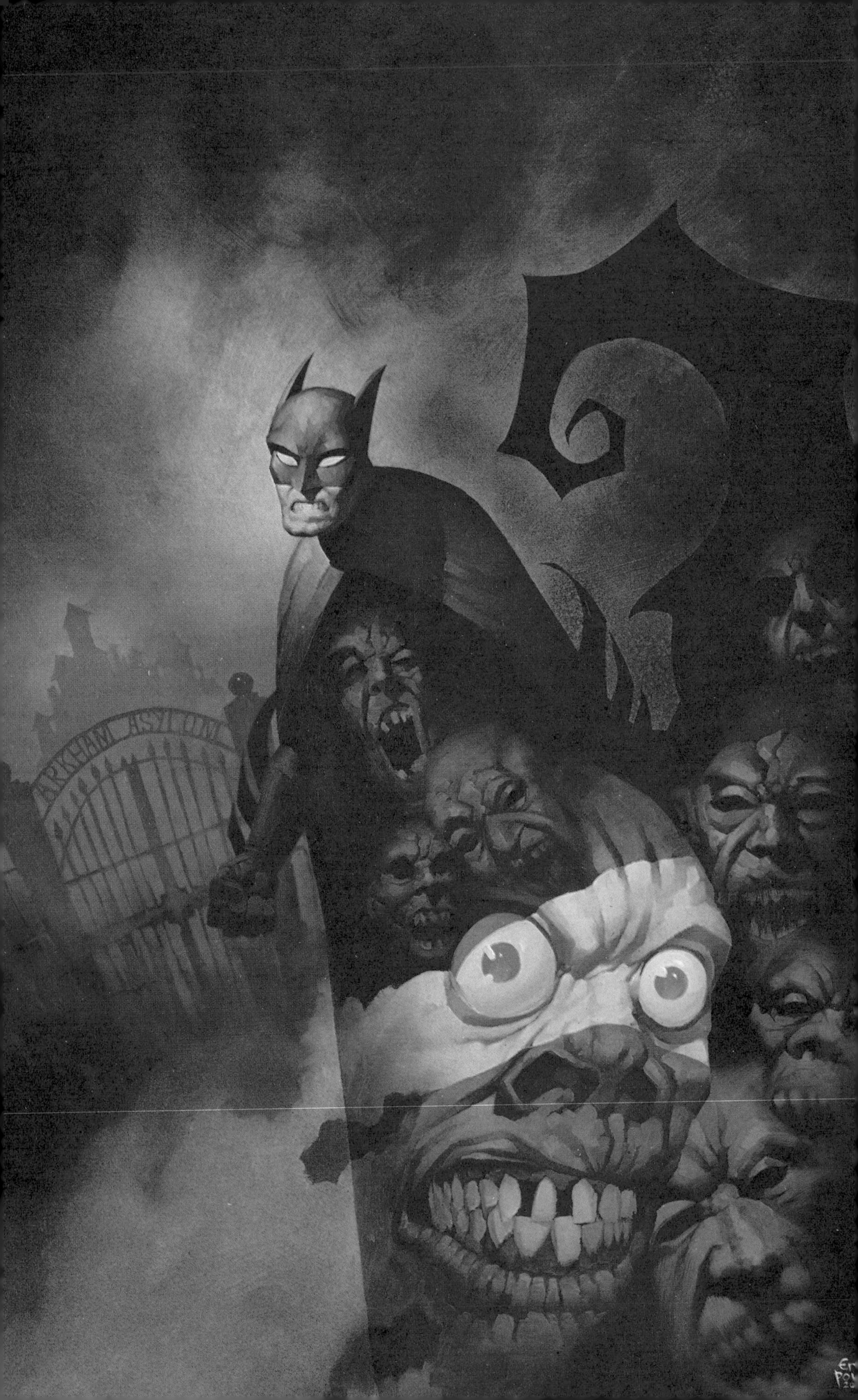
ARKHAM ASYLUM

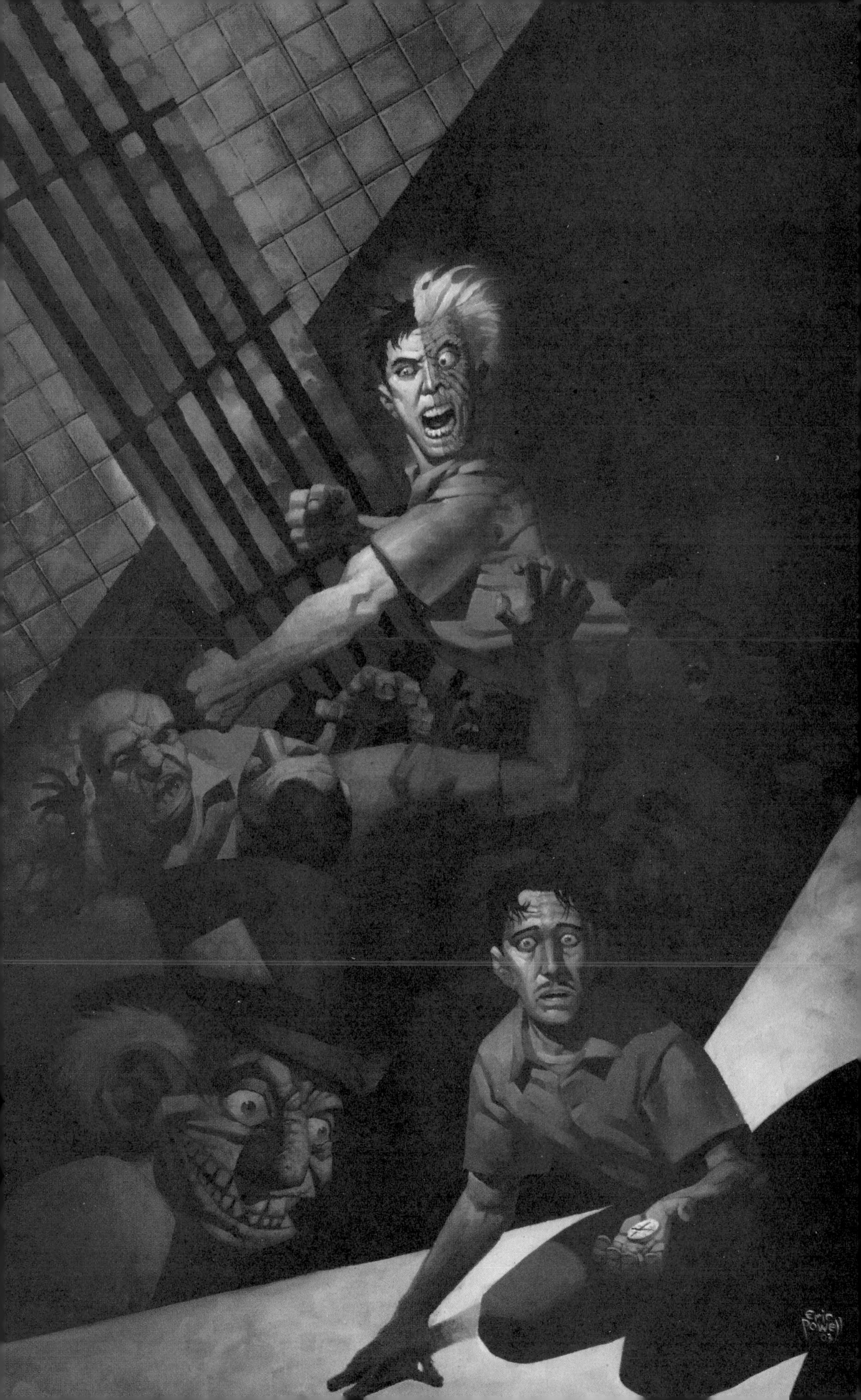
Eric Powell

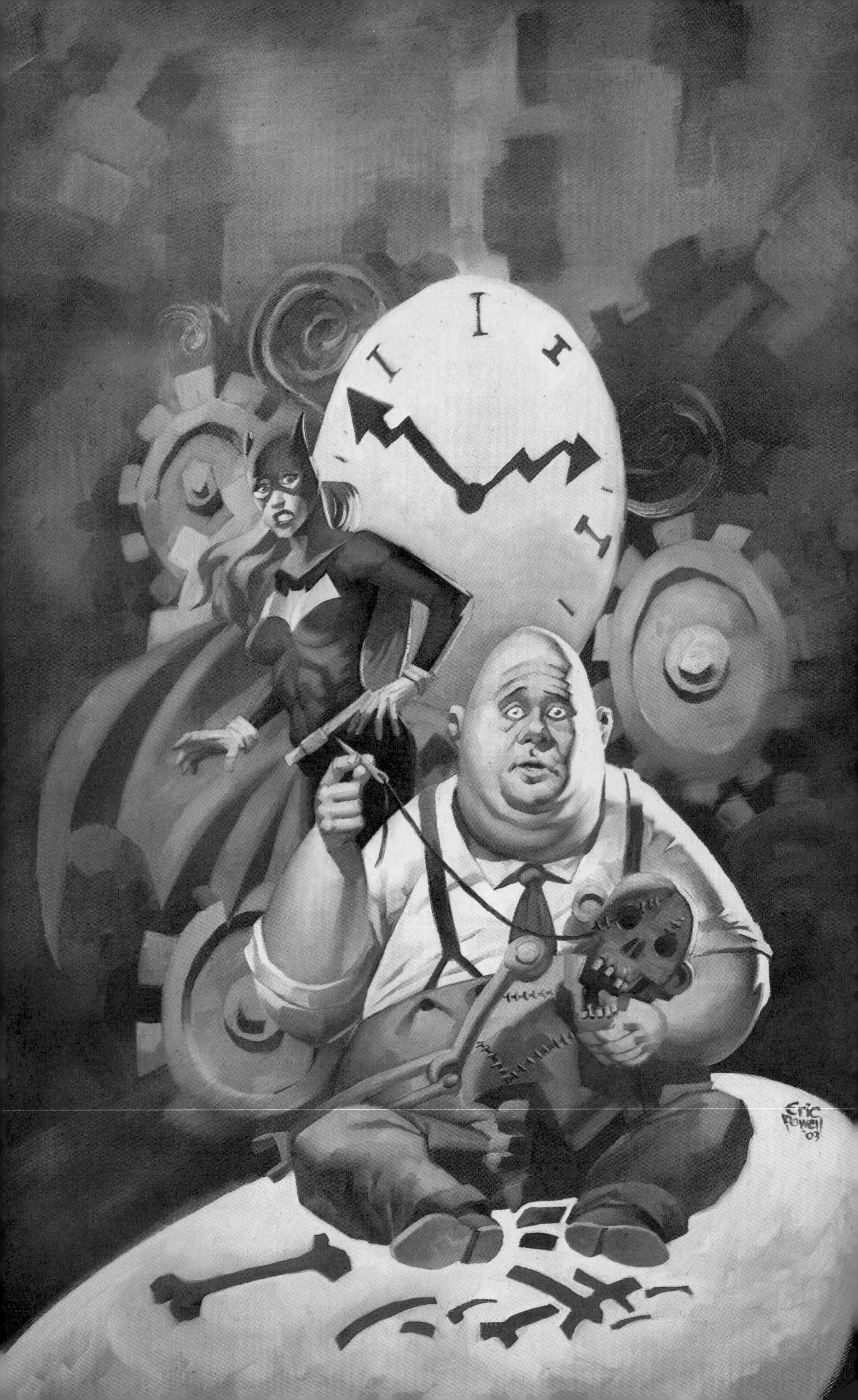
Eric Powell '03

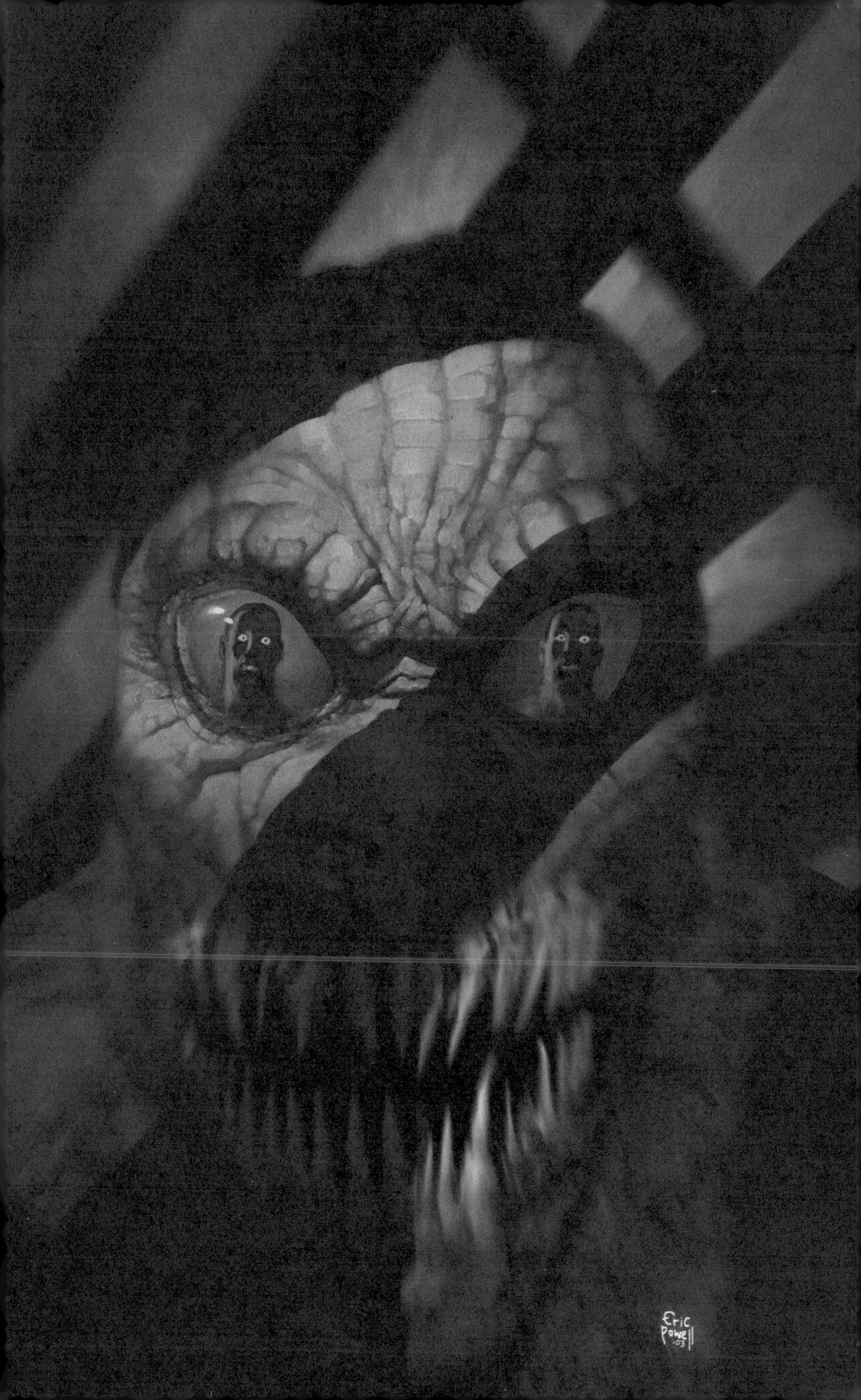
Eric Powell '03

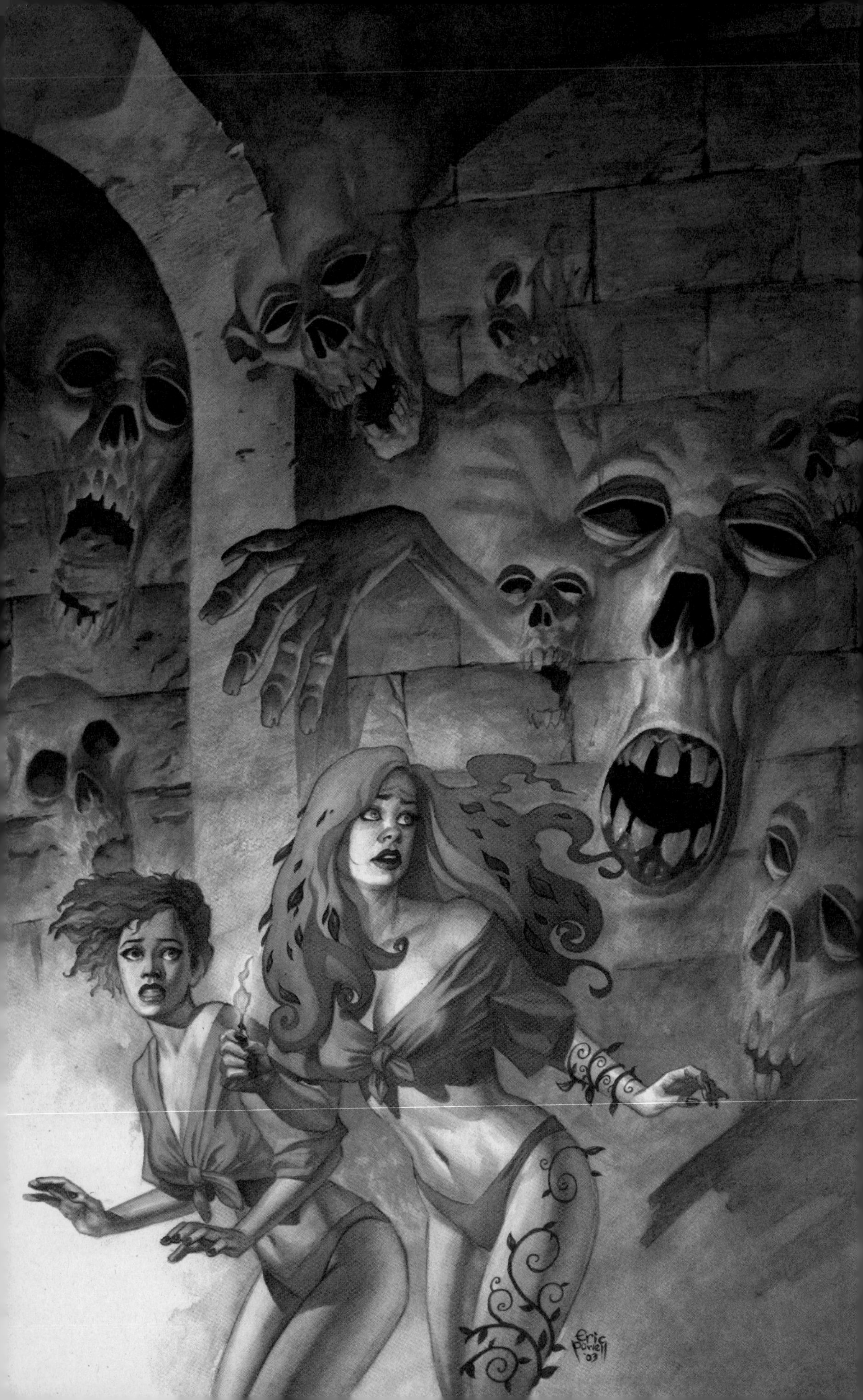
Eric Powell '03

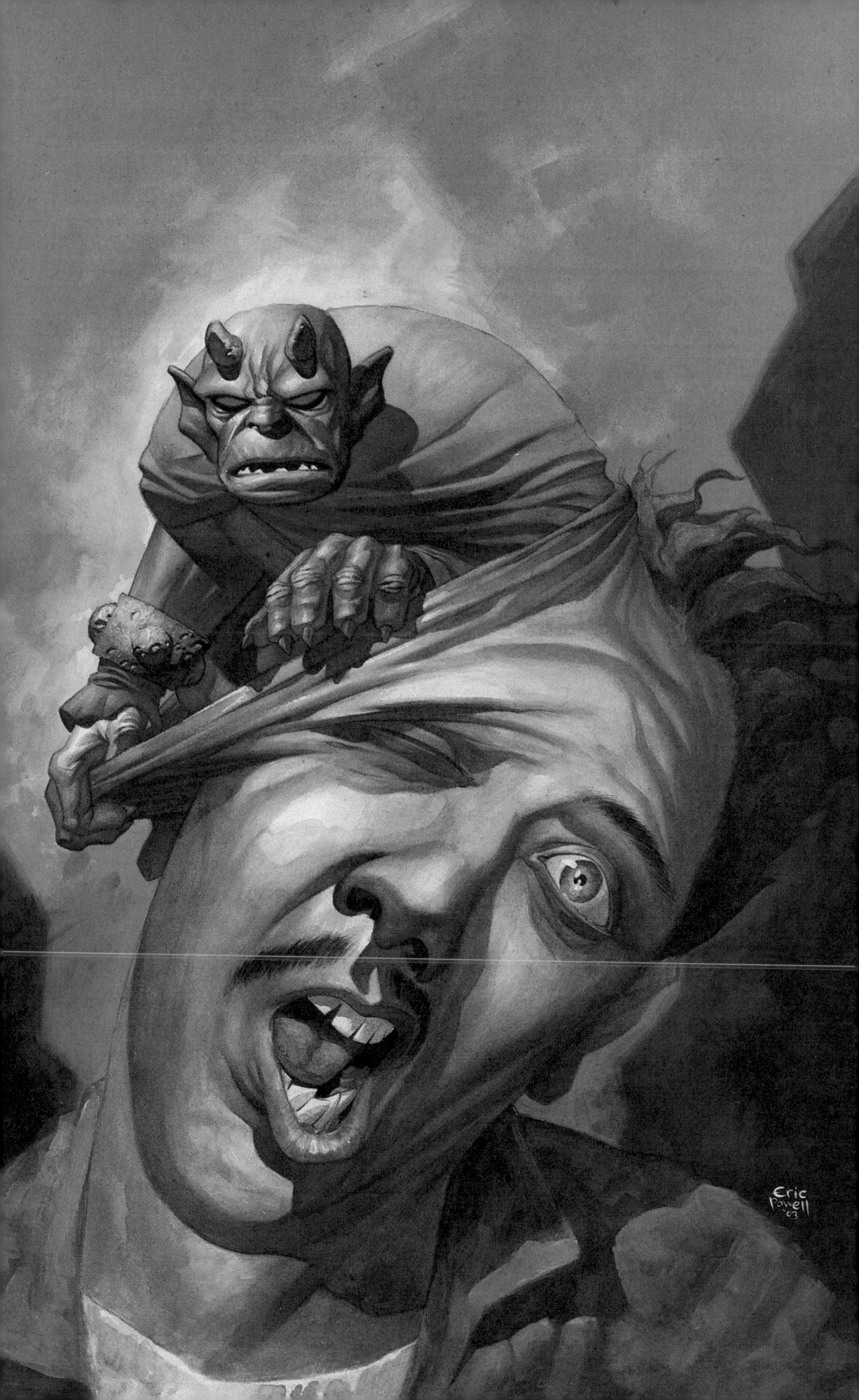
Eric Powell '03

B A T M A N
THE QUEST FOR JUSTICE CONTINUES IN THESE BOOKS FROM DC:

FOR READERS OF ALL AGES

THE BATMAN ADVENTURES
K. Puckett/T. Templeton/
R. Burchett/various

BATMAN BEYOND
Hilary Bader/Rick Burchett/
various

BATMAN: THE DARK KNIGHT ADVENTURES
Kelley Puckett/Mike Parobeck/
Rick Burchett

BATMAN: WAR ON CRIME
Paul Dini/Alex Ross

GRAPHIC NOVELS

BATMAN: ARKHAM ASYLUM
Suggested for mature readers
Grant Morrison/Dave McKean

BATMAN: BLOODSTORM
Doug Moench/Kelley Jones/
John Beatty

BATMAN: THE CHALICE
Chuck Dixon/John Van Fleet

BATMAN: CRIMSON MIST
Doug Moench/Kelley Jones/
John Beatty

BATMAN/DRACULA: RED RAIN
Doug Moench/Kelley Jones/
Malcolm Jones III

BATMAN: FORTUNATE SON
Gerard Jones/Gene Ha

BATMAN: HARVEST BREED
George Pratt

BATMAN: THE KILLING JOKE
Suggested for mature readers
Alan Moore/Brian Bolland/
John Higgins

BATMAN: NIGHT CRIES
Archie Goodwin/Scott Hampton

BATMAN: NINE LIVES
Dean Motter/Michael Lark

BATMAN: SON OF THE DEMON
Mike Barr/Jerry Bingham

**CATWOMAN:
SELINA'S BIG SCORE**
Darwyn Cooke

COLLECTIONS

BATMAN: A DEATH IN THE FAMILY
Jim Starlin/Jim Aparo/
Mike DeCarlo

BATMAN: A LONELY PLACE OF DYING
Marv Wolfman/George Pérez/
various

BATMAN BLACK AND WHITE Vols. 1 & 2
Various writers and artists

BATMAN: BRUCE WAYNE — MURDERER?
Various writers and artists

BATMAN: BRUCE WAYNE — FUGITIVE Vol. 1
Various writers and artists

BATMAN: BRUCE WAYNE — FUGITIVE Vol. 2
Various writers and artists

BATMAN: CATACLYSM
Various writers and artists

BATMAN: CHILD OF DREAMS
Kia Asamiya

BATMAN: DANGEROUS DAMES & DEMONS
Dini/Timm/various

BATMAN: THE DARK KNIGHT RETURNS
Frank Miller/Klaus Janson/
Lynn Varley

BATMAN: THE DARK KNIGHT STRIKES AGAIN
Frank Miller/Lynn Varley

BATMAN: DARK KNIGHT DYNASTY
M. Barr/S. Hampton/G. Frank/
S. McDaniels/various

BATMAN: DARK VICTORY
Jeph Loeb/Tim Sale

BATMAN: EVOLUTION
Rucka/Martinbrough/Mitchell/
various

BATMAN: GOTHIC
Grant Morrison/Klaus Janson

BATMAN: HAUNTED KNIGHT
Jeph Loeb/Tim Sale

BATMAN/HUNTRESS: CRY FOR BLOOD
Rucka/Burchett/T. Beatty

**BATMAN IN THE FIFTIES
BATMAN IN THE SIXTIES
BATMAN IN THE SEVENTIES**
Various writers and artists

**THE KNIGHTFALL Trilogy
BATMAN: KNIGHTFALL Part 1:
Broken Bat
BATMAN: KNIGHTFALL Part 2:
Who Rules the Night**

BATMAN: KNIGHTFALL Part 3: KnightsEnd
Various writers and artists

BATMAN: THE LONG HALLOWEEN
Jeph Loeb/Tim Sale

BATMAN: NO MAN'S LAND Vols. 1 - 5
Various writers and artists

BATMAN: OFFICER DOWN
Various writers and artists

BATMAN: PRODIGAL
Various writers and artists

BATMAN: STRANGE APPARITIONS
S. Englehart/M. Rogers/
T. Austin/various

BATMAN: SWORD OF AZRAEL
Dennis O'Neil/Joe Quesada/
Kevin Nowlan

BATMAN: TALES OF THE DEMON
Dennis O'Neil/Neal Adams/
various

BATMAN: VENOM
Dennis O'Neil/Trevor Von Eeden/
various

BATMAN VS. PREDATOR: THE COLLECTED EDITION
Dave Gibbons/Andy Kubert/
Adam Kubert

BATMAN: YEAR ONE
Frank Miller/David Mazzucchelli

BATMAN: YEAR TWO — FEAR THE REAPER
Barr/Davis/McFarlane/various

BATGIRL: A KNIGHT ALONE
Puckett/D. Scott/Turnbull/
Campanella/various

BATGIRL: SILENT RUNNING
Puckett/Peterson/D. Scott/
Campanella

BIRDS OF PREY
Various writers and artists

BIRDS OF PREY: OLD FRIENDS, NEW ENEMIES
Dixon/Land/Geraci/various

CATWOMAN: THE DARK END OF THE STREET
Brubaker/Cooke/Allred

THE GREATEST BATMAN STORIES EVER TOLD Vol. 1
Various writers and artists

THE GREATEST JOKER STORIES EVER TOLD
Various writers and artists

NIGHTWING: A KNIGHT IN BLÜDHAVEN
Dixon/McDaniel/Story

NIGHTWING: ROUGH JUSTICE
Dixon/McDaniel/Story

NIGHTWING: LOVE AND BULLETS
Dixon/McDaniel/Story

NIGHTWING: A DARKER SHADE OF JUSTICE
Dixon/McDaniel/Story

NIGHTWING: THE HUNT FOR ORACLE
Dixon/Land/Guice/Zircher/various

ROBIN: FLYING SOLO
Dixon/Grummett/P. Jimenez/
various

ROBIN: YEAR ONE
Dixon/S. Beatty/Pulido/
Martin/Campanella

ARCHIVE EDITIONS

BATMAN ARCHIVES Vol. 1
(DETECTIVE COMICS 27-50)
BATMAN ARCHIVES Vol. 2
(DETECTIVE COMICS 51-70)
BATMAN ARCHIVES Vol. 3
(DETECTIVE COMICS 71-86)
BATMAN ARCHIVES Vol. 4
(DETECTIVE COMICS 87-102)
BATMAN ARCHIVES Vol. 5
(DETECTIVE COMICS 103-119)
All by B. Kane/B. Finger/D. Sprang/
various

BATMAN: THE DARK KNIGHT ARCHIVES Vol. 1
(BATMAN 1-4)
BATMAN: THE DARK KNIGHT ARCHIVES Vol. 2
(BATMAN 5-8)
BATMAN: THE DARK KNIGHT ARCHIVES Vol. 3
(BATMAN 9-12)
All by Bob Kane/Bill Finger/various

BATMAN: THE DYNAMIC DUO ARCHIVES Vol. 1
(BATMAN 164-167,
DETECTIVE COMICS 327-333)
B. Kane/Giella/Finger/Broome/
Fox/various

WORLD'S FINEST COMICS ARCHIVES Vol. 1
(SUPERMAN 76,
WORLD'S FINEST 71-85)
B. Finger/E. Hamilton/C. Swan/
Sprang/various

TO FIND MORE COLLECTED EDITIONS AND MONTHLY COMIC BOOKS FROM DC COMICS,
CALL 1-888-COMIC BOOK FOR THE NEAREST COMICS SHOP OR GO TO YOUR LOCAL BOOK STORE.

Visit us at www.dccomics.com

BM0012